To Victor and Janet Bignell

Jonathan Bignell

Media semiotics

AN INTRODUCTION

Manchester University Press

Manchester and New York

distributed exclusively in the USA by St. Martin's Press

Published by Manchester University Press
Oxford Road, Manchester M13 9NR, UK
and Room 400, 175 Fifth Avenue, New York, NY 10010, USA

Distributed exclusively in the USA
by St. Martin's Press, Inc., 175 Fifth Avenue, New York,
NY 10010, USA

British Library Cataloguing-in-Publication Data
A catalogue record is available from the British Library

Library of Congress Cataloging-in-Publication Data
Bignell, Jonathan.
    Media semiotics : an introduction / Jonathan Bignell.
        p.   cm.
    Includes bibliographical references (p.   ) and index.
    ISBN 0–7190–4500–2. — ISBN 0–7190–4501–0 (pbk.)
    1. Mass media. 2. Semiotics. I. Title.
    P91.B54   1997
    302.23'014—dc20   96–34390

7 ISBN 0 7190 4500 2 *hardback*
        0 7190 4501 0 *paperback*   1001185947

First published 1997
01 00 99 98 97   10 9 8 7 6 5 4 3 2 1

Typeset in Great Britain
by Northern Phototypesetting Co Ltd, Bolton
Printed in Great Britain
by Biddles Ltd, Guildford and King's Lynn

Contents

List of illustrations

Preface

The desire to write this book has come mainly from my experience of teaching a course called 'Media Semiotics' in the Department of English at the University of Reading. Each year a group of undergraduates has explored and grappled with semiotic theories in relation to words, still images and moving images in a range of contemporary media. As each group has taken the course with me, at least one person has always asked whether there is one really useful book that I can recommend. Such a book would introduce the key theoretical issues, demonstrate how they can be applied, discuss the various problems which media material presents to theories that take their cue from semiotics, and outline the shortcomings of semiotic analysis as well as its strengths. I have tried to achieve these objectives in this book, but it has not been easy to do so in a single volume and I hope that readers will also go on to use some of the other books I have quoted from and referred to.

A number of people deserve my thanks, but not all of them can be individually named here. It was Stephen Heath who first inspired my interest in semiotics as an undergraduate. Later, as a postgraduate student, my supervisor Stuart Laing both supported and challenged my semiotic approach to the media and to literature. My colleagues at the University of Reading have supported and encouraged me, not only during the writing of this book but over my years as a lecturer. I am also grateful for a term without teaching commitments which was very valuable in getting the first draft done. This project would not have existed without my interaction with both undergraduate and postgraduate students. I would like to thank Tania Christidis for our discussions of semiotic theory, and Ian Stewart for opening my eyes to the role of semiotics in the curriculum of Sandhurst Miltary Academy. My thanks to all those students who have taken my course in Media Semiotics over the last six years, especially in 1995 and 1996 when parts of this book were used as teaching materials.

I would like to thank those people who helped me to obtain the illustrations in this book, particularly Bobbie Mitchell of BBC Picture Archives, Nicky Owen formerly of TBWA, and Dave Sutcliffe for photographing three of the illustrated items. For copyright permissions, I gratefully acknowledge TBWA for the Wonderbra advertisement,

DMP DDB Needham for the VW Golf Estate advertisement photographed by Malcolm Venville, Mirror Syndication International for
the front page of the *Daily Mirror*, Times Newspapers Limited for the
front page of *The Times*, Popperfoto/Reuters for the photographs on
the front page of *The Times*, BBC Picture Archives for the stills from
BBC News, *One Foot in the Grave*, *Harry Enfield's Television Programme*, and *You Decide – with Paxman*. Finally, *Four Weddings and
a Funeral* photographs by Stephen Morley are reprinted by kind permission of Polygram Filmed Entertainment, and were supplied by
BFI Stills.

My thanks also go to Anita Roy and her successors for the enthu-
siastic support for this book at Manchester University Press. I am
grateful to Mike Cormack of the University of Stirling for his helpful
comments on the original proposal, and to Sean Cubitt of Liverpool
John Moores University for his careful reading of the manuscript. Lib
Taylor has lived with this book for almost as long as I have, and I
thank her for her support, encouragement and love.

Introduction

Every day we encounter and make use of a huge variety of media. Some of them fall into the category habitually referred to as 'the media', like newspapers, magazines, television, cinema or radio. All of these are obviously communications media, which make available a wide range of messages and meanings. But the term 'media' refers more widely to all those things which are channels for communicating something. If we widen the term 'media' to include anything which is used as a channel for communicating meanings, a large part of our experience of the world involves interactions with media. Walking down the street, all kinds of messages are being generated for us by, for instance, shop signs, posters, and traffic lights. Even the people passing by are generating meanings by virtue of the kind of clothes they are wearing, or their hairstyles. Meanings are being made everywhere, through a huge variety of different channels of communication, a huge variety of media. Since media in this broad sense are so important to the experience of living in society, it is clearly both useful and interesting to find a way of understanding how these media are meaningful to us.

In recent times, one of the most powerful and influential ways of thinking about media has been the approach known as semiotics (or semiology). The names semiotics and semiology derive from the ancient Greek word *sēmeion*, which means 'sign'. Semiotics or semiology is a way of analysing meanings by looking at the signs (like words, for instance, but also pictures, symbols etc.) which communicate meanings. Because society is so pervaded by media messages, semiotics can contribute to far more than our understanding of 'the media' in the narrow sense of mass-media texts like those discussed in the following pages. The power of the semiotic approach lies partly in its applicability to the much wider field of meaning-making which includes, for instance, fashion, theatre, computer games, literature and architecture. But this book has been written primarily for students of the media, for use as part of courses in Media Studies, Cultural Studies, or

Communications Studies for instance. Therefore this book deals with the semiotic approach partly by conducting critical analyses of recent material in 'the media' of advertising, magazines, newspapers, television and cinema. The analyses of these different kinds of written and audiovisual materials are used to introduce, discuss and evaluate semiotic methods, and to show how this method can be extended or challenged by other approaches.

My primary focus is on how semiotics can be used in the study of the media, because of the assumption that meanings in the media are communicated by signs, and because the question of how signs work is what semiotics is concerned with. Semiotics was first developed as a way of understanding how language works, and language is the medium which we use most often. We use language to communicate by speaking and by writing, and much of 'the media' uses language either as their primary medium of communication, or to support other media of communication like pictures, for instance. Semiotic analysis has been extended to the analysis of other non-linguistic media of communication, but chapter one takes up the initial linguistic focus of semiotics by explaining its approach to language and then to visual signs. The chapters which follow build on these foundations and explore how semiotics can be used in the study of advertising, magazines, newspapers, television, and cinema. Like every analytical method, semiotics makes use of some technical language, has drawn on insights which come from other related disciplines, and has evolved and changed over time. In this book, some of the terminology of semiotics is explained, some ideas which it has borrowed from other disciplines are discussed, and some developments of semiotics in response to new challenges and difficulties are assessed.

This book assumes no prior knowledge about semiotics. It does assume a basic familiarity with the kinds of media found in British and American culture. It will be enough to have noticed some advertisements, to have read some newspapers, read some magazines, watched some television, and been to the cinema. As I have already hinted, this book is not just an introduction to media semiotics, it is a critical introduction. Key ideas from semiotic approaches to the media are discussed in the chapters which follow, but these ideas are also tested out, modified, and their limitations explored. There is no perfect analytical method for studying the media since different theoretical approaches define their tasks, the objects they study, or the questions they ask in different ways. For instance, at one extreme it could be argued that meanings in the media can be understood by doing a very detailed analysis of media texts (like newspapers or television programmes). At the other extreme, it could be argued that meanings in the media can be understood by asking individuals how they interact with media in localised and specific ways. These two positions are oversimplified caricatures of, respectively, a very rigid kind of semiotic analysis known as structuralism, and a recently fashionable kind of research known as ethnography. Clearly, each of them takes a quite different approach to what appears to be the same issue.

This book takes a position somewhere between those two extremes. These are the five basic assumptions which underlie my approach to meanings in the media. The patterns and structures of signs in media texts condition the meanings which can be communicated and read. The signs in media texts are read in relation to other signs and other texts in a social and cultural context. Each medium has features specific to it and features which are shared with other media. Texts and media position their audiences in particular ways. Audiences understand and enjoy the media in different and diverse ways. The negotiation of meanings between media and audiences are important in establishing terms through which we understand ourselves and our culture. These assumptions form the basis of the issues which are explored and discussed in the chapters which follow, though the weight given to each of them varies. This often reflects the different emphases of academic approaches to the different media because the study of the media is not a homogeneous subject, though there are overlaps between currents of critical thinking as well as relatively discrete areas. In writing this book, I have aimed to maintain a consistent focus on semiotic analysis, while at the same time acknowledging other ways of studying the media to some extent. Some of these different academic approaches (like psychoanalytic criticism) add weight to semiotics, while others (like ethnographic research) are virtually opposed to it.

There are alternative ways in which this book could have been organised, around theoretical issues for instance, or by following the history of developments in a particular field of study. I have chosen the present structure because it seems the clearest for a teaching and learning context. The order and emphases of each chapter should enable the reader to gain an understanding of critical discourses developed in semiotics for each medium and to pick up the common conceptual strands which link the study of these media together. In a similar way, challenges to semiotics are gradually posed as the book proceeds, and exemplified in relation to particular examples and cases in the various media which my chapters discuss. Each chapter has a section at the end called *Sources and further reading*, which notes important and accessible works for the reader who wishes to follow up both semiotic studies of the relevant medium and also cites some works which are critical of semiotics. For greater clarity and ease of use, I have collected the majority of references together in these sections, rather than citing a mass of books in the text itself. A section called *Suggestions for further work* also appears at the end of each chapter, with seven tasks and questions which encourage readers actively to make use of semiotics and other approaches to the media which are relevant to the issues raised in the chapter.

1

Signs and myths

The semiotic point of view

Semiotics originates mainly in the work of two men, Ferdinand de Saussure, and Charles Peirce. Their ideas are quite closely related, but exhibit some differences, so I am going to explain some of their major insights separately in this chapter, and then indicate the kind of synthesis between them which is referred to as simply 'semiotics' in this book. Saussure was an academic who taught linguistics at the University of Geneva in the early years of this century. His *Course in General Linguistics* (1974) was published in French in 1915, three years after his death. Saussure's book is a reconstruction of a series of lectures that he gave on language, assembled from the notes taken by his students and jottings discovered by his colleagues. The book explains his ground-breaking view of language, and was a major contribution to the discipline of linguistics. But Saussure viewed linguistics as only one part (though a privileged part) of a much broader science which he predicted would one day exist, a science which he called semiology. Saussure believed that language is made up of signs (like words) which communicate meanings, and that all kinds of other things which communicate meanings could potentially be studied in the same way as linguistic signs.

Semiotics or semiology, then, is the study of signs in society, and while the study of linguistic signs is one branch of it, it encompasses every use of a system where something (the sign) carries a meaning for someone. Much of this book is concerned with the semiotic analysis of language, but much of it is also concerned with non-linguistic things (like photographs, for instance) which carry meanings for someone. The same semiotic approach

Not just language

can be used to discuss language-based media and image-based media, because in either case we find signs which carry meanings. Since language is the most fundamental and pervasive medium for human communication, semiotics takes the way that language works as the model for all other media of communication, all other sign systems. That is the way in which this book proceeds; explaining some of semiotics's insights into how language works, and expanding this semiotic method to other media in society.

It is usual to assume that words and other kinds of sign are secondary to our perception and understanding of reality. It seems that reality is out there all around us, and language usefully names real things and the relationships between them. By contrast, Saussure proposed that our perception and understanding of reality is constructed by the words and other signs which we use in a social context. This is a very surprising and revolutionary argument, because it implies that signs shape our perceptions, rather than reflecting a reality which was already out there. From this point of view, words are not labels which are attached to things that already exist in a pre-given 'natural' state. Nor are they labels attached to ideas which already existed in the human mind before language came along. Instead, Saussure showed that language and the other communication systems which we collectively use, provide the conceptual framework in and through which reality is available to us. This reverses the common-sense view that reality exists before language gives words to it. Instead, the language system we use creates our concepts of reality. We cannot think or speak about something for which there are no words in our language.

At the same time as language and sign systems shape our reality, they also provide the means for communicating about this reality. A system of signs which works in this way has to be thought of as a medium in a more extended sense than the way that a medium is conventionally thought of. A medium is conventionally something which acts as a channel, passing something from one place to another. But if language and other sign systems are not simply channels, if they give form and meaning to thought or experience instead of just naming what was already there, then there is nothing which exists before signs and

media communicate thought and experience. Rather than thinking of signs and media as channels which translate pre-existing
thought and reality into communicable form, signs and media
are the only means of access to thought or reality which we
have.

This is one reason why Saussure's work is so important.
Although Saussure never made this leap, his semiotic method,
showing how we are surrounded by and shaped by sign systems,
leads to the realisation that consciousness and experience are
built out of language and the other sign systems circulating in
society that have existed before we take them up and use them.
Language was already there before we were born, and all of our
lives are lived through the signs which language gives us to
think, speak and write with. All of our thought and experience,
our very sense of our own identity, depends on the systems of
signs already existing in society which give form and meaning to
consciousness and reality. We tend to think of ourselves as individuals, whole beings who are not divided, and who are the
unique subjects of our own life experience. But semiotics shows
that this impression is created by the language which gives us
the word 'I' to refer uniquely to ourselves, and gives us the words
which divide up our reality in particular ways.

We shall be returning to these complex ideas about the self
and reality later in this book, and testing them out in relation to
some concrete examples. But perhaps it is already evident at this
stage that thinking about signs, media and meaning in semiotic
terms will have large implications for the ways in which the self,
identity, reality and society are understood. Before getting too
carried away by the general thrust of these ideas, we need to be
specific about how Saussure's view of language works. In doing
this, some of the recurring semiotic terminology used later in this
book can be explained, and we can also move from thinking
mainly about language to considering visual signs with the help
of some ideas developed by the American philosopher, Charles
Peirce.

Sign systems

Saussure's first move was to set limits to the variety of tasks

which his study of language might involve. Instead of considering language from a psychological, sociological, or physiological
point of view, he decided to focus on a clearly defined object of
study: the linguistic sign. He showed that the linguistic sign is
arbitrary. The linguistic sign 'cat' is arbitrary in that it has no
connection either in its sound, or its visual shape, with what cats
are really like. In another language, the sign for cat will be different from the linguistic sign in English (e.g. French uses *chat*).
Clearly, there must be a kind of agreement among the users of
our language that the sign 'cat' shall refer to a particular group
of furry four-legged animals. But this agreement about signs is
not consciously entered into, since we learn how to use language
so early in our lives that there can be no deliberate choice available to us. Language has always been there before we arrived on
the scene. Even if I perversely decided to adopt another sign for
what we call a cat, like 'yorup' for instance, this sign would be
entirely useless since no-one else would understand me. The
capacity of linguistic signs to be meaningful depends on their
existence in a social context, and on their conventionally
accepted use in that social context.

Each linguistic sign has a place in the whole system of language (in Saussure's original French, *langue*), and any example
of actual speech or writing (in French, *parole*) uses some particular elements from the system. This distinction is the same as
that between, for instance, the system of rules and conventions
called chess, and the particular moves made in an actual game
of chess. Each individual move in chess is selected from the whole
system of possible chess moves. So we could call the system of
possible chess moves the *langue* of chess. Any individual move in
a game of chess would be *parole*, the selection of a move from the
whole set of possible moves allowed in the *langue* of chess.

The same distinction can be made about language. In English,
there is a huge range of meaningful utterances which a speaker
(or writer) can make. In order for an utterance to be meaningful, it has to conform to the system of rules in the English language. The whole system of rules governing which utterances
are possible is the *langue* of English, and any utterance that is
actually made is an example of *parole*. *Langue* is the structure of
rules which can be partially glimpsed in any concrete example of

parole. The linguistic signs of *parole* are only meaningful if they are used in accordance with the rules of *langue*. The first two important ideas from Saussure then are that first, linguistic signs are arbitrary and agreed by convention, and second that language is a system governed by rules, where each instance of speech or writing involves selecting signs and using them according to these rules.

Every sign in *langue* acquires its value by virtue of its difference from all the other signs in *langue*, the language system. We recognise the sign 'cat' by its difference from 'bat' or 'cap' or 'cot' or 'top'. Saussure described language as a system which has no positive terms, and by this he meant that signs have no special right to mean something in particular and not something else. Instead, signs acquire their potential meaningfulness by contrasting themselves with what they are not. 'Cat' is not 'bat' or 'cot'. So language is a system of differences between one sign and all others, where the difference between one sign and the others allows distinctions of meaning to be made. At any point in time it is the difference of one sign from all other existing signs which allows that sign to work. So no sign can have meaning except inasmuch as it is differentiated from the other signs in *langue*. 'Cat' works as a sign by being different from 'bat', rather than by any internal property of the sign 'cat' itself.

Written or spoken languages are only one example of what Saussure believed to be the feature which characterises the human animal: that we make use of structures of signs which communicate meanings for us. Just as language can be investigated to discover how *langue* is structured as a system, allowing us to communicate with linguistic signs, the same kind of investigation can be carried out on any medium in which meanings are generated by a system of signs. Linguistics shows the way in which semiotics will operate, seeking to understand the system of *langue* which underlies all the particular instances of *parole* in which this signifying system is used. Semioticians search for the systems which underlie the ability of signs like words, images, items of clothing, foods, cars, or whatever to carry certain meanings in society.

The systems in which signs are organised into groups are called codes. This is a familiar term, for instance in the phrase

'dress codes'. In our society, the dress code which governs what
men should wear when going to a formal wedding includes items
like a top hat and a tail jacket. These items of clothing are signs
which can be selected from the almost infinite *langue* of male
clothing, from the code of male formal dress, and they communicate a coded message of 'formality'. By contrast, a man might
select jogging shorts, training shoes and a baseball cap to go to
the local gym. These clothing signs belong to a different dress
code, and communicate a message of 'informality'. In the case of
dress codes, it is possible to select the clothing signs which we
use in order to communicate particular messages about ourselves. Even when clothes perform practical functions (like the
loose and light clothes worn to play sports) codes still give social
meanings to our choices, like codes of fashionableness and codes
governing what men may wear versus what women may wear.
In the same way, there are linguistic codes within the whole
system of *langue*, which divide language up just as clothes are
divided up into coded sets of signs. There are linguistic codes
appropriate for talking to babies, talking to royalty, writing job
applications, or writing love poems.

The message conveyed by linguistic signs often has much to
do with how they can be used as part of coded ways of speaking
or writing. Similarly, a television sequence of a newsreader
behind a desk is a message which gains its authority by drawing
on recognisable codes, while different codes constrain the way
we might interpret a sequence showing cowboys shooting at
each other on the main street of a western town. As we begin to
address different kinds of sign in different media, the concept of
a code becomes very useful in dividing signs into groups, and
working out how the meaning of signs depends on their membership of codes. Individual linguistic signs become meaningful
because of their difference from all other linguistic signs. But the
significance of individual signs often depends on which code
groupings they belong to: our understanding of a sign often
depends on recognising that it belongs to a code which has particular meaning for us.

Components of the sign

Saussure drew a distinction between the evolution of linguistic signs through time, called 'diachronic' linguistics, and the study of signs existing at a given point in time, called 'synchronic' linguistics. From a diachronic point of view, we might investigate the way that a particular sign like 'thou' used to be used in ordinary language but is now used only in religious contexts. But from a synchronic point of view, it is the place of 'thou' in our own historical moment that is of interest, not how it has gained its current role in our language. The linguists who preceded Saussure had concentrated on diachrony, the development of language over time, and Saussure argued that this approach was useless for giving us an understanding of how language works for the people who actually use it. For a community of language users, it is the system and structure of the current language, *langue*, which makes articulation meaningful, and not the history of how signs have come to take the form they have now. His emphasis on synchrony enabled him to show how signs work as part of a structure that is in place at a given point in time. The same emphasis on synchronic analysis works for any other communication method where signs contrast one with another. For instance, denim jeans used to be work-clothes, and were clothing signs in a code of clothes for manual labour. Today, jeans are a sign whose meaning is 'casual style' or 'youthfulness', signs belonging to a style code of everyday dress in contrast to suit trousers, which signify 'formality' and belong to a different dress code. The coded meaning of jeans depends much more on their relationship with, and difference from, other coded signs in the clothing system today, rather than their meaning depending on the history of jeans. Synchronic analysis reveals more about the contemporary meaning of jeans than diachronic analysis.

In his analysis of linguistic signs, Saussure showed that there are two components to every sign. One is the vehicle which expresses the sign, like a pattern of sound which makes up a word, or the marks on paper which we read as words, or the pattern of shapes and colours which photographs use to represent an object or person. This vehicle which exists in the material world is called the 'signifier'. The other part of the sign is called the 'signified'. The signified is the concept which the signifier calls forth when we perceive it. So when you perceive the sign 'cat' written on this page, you perceive a group of marks, the letters 'c', 'a', and 't', which are the signifier. This signifier is the vehicle which immediately calls up the signified or concept of cat in your mind. The sign is the inseparable unity of the signifier with the signified, since in fact we never have one without the other.

This stage of the explanation of the sign says nothing about any real cat out there in reality: the sign 'cat' is made up of two entities, signifier and signified, which are joined together in the minds of language users. The sign 'cat' does not refer to any particular cat, but to a mental concept. It is perfectly possible to use a sign, like 'God' which does not relate to any observable thing out there in the real world. Many linguistic signs, like nouns, clearly relate to actual things, like cats, which could be observed in reality. The actual things which signs refer to are called 'referents', so the referent of the sign 'cat' which I speak when talking to my own cat has my particular cat as its referent. If I write a note to my neighbours when I leave for a holiday, saying 'Please feed cat', it is clear from the context that my cat is the referent of the sign, but the sign 'cat' could refer to any cat. And just as the English language arbitrarily connects the signifier 'c', 'a', 't' with the signified 'cat' in our minds, so too the language arbitrarily connects the whole sign 'cat' with a particular sort of living creature, the real cats which can be referents of this sign.

Once Saussure had divided the sign into signifier and signified, it became possible to describe how language divides up the world of thought, creating the concepts which shape our actual experience. This can be illustrated by a simple comparison between signs in different languages. In English, the signifier 'sheep' is joined to a particular signified, the concept of a certain type of animal, and the signifier 'mutton' is joined to the signified of the meat of this animal. In French, the signifier *mouton* draws no distinction between the signified animal and its meat. So the meaning of 'mutton' in English is sustained only by its difference from 'sheep'. Meaning is only generated by the relationships between signifiers, and the signified is shaped by the signifier (not the other way around). The signifieds or concepts in our minds are shaped by the signifiers that our language provides for us to think and talk with. In English we have only one signifier for the signified colour white, so the signified concept of whiteness is indivisible, one single thing. But we can conceive of a language where there are several words subdividing whiteness into several distinct colours. For speakers of such a language our signified white would not be one colour but several different and separate colours, just as for us, redness is divided into the distinctly different colours scarlet, crimson, vermilion, etc. The systems which structure our language also shape our experience of reality, as indicated at the beginning of this chapter. This surprising reversal of common-sense comes logically from Saussure's thinking about the components of the linguistic sign.

Sequences of linguistic signs

One of the distinctions between linguistic signs and other kinds of sign is that language is always dependent on time. In a written or spoken articulation, one sign must come before the next, and the articulation is spread out over time. In photographs, paintings, or an outfit of clothes, each sign is present at the same time as the others: the signs are distributed across space rather than time. In film or television for example, both space and time are involved, since the shapes on the screen are next to other shapes in the same space, while the image changes over time as the film progresses.

When signs are spread out in a sequence over time, or have an order in their spatial arrangement, their order is obviously important. In a sentence like 'The dog bites the man', meaning unfolds from left to right along the line of the sentence, as we read the words in sequence one after another. This horizontal movement is called the 'syntagmatic' aspect of the sentence. If we reverse the order into 'The man bites the dog', the meaning is obviously different. Each linguistic sign in the syntagm could also be replaced by another sign which is related to it, having perhaps the same grammatical function, a similar sound, or relating to a similar signified. These sets of related signs are called 'paradigms'. We could replace 'dog' with 'cat' or 'beast', and replace 'bites' with 'fights' or 'kicks' or 'chews'. Each different selection from these paradigms would alter the meaning of the syntagm.

So an important aspect of how language makes meaning must be that each linguistic sign is surrounded by paradigms of associated signs that are not present. Explaining the meaning of an instance of *parole* must involve noting the way that the syntagmatic ordering of signs affects meaning, and the way that the signs not selected from a particular paradigm shape the meaning of the sign that has been selected. As a general principle, every sign that is present must be considered in relation to other signs present in the structure of the articulation, and every sign present has meaning by virtue of the other signs which have been excluded and are not present in the text.

Visual signs

Most of the account of linguistic signs above comes directly from Saussure, but some of the principles and terms which we shall need in the chapters that follow derive from the semiotic work of the American philosopher Charles S. Peirce (1958). In particular, the semiotic analysis of images and other non-verbal signs is made much more effective by some of Peirce's distinctions. Although language is the most striking form of human sign production, the whole of our social world is pervaded by messages which contain visual as well as linguistic signs, or which are exclusively visual. Gestures, dress codes, traffic signs, advertising images, newspapers, television programmes and so on are all kinds of media which use visual signs. The same principles underlie the semiotic study of visual signs and linguistic signs. In each case, there is a material signifier, which expresses the sign, and a mental concept, a signified, which immediately accompanies it. Visual signs also belong to codes, are arranged in syntagms, and selected from paradigms. In the last few pages, I have used some examples of visual signs along with linguistic ones, to suggest that they can be approached in similar ways.

We have already seen how linguistic signs are arbitrary, since there is no necessary connection between the signifier 'cat' on this page and the signified concept of cat in our minds, and nor is there any connection except a conventional one for English speakers between the whole sign 'cat' and its referent, the kind of furry four-legged animal which is sitting next to my desk. The relationship of signifier to signified, and of sign to referent, is entirely a matter of the conventions established by *langue* in general, and in this case by the English language in particular. This type of sign, characterised by arbitrariness, Peirce calls the 'symbolic' sign.

But a photograph of a cat looks recognisably like a specific cat. The arrangement of shape and colour in the photograph, the signifier which expresses the signified 'cat', has a close resemblance to its referent, the real cat which the photograph represents. In a photograph, the signifier is the colour and shape on the flat surface of the picture. The signified is the concept of a cat which this signifier immediately calls up. The referent is the cat which was photographed. Just as my cat is white with some black and orange patches, so a photograph of my cat will faithfully record these different shapes and colours. This kind of sign, where the signifier resembles the referent, Peirce calls an 'iconic' sign. We shall encounter iconic signs in our exploration of the semiotics of various visual media. Unlike the case of linguistic signs, iconic signs have the property of merging the signifier, signified and referent together. It is much more difficult to realise that the two components of the photographic sign plus their referent are three different things. It is for this reason that photographic media seem to be more realistic than linguistic media, and we shall be exploring this issue in greater depth later.

When a cat is hungry and miaows to gain our attention, the sound it makes is a way of pointing out its presence, asking us to notice it, and Peirce called this kind of sign 'indexical'. Indexical signs have a concrete and often causal relationship to their signified. The shadow cast on a sundial tells us the time, it is an indexical sign which is directly caused by the position of the sun, and similarly smoke is an index of fire, a sign caused by the thing which it signifies. Certain signs have mixed symbolic, indexical and iconic features. For instance, a traffic light showing red has both indexical and symbolic components. It is an indexical sign pointing to a traffic situation (that cars here must wait), and using an arbitrary symbolic system to do this (red arbitrarily signifies danger and prohibition in this context).

Connotation and myth

The rest of this chapter deals with semiotic ideas which are found
in the work of the French critic Roland Barthes. His ideas build
on the foundations outlined so far, and take us closer to the semiotic analysis of contemporary media. Because we use signs to
describe and interpret the world, it often seems that their function
is simply to 'denote' something, to label it. The linguistic sign
'Rolls-Royce' denotes a particular make of car, or a photographic
sign showing Buckingham Palace denotes a building in London.
But along with the denotative, or labelling function of these signs
to communicate a fact, come some extra associations which are
called 'connotations'. Because Rolls-Royce cars are expensive and
luxurious, they can be used to connote notions of wealth and
luxury. The linguistic sign 'Rolls-Royce' is no longer simply denoting a particular type of car, but generating a whole set of connotations which come from our social experience. The photograph
of Buckingham Palace not only denotes a particular building, but
also connotes notions of royalty, tradition, wealth and power.
     When we consider advertising, news, and TV or film texts, it
will become clear that linguistic, visual, and other kinds of sign
are used not simply to denote something, but also to trigger a
range of connotations attached to the sign. Barthes calls this
social phenomenon, the bringing together of signs and their connotations to shape a particular message, the making of 'myth'.
Myth here does not refer to mythology in the usual sense of traditional stories, but to ways of thinking about people, products,
places, or ideas which are structured to send particular messages
to the reader or viewer of the text. So an advertisement for shoes
which contains a photograph of someone stepping out of a Rolls-
Royce is not only denoting the shoes and a car, but attaching the
connotations of luxury which are available through the sign
'Rolls-Royce' to the shoes, suggesting a mythic meaning in
which the shoes are part of a privileged way of life.
     Myth takes hold of an existing sign, and makes it function as
a signifier on another level. The sign 'Rolls-Royce' becomes the
signifier attached to the signified 'luxury'. It is as if myth were a
special form of language, which takes up an existing sign system
and makes a new sign system out of it. As we shall see, myth is

not an innocent language, but one that picks up existing signs and their connotations, and orders them purposefully to play a particular social role.

Wrestling and *Julius Caesar*

In 1957 the French lecturer and critic Roland Barthes published a book called *Mythologies* (1973). It consisted of short essays, previously published in French magazines, which dealt with a wide variety of cultural phenomena, from wrestling matches to Greta Garbo, from Citroën's latest car to steak and chips. These essays on aspects of contemporary French culture sought to look beyond the surface appearance of the object or practice which they discussed, and to decode its real significance as the bearer of particular meanings. What Barthes did was to read social life, with the same close attention and critical force that had previously been evident only in the study of 'high art', like literature, painting or classical music. *Mythologies* uses semiotics as the predominant means of analysing aspects of everyday culture.

The book concluded with an essay called 'Myth Today', which drew together the implications of the semiotic method Barthes was using in his short essays, and showed why his reading of social life was significant. *Mythologies* had a huge impact in France, and later in the English-speaking world, and opened up everyday popular culture to serious study. This section is devoted to the discussion of two of the short essays in *Mythologies*, and more fully discusses the essay 'Myth Today' which provides a general framework for the study of popular culture. Many of the analytical methods and critical concepts in 'Myth Today' recur in later chapters of this book.

The first essay in *Mythologies* is 'The World of Wrestling'. Barthes discusses the meaning of the rather seedy wrestling matches which at that time took place in small auditoria around Paris. Something fairly similar can be seen today in the televised WWF wrestling from the United States, where exotically-named and colourfully-clad wrestlers perform very theatrically. The modern television form of this type of wrestling is much more glossy and widely marketed than the backstreet entertainment Barthes discusses, however. Who wins and who loses in these

wrestling contests is insignificant compared to the excessive pos-
turing and the dramatic incidents which are displayed in the
bouts and in the stadium by the wrestlers. This form of wrestling
is not only popular enough to be televised recently, but has also
given rise to spin-off products: a TV cartoon featuring star
wrestlers, toy action figures, T-shirts and other clothing, and
computer games. Clearly, something about this theatrical
wrestling spectacle has been significant and popular, in 1950s
Paris and in Britain, and in the United States today.

Barthes describes wrestling as a theatrical spectacle rather
than a sport. The spectators, he finds, are interested primarily in
the powerful emotions which the wrestlers simulate. These can
be clearly read in their gesture, expression and movement, which
are so many coded signs signifying inner passions. Wrestling
becomes a kind of melodrama, a drama using exaggerated physical signs, and is characterised by an emphasis on emotion and
questions of morality. Here Barthes describes some of the physical signs made by the wrestlers, and it is easy to read their connotations, since they belong to a very clear code:

> Sometimes the wrestler triumphs with a repulsive sneer while
> kneeling on the good sportsman; sometimes he gives the crowd a
> conceited smile which forebodes an early revenge; sometimes,
> pinned to the ground, he hits the floor ostentatiously to make evi-
> dent to all the intolerable nature of his situation. (1973: 18)

For Barthes, wrestling is like ritual, pantomime, or Greek
tragedy, where what is important is to see some struggle being
played out by actors who do not represent realistic individual
characters, but ideas or moral positions. The 'bad-guy' wrestler,
the 'bastard' as Barthes calls him (1973: 17), appears to fight
cruelly and unfairly, but is pursued by his opponent despite the
bastard's attempt to hide behind the ropes of the wrestling ring,
and is deservedly punished. The spectators enjoy both the outra-
geous cheating and cruelty of the bastard, and also the eventual
punishment of the bastard by the good-guy wrestler. All of this
drama is communicated by the physical signs made by the
wrestlers, and these signs belong to a code which is familiar to
the audience. The audience's pleasure comes from reading and
enjoying the wrestlers' coded signs.

Whether the good wrestler wins or not, the bout will have made Good and Evil easily readable through the medium of the coded signs the wrestlers use to communicate their roles and their emotions to the crowd. Grins, sneers, gestures and ways of moving, etc. are all indexical signs which connote triumph, revenge, innocence, viciousness or some other meaning. A grin would be an index of triumph, hitting the floor an index of submission in defeat, for instance. The wrestlers combine these signs together in syntagms and exaggerate them, so that there can be no doubt about how to read their connotations. The wrestling bout is much more like a pantomime than a fight, because highly coded signs are being presented for the enjoyment of the audience. Barthes's conclusion is that wrestling makes our confusing and ambiguous world intelligible, giving clearly readable meanings to the struggle between moral positions represented by the wrestlers. Wrestling for Barthes is a system of coded signs, a visual spectacle in which a highly theatrical and controlled version of reality is presented to us without ambiguity. Once we look beyond the surface of wrestling, where it can appear to be a rather silly and pointless spectacle, we find that wrestling is a way of communicating about morality and justice, transgression and punishment, through signs which belong to a code. Wrestling is a medium which speaks about our culture in a highly codified (and entertaining) form.

The second example of Barthes's project in *Mythologies* brings his work closer to the focus of this book: signs in the mass media. The second short essay in the volume is 'Romans in Films', and refers to the 1952 film *Julius Caesar*, based on Shakespeare's play and starring Marlon Brando. Once again Barthes produces a surprisingly analytical discussion of something apparently undeserving of serious study. The essay is not only about a Hollywood film (rather than an 'art' film, for instance), but it also focuses on only two details of the film: the haircuts of the actors, and the fact that almost everyone sweats in the film. Barthes considers these two details as symptoms of how the film adopts coded signs whose connotations communicate the film's underlying themes. The images of people on the screen are iconic signs, resembling the actors. The images of the film belong to a syntagm, the film narrative which unfolds through time from the beginning to the end.

In *Julius Caesar*, Barthes notes, 'all the characters are wearing fringes', and none of them are bald (1973: 26). This particular hairstyle works as a sign, whose connotation is 'Roman-ness'. Despite the American accents of the actors, and the fact that the film is based on a play written in the Renaissance, this hair sign enables the actors to persuade us of the consistency and believability of the classical setting. 'Romans are Romans thanks to the most legible of signs: hair on the forehead' (1973: 26). The film's impression of authenticity is conveyed in part, Barthes suggests, by this coded way of representing Roman-ness, so that the sign appears natural and intelligible, perhaps not even noticeable. The point is not whether Romans really had fringes or not. Rather, the hairstyle is a conventional sign belonging to a code of Roman-ness which the film uses, and which is both recognisable and consistent.

The soldiers, the labourers and the conspirators against Caesar all sweat in the film. Barthes argues that this is also a sign. 'Everyone is sweating because everyone is debating something within himself' (1973: 27). The sweat is therefore an indexical sign of moral feeling, the struggle in the minds of the characters about what they should do. This internal struggle apparently makes the characters sweat, and we read the sweat as an indexical sign of moral struggle. The only man who does not sweat is Julius Caesar himself, and Barthes argues that this is because he is the object of the conspiracy. Caesar does not have a moral dilemma in the same way as Brutus and the others who are plotting to kill Caesar. Sweating, like hairstyle, appears to be 'natural' in the film, perhaps scarcely noticeable, but it is a sign used in a meaningful way to signify that the film narrative is presenting a tragic psychological drama. Like hairstyle, this use of sweat as a sign depends on its belonging to a code recognised in our culture. Sweating and having fringes are coded signs whose connotations enable us to read the meaning of the film.

As a general conclusion at the end of 'The Romans in Films', Barthes criticises this kind of use of signs. Hairstyle and sweating are not foregrounded, made clear to the viewer as being coded signs (unlike the self-conscious display by the wrestlers). Barthes shows that these signs can be seen as a coherent and meaningful system once they are closely investigated, but a straightforward viewing of the film would be unlikely to pick them out. Watching wrestling is pleasurable largely because of the audience's knowledge of the codes which are being used, and the way that the wrestlers exaggerate their signifying actions, making the codes they use evident. The coded signs in *Julius Caesar* are not made evident in this way. In the film, the sign 'remains on the surface, yet does not for all that give up the attempt to pass itself off as depth. It aims at making people understand (which is laudable) but at the same time suggests that it is spontaneous (which is cheating)' (1973: 28). These signs conceal the fact that they are part of a conventional code for representing Roman-ness, even though they are a crucial part of the film's meaningfulness.

Myth and social meanings

Having looked briefly at two of Barthes's short essays in *Mythologies*, the rest of this section explains and discusses the longer essay which concludes the volume, 'Myth Today'. In it, Barthes draws together some of the more general critical points which his analyses of cultural products have led him to, and explains a coherent method for going on to study more aspects of social life. Many of the methods used, and issues addressed, in 'Myth Today' will appear in the following chapters of this book, though they will often require some development or criticism when they are applied to the different media covered there.

At the beginning of 'Myth Today', Barthes declares that 'myth is a type of speech' (1973: 109). We saw above that wrestling can be regarded as a medium in which messages about morality and behaviour are communicated though a theatrical type of entertainment. The moves, gestures and expressions in wrestling are a form of coded communication through signs, used self-consciously by the wrestlers. Wrestling, as it were, speaks to us about our reality. On one level, the wrestlers' gestures signify 'defeat' or 'helplessness'. They are signs for emotional or moral attitudes. But on another level, more abstractly, the whole wrestling match is itself a sign. It represents a moral terrain in which there is a crude and 'natural' form of justice. The 'bastard' is made to pay for his cheating and cruelty, and the match shows the spectators an exciting yet ordered world, compensating for the ordinariness and disorder of reality. The wrestling match makes this 'natural' world intelligible by putting it on stage in the artificial form of the match itself.

But is this moral world natural, common-sense, unchangeable? It is not, Barthes argues, and instead the wrestling-match, with its moral structures and positions represented by the wrestlers, merely makes it seem as if it were natural. Wrestling, and morality, are both products of a specific culture (west European pseudo-Christian culture). They are both tied to a certain historical period, and to a particular way of organising society in a particular place. The meanings of wrestling are not natural but cultural, not given but produced, not discovered but worked for, not real but mythical. In the same way, the Romans in *Julius Caesar* are made intelligible to the audience by a set of conventional signs, whose aim is to produce a myth of Roman-ness, a historical and psychological realism based not on reality but on convention. Myth, as Barthes uses the term, means things used as signs to communicate a social and political message about the world. The message always involves the distortion or forgetting of alternative messages, so that myth appears to be exclusively true, rather than one of a number of different possible messages.

The study of these myths, mythology, is part of the 'vast science of signs' which Saussure predicted, and called 'semiology' (or semiotics) (Barthes 1973: 111). Reading the messages in myth involves identifying the signs which it uses, and showing how they are built by means of codes into a structure which communicates particular messages and not others. This can be explained by discussing the main example Barthes uses in 'Myth Today'. Barthes imagines himself at the barber's, looking at the cover of an edition of the French glossy magazine *Paris-Match*. On the cover is a photograph of a black soldier in uniform, who is saluting the French flag. The signifiers, the shapes and colours in the photograph, can be easily read as meaningful iconic signs, which communicate the message 'a black soldier is giving the French salute'. But the picture has a greater signification, which goes beyond what it denotes. The picture signifies that

> France is a great empire, that all her sons, without any colour discrimination, faithfully serve under her flag, and that there is

no better answer to the detractors of an alleged colonialism than the zeal shown by this Negro in serving his so-called oppressors. (Barthes 1973: 116)

A set of iconic signs which already possess a meaning ('a black soldier is giving the French salute') becomes the basis for the imposition of an important social message, that French imperial rule is fair and egalitarian. This social message is myth, and a controversial one when Barthes wrote the essay in the 1950s. France's empire was disintegrating, and there was brutal military conflict in France's North African colony of Algeria where Algerians fought and campaigned for independence. The crisis was the main political issue in France, and extensively debated in the media. The mythic signification of the picture on *Paris-Match*'s cover argues in favour of colonial control, without appearing to do so.

The myths which are generated in a culture will change over time, and can only acquire their force because they relate to a certain context. In myth, the context and history of the signs are narrowed down and contained so that only a few features of their context and history have a signifying function. Where the photograph was taken, the name and life experience of the soldier, who it was that took the photograph, are all historical and contextual issues which are irrelevant and neglected once the photographic sign is used as the signifier to promote the myth of French imperialism. Instead, the mythic signification invokes other concepts, like the history of France as a colonial power, the contemporary conflict over Algeria, and issues of racial discrimination. What myth does is to hollow out the signs it uses, leaving only part of their meaning, and to invest them with a new signification which directs us to read them in one way and no other. The photograph of the black soldier saluting makes the reader aware of the issue of French colonialism, and asks him or her to take it for granted that black soldiers should be loyal to the French flag, that colonial rule is perfectly reasonable.

This is not the only way to read the mythic image of the soldier, though it is the reading which appears most 'natural'. Barthes suggests three ways of reading the photograph. First, the photograph could be seen as one of a potentially infinite number of possible images which support the myth of French imperialism. The black soldier is just one example of French imperialism in this case. Thinking of the image in this way, Barthes suggests, is how a journalist would think of it. Seeking to present a certain mythic signification on the cover of the magazine, the journalist would look for a suitable photograph which gives a concrete form to this abstract concept, and creates the mythic signification.

Alternatively, a mythologist like Barthes himself, or someone using the semiotic methods discussed here, would 'see through' the myth. This critical reader would note the way that the black soldier has had his meaning emptied out of the photograph, except that he is an alibi, a justification, for the mythic signification. The rightness and naturalness of France's colonial power is the dominant signification of the photograph, but one which the semiologist is able to explain and unmask. The myth of French imperialism has been imposed on the photograph, but the mythologist is able to separate the photograph from the myth, the sign from the signification, to undo the effect which the myth aims to produce. The mythologist 'deciphers the myth, he understands a distortion' (Barthes 1973: 128).

Thirdly, an uncritical reader noticing the cover of *Paris-Match* but not analysing it, would simply receive the mythic signification as an unremarkable and natural fact. The photographic sign would seem to just show France's imperialism (translated, confusingly, as 'imperiality') as a natural state of affairs, hardly worth commenting on. The black soldier saluting would seem to be 'the very presence of French imperiality' (Barthes 1973: 128). The photograph in this case is neither an example chosen to illustrate a point, nor a distortion trying to impose itself on us. Instead, 'everything happens as if the picture naturally conjured up the concept, as if the signifier gave a foundation to the signified: the myth exists from the precise moment when French imperiality achieves the natural state' (Barthes 1973: 129–130). For Barthes, the function of myth is to make particular ideas, like France's colonial rule of other countries, seem natural. If these ideas seem natural, they will not be resisted or fought against. Myth makes particular social meanings acceptable as the common-sense truth about the world. The function of the criticism and analysis of myth must then be to remove the impression of naturalness by showing how the myth is constructed, and showing that it promotes one way of thinking while seeking to eliminate all the alternative ways of thinking.

Myth and ideology

The analysis of myth to reveal its selectiveness and distortion is obviously political in the broadest sense. Every political view, even if it does not acknowledge the fact, is a representation of an existing state of affairs which implies that changes of certain kind, with a certain purpose, should be made. In Barthes's work, and in the work of many semiotic critics, the analysis of culture and society is carried out from a left-wing perspective, and often closely tied to Marxist ideas. In 'Myth Today', the later sections of the essay take up the methods of semiotic analysis which have been discussed so far, and relate them to a general political analysis of society. The key concept in this analysis is 'ideology', which will be discussed further in subsequent chapters of this book as it relates to the study of the media. An ideology is a way of perceiving reality and society which assumes that some ideas are self-evidently true, while other ideas are self-evidently biased or untrue. Ideologies are always shared by the members of a group or groups in society, and one group's ideology will always conflict with another's. Some of the arguments about ideology which are advanced by Barthes and others will be subject to criticism later as we investigate their usefulness in relation to concrete examples of contemporary media texts. In particular, I shall argue that an ideology is not necessarily a false consciousness of reality. But first, it is important to see how Barthes's analysis of myth is connected to the concept of ideology.

Barthes proposes that myth serves the ideological interests of a particular group in society, which he terms 'the bourgeoisie' (1973: 137). This term refers to the class of people who own or control the industrial, commercial, and political institutions of the society. It is in the interests of this class to maintain the stability of society, in order that their ownership, power and control can remain unchanged and unchallenged. Therefore, the current ways of thinking about all kinds of questions and issues, which

allow the current state of economic and political affairs to continue unchallenged, need to be perpetuated. Although the existing state of society might sometimes be maintained by force, it is
most effective and convenient to maintain it by eliminating oppositional and alternative ways of thinking. The way that this is
done is by making the current system of beliefs about society, the
'dominant ideology', seem natural, common-sense and self-evident.

The dominant ideology of a society is subject to change as the
economic and political balance of power changes. Ideology then,
is a historically contingent thing. If we look back, say, two hundred years, some features of the dominant ideology have obviously changed. Two hundred years ago, it would have been
'self-evident' that black people were inferior to whites, that
women were weaker than and inferior to men, that children
could be employed to do manual labour. These ideas were made
to seem natural, common-sense. Today, each of these ideological
views has been displaced. The ideology of today is different, but
not necessarily any less unjust. However, it would by definition
be difficult to perceive that current ideologies need to be changed,
since the function of ideology is to make the existing system
appear natural and acceptable to us all. Myth, for Barthes, is a
type of speech about social realities which supports ideology by
taking these realities outside of the arena of political debate.

> In the case of the soldier-Negro, for example, what is got rid of is
> certainly not French imperiality (on the contrary, since what
> must be actualised is its presence); it is the contingent, historical,
> in one word: fabricated, quality of colonialism. Myth does not
> deny things, on the contrary, its function is to talk about them;
> simply, it purifies them, it makes them innocent, it gives them a
> natural and eternal justification, it gives them a clarity which is
> not that of explanation but that of a statement of fact. If I state
> the fact of French imperiality without explaining it, I am very
> near to finding that it is natural and goes without saying: I am
> reassured. (Barthes 1973: 143)

The function of the photograph of the black soldier saluting the
flag is to make French imperialism ('imperiality' in the quotation)
seem like a neutral fact. It discourages us from asking questions
or raising objections to colonialism. It serves the interests of a

dominant ideology. The way that it is able to do this is by functioning as myth, presenting a historically specific situation as a natural and unremarkable one. Today, nearly thirty years after Barthes published *Mythologies*, colonial rule is regarded by most people as an outdated and embarrassing episode in European history. It is much easier to see how myths like French imperialism are constructed once they become distanced from the prevailing ideology. When analysing contemporary examples of myth in the media, the task of the mythologist in analysing the semiotic construction of myth becomes more difficult, since the very naturalness and self-evident quality of myth's ideological messages have to be overcome.

Semiotic methods are not always used to analyse cultural meanings from a left-wing point of view. British Army officers in training at Sandhurst Military Academy are taught semiotics as part of a course on media coverage of wars. Understanding media semiotics is useful to them when they have to deal with media reporting of military conflicts they are involved in, so that mythic meanings appropriate to the British Army's ideological view of the situation can be more effectively presented and made to appear natural, common-sense. Advertising agencies in continental Europe (e.g. Italy) and a few in Britain use semiotics to design more effective advertisements. Just as Barthes argued that a photographer might look for an image which conveys the myth of French imperialism, advertising copywriters might look for linguistic and visual signs which support the mythic meanings of a product.

Both verbal and visual signs are used in ads to generate messages about products and their users, and semiotics can provide a framework for precise discussion of how these signs work. But it will also become clear that advertisements have a highly ideological role, since 'by nature' they are encouraging their readers to consume products, and consumption is one of the fundamental principles of contemporary culture, part of our dominant ideology. In advertisements, consumption is naturalised and 'goes without saying'. In order to accomplish this ideological effect, we will see that advertisements make use of myth, attempting to attach mythic significations to products by taking up already-meaningful signs in a similar way to the photograph on the cover of *Paris-Match*. The investigation of advertisements will involve further discussion of myth and ideology, and introduce some of the problems with the concepts of myth and ideology which have not so far been addressed.

Sources and further reading

The theories of the sign in Saussure (1974) and Peirce (1958) are considerably more complex than the outlines of them in this chapter. For other explanations and discussions of the sign, see Culler (1976), and from a linguistic and literary perspective Hawkes (1983) and Eagleton (1983), and from a media studies perspective Fiske (1982) and Branston and Stafford (1996).

Barthes (1973) contains many entertaining short essays in addition to those discussed in this chapter and is not too difficult, although some of his references to French culture and theorists may be obscure to a present-day reader. Two books which analyse aspects of culture in a similar way are Blonsky (1985) and Hebdige (1988), and Masterman (1984) contains short essays discussing myth and social meaning with reference to television. Barthes's work is discussed by Culler (1983) and Lavers (1982).

Suggestions for further work

1   Make a selection of road signs from the Highway Code or from observation of your local area. Which features of the signs are iconic, indexical or symbolic? (Some may be combinations of these.) Why do you think these signs were selected?
2   Analyse the front and back covers of this book and two others you are using on your course, or two others you use in different contexts (like cookbooks or leisure reading). What is denoted and connoted by the signs you find, and why?
3   Note the clothing, hairstyles and other adornments of two people you encounter. What do these signs connote, and what knowledge of cultural codes do you need in order to read the connotations?
4   Barthes argues that 'Roman-ness' is signified by hair on the forehead in the film of *Julius Caesar*. What other conventionalised signs for historical and cultural identities have you encountered in the media? Do they encode mythic meanings about the culture?
5   There are cultural codes governing the 'natural' combinations of foods in each course in a meal (paradigmatic choices), or the order

of courses in a meal (syntagmatic choices). How do the cultural codes of foods and eating with which you are familiar differ from those of other cultures (for example, Indian, Chinese, French) whose foods you have sampled?

6   Analyse the layout, décor, music, staff uniforms, displays, etc. in your local supermarket. What do these signs connote about the social roles of the shopper, the staff and the shop?

7   Analyse the physical attributes, accessories and packaging of dolls and action figures like Cindy, Barbie, Action Man and G. I. Joe. In what ways do their connotations encode ideological assumptions about each gender?

2

Advertisements

Introduction

This chapter introduces the semiotic study of advertisements. The combination of linguistic signs with visual, often photographic signs in ads allows us to explore the terms and ideas outlined in the previous chapter, and to begin to question them. The discussion of advertisements here is mainly focused on magazine ads, and I have made this decision for several reasons, some of them pragmatic and some academic. Ads in magazines often take up a whole two-page spread, and can be thought of, for the moment, as relatively self-contained. Two ads are reproduced as illustrations in this chapter so you can see the ad I am discussing, whereas TV or cinema ads, for instance, are composed of a syntagmatic sequence of images, sounds and words. It is much harder to get a grip on these syntagms of moving images when you cannot see and hear them in their original form. The ads discussed here appear in magazines, and a particular genre of magazine is the subject of my next chapter. So the context of ads like those discussed here can be more fully explained in chapter three. There have been several influential academic books dealing with ads from a semiotic point of view. So my focus on magazine ads allows me to introduce some of the key findings which have previously emerged from semiotic work on ads, and identify some of the problems which semiotic analysis has encountered.

The beginning of this chapter gives a very broad overview of advertising as an industry and of the socio-economic functions of ads. Then we move on to the types of signs and codes which can be found in ads themselves, and consider a theoretical model of how ads are read. The remaining part of the chapter deals with the problems which semiotic analysis faces when it attempts to justify its findings and apply them to the experience of real readers of ads, rather than using an abstract theoretical model of what readers do. I shall be using the two ads reproduced in this book to show how semiotic methods can be applied to ads, and to point out how semiotic methods often have to reduce the complexity of what reading an ad is really like.

The advertising business

Advertising is very common and is found in a range of media. If we begin to list the places where advertisements are found, it soon becomes obvious that they are both widespread and diverse. Ads are found in magazines, and in local and national newspapers, where we encounter brief 'small ads' which are mainly linguistic, and much larger 'display ads' placed by businesses, comprising images and words. There are small posters on walls, in shop windows, on railway platforms, and huge poster hoardings next to roads and railway lines. There are advertisements on radio, on television and on film. All these kinds of advertisement are usually recognisable as ads and not something else, but there are other more subtle kinds of advertisement. We will note later in this book, in the chapters dealing with television and cinema, how sponsorship, the placement of products in fictional narrative settings, and products 'tying in' with films and TV programmes, can also fulfil advertising functions. In the next chapter, we will encounter self-contained advertisements in the pages of women's magazines, as well as advertisements embedded in editorial material, and advertisements for the magazines themselves within their pages. As we shall see, it can be difficult to determine what is an ad and what is not.

With all of this advertising going on, it is not surprising that the advertising industry is economically significant in modern developed societies. The weekly newspaper of the British advertising industry, *Campaign*, reported some of the results of a survey by the UK Government's Central Statistical Office (9 December 1994: 2) which showed just how major an industry advertising has become. By the second quarter of 1994, the annual turnover of UK advertising and market research companies was £770 million. The British advertising industry employs about forty-five thousand people, and is part of the 'service' sector of the economy (as opposed to manufacturing). The service sector employs fifteen million people in Britain and accounts for about 80 per cent of national wealth. Advertising was one of the four fastest-growing service industries in 1994, and is highly professionalised and competitive. The people who work in the advertising business are very often highly creative and well educated. Many of them have studied semiotics as part of their formal education, and there is even a British advertising agency called Semiotic Solutions, which uses semiotic methods to design advertisements. While semiotic analysis has been used in the past for a critique of advertising, it can also be used in the industry to help make ads more effective.

Companies spend very large amounts of money on advertising. It is not unusual for a large manufacturer or financial corporation to spend several million pounds on advertising in Britain each year. But it is not only businesses that buy advertising; government agencies for instance, also advertise. Campaigns against cigarette smoking, drug use, or drink driving, and campaigns promoting healthy exercise, are examples of government-funded advertising. There are several different ways in which advertising campaigns are produced. Probably the most common model is for a company to employ an advertising agency, which will propose a campaign plan involving ads in one or more media, and perhaps other promotional activities like mailings direct to potential customers. Space for the ads will be bought from magazine publishers, newspapers, or TV companies for instance, for a specific placing and length of time. Publications which feature advertisements are therefore able to charge advertisers a considerable sum to place advertising material before their readers. Advertising is a significant commercial activity, and is evidently thought to be effective enough to warrant large financial commitments. The central issues considered in this chapter are how semiotic analysis can explain the ways ads work, and how effective semiotics can be in accounting for their meanings.

Analysing advertising

The semiotic analysis of advertising assumes that the meanings of ads are designed by their creators to move out from the page or screen on which they are carried, to shape and lend significance to our experience of reality. We are encouraged to see ourselves, the products or services which are advertised, and aspects of our social world, in terms of the mythic meanings which ads draw on and help to promote. As we saw in the last chapter, Barthes discussed the mythic meanings of the front cover of *Paris-Match*, and showed that signs and codes were used to represent French colonial rule as natural and self-evident. This process of naturalising colonial rule had an ideological function. The legitimacy of French colonialism was a political stance which the mythic meaning encoded in the photograph made neutral and scarcely noticeable. The photograph worked to support the ideological view that colonialism was normal, natural and uncontroversial. In the same way, the semiotic analysis of the signs and codes of advertisements has also often been used to critique the mythic structures of meaning which ads work to communicate. In her classic study of the semiotics of advertisements, Judith Williamson declares that advertising 'has a function, which is to sell things to us. But it has another function, which I believe in many ways replaces that traditionally fulfilled by art and religion. It creates structures of meaning' (Williamson 1978: 11–12). As well as just asking us to buy something, Williamson argues that ads ask us to participate in ideological ways of seeing ourselves and the world.

In fact many contemporary ads do not directly ask us to buy products at all. This kind of 'hard sell' has been replaced by a more diffuse range of functions. Ads often seem more concerned with amusing us, setting a puzzle for us to work out, or demonstrating their own sophistication. The aim of ads is to engage us in their structure of meaning, to encourage us to participate by decoding their linguistic and visual signs and to enjoy this decoding activity. Ads make use of signs, codes, and social myths which are already in circulation, and ask us to recognise and often to enjoy them. At the same time that we are reading and decoding the signs in ads, we participate in the structures of meaning that ads use to represent us, the advertised product, and society. Many previous studies of the semiotics of advertising use semiotic methods as part of a critique of advertising's role in perpetuating particular mythic meanings which reinforce a dominant ideology.

Analysing ads in semiotic terms involves a number of 'unnatural' tasks. In order to study them closely, we need to separate ads from the real environment in which they exist, where they often pass unnoticed or without analysis. We need to identify the visual and linguistic signs in the ad, to see how the signs are organised by paradigmatic and syntagmatic selection, and note how the signs relate to each other through various coding systems. We need to decide which social myths the ad draws on, and whether these myths are reinforced or challenged. These are the main tasks which semiotic analysts of advertisements have concentrated on in the past, and which this chapter will explain. But since we cannot be certain that ads are read in the same way by all readers, we also need to examine two limiting factors which will complicate our ability to be sure of our findings. The first limiting factor is the potential ambiguity of the meanings of signs, and the second is that real readers of ads might decode signs differently, with a range of different results. These two limiting factors pose challenges to the semiotic methods outlined above, and we shall need to assess their importance later in this chapter. At this point, it is necessary to show how semiotic analysis has proceeded until quite recently.

The semiotic critique of ads   (Saussure)

The first step in analysing an advertisement is to note the various signs in the advertisement itself. We can assume that anything which seems to carry a meaning for us in the ad is a sign. So linguistic signs (words) and iconic signs (visual representations) are likely to be found in ads, as well as some other non-representational signs like graphics. At first sight, most of these signs simply seem to denote the things or people which the images represent, or to denote the referents of the linguistic signs. But the signs in ads very rarely just denote something. The signs in ads also have connotations, meanings which come from our culture, some of which we can easily recognise consciously, and others which are unconsciously recognised and only become clear once we look for them. Let us take a hypothetical example which reproduces the features of a large number of ads. A picture of a beautiful female model in a perfume ad is not simply a sign denoting a particular person who has been photographed. The picture of the model is also a sign which has connotations like youth, slimness, health, etc. Because the sign has these positive connotations, it can work as the signifier for the mythic signified 'feminine beauty'. This concept belongs to our society's stock of positive myths concerning the attributes of sexually desirable women. The ad has presented us with a sign (the photographed model) which itself signifies a concept (feminine beauty). This concept of feminine beauty is what Barthes would describe as a mythic meaning.

As in the case of Barthes's black soldier saluting the flag, it does not matter who the model is, who the photographer was, where the picture was taken, and so on. The only significant attribute of the photographed model is that she exhibits the physical qualities which enable her to function as a signifier for the mythic meaning 'feminine beauty'. The photographic sign has been emptied of its meaning except inasmuch as it leads the reader of the ad towards comprehending the myth. In analysing the signs in ads, we pass from the sign's denotative meaning to its connotative meanings. These connotative meanings are the ingredients of myth, the overall message about the meaning of the product which the ad is constructing by its use of the photographed model. The ad works by showing us a sign whose mythic meaning is easily readable (the photographed model is a sign for feminine beauty) and placing this sign next to another sign whose meaning is potentially ambiguous (the name of the perfume, for instance). The mythic meaning 'feminine beauty' which came from the photographic sign (the model) is carried over onto the name of the perfume, the linguistic sign which appears in the ad. So the name of the perfume becomes a linguistic sign that seems to connote feminine beauty as well. The product has been endowed with a mythic meaning.

This short hypothetical example gives a sense of how the semiotic analysis of ads works at a basic level. We identify the signs

in the ad, try to decide which social myths the connotations of
the ad's signs invoke, and see how these mythic meanings are
transferred to the product being advertised. The next step is to
consider how the mythic meaning constructed in the ad relates
to our understanding of the real world outside the ad. In other
words, we need to ask what the ideological function of the ad
might be. Our hypothetical perfume ad invited us to recognise
the connotations of the signs in the ad, and to transfer these connotations to the product being advertised. The perfume became
a sign of feminine beauty, so that buying the product for ourselves (or as a present for someone else) seems to offer the wearer
of the perfume a share in its meaning of feminine beauty for herself. As Williamson argued: 'The technique of advertising is to
correlate feelings, moods or attributes to tangible objects, linking
possible unattainable things with those that are attainable, and
thus reassuring us that the former are within reach' (Williamson
1978: 31). Buying and using the product (an attainable thing)
gives access to feminine beauty (a social meaning). To possess
the product is to 'buy into' the myth, and to possess some of its
social value for ourselves.

Ideology in ads

Our hypothetical perfume ad, by placing the photographed
woman next to the product, actively constructs a relationship
between the woman and the product. It does this by placing an
iconic sign (the photographed woman) and a linguistic sign (the
name of the perfume) next to each other. It is this relationship
between one sign and another which is important for the meaning of the ad, since the relationship involves the sharing of the
mythic meaning 'feminine beauty' by both the product and the
photographed model. The ad is constructed to make this sharing of the same mythic meaning appear automatic and unsur-
prising, whereas in fact it only exists by virtue of the ad's
structure. So one point that a semiotic critic of ads would make
is that the ad conceals the way that it works. Perfume ads do
not literally announce that a perfume will make you seem beautiful (this claim would be illegal in many societies anyway).
Instead this message is communicated by the structure of signs

in the ad, by the way that we are asked to decode the ad's mythic meaning.

It is worth considering what [∧ women] would happen to the meaning of the ad if a different type of model had been photographed. We could list the different attributes of different photographic models, like youthful/mature, underweight/overweight, above average height/below average height, etc. The positive connotations of our hypothetical woman used as a sign in a perfume ad derive from the positive connotations in our culture of the first sign in each of these pairs of opposites when they are applied to women in ads. The mythic meaning of 'feminine beauty' is much more likely to be perceived by the reader of the ad if the photographic sign calls on our social prejudices in favour of images of young, slim and tall women as signifiers of beauty. The iconic sign of the model can signify beauty because she is not elderly, overweight or below average height.

The ad presupposes that we can read the connotations of photographed women as if they were signs in a kind of restricted language, a code. Just as language works by establishing a system of differences, so that cat is not dog, red is not blue, youthful is not elderly, ads call on systems of differences which already exist in our culture, and which encode social values. One of the reasons I chose to discuss a hypothetical perfume ad featuring an iconic sign denoting a beautiful woman was that the example is controversial. Feminists have been critiquing ads and many other media texts for over three decades showing that iconic signs denoting women in the media very often perpetuate oppressive ideological myths about real women. By calling on the positive social value of youth, slimness and tallness, for instance, our perfume ad could be described as supporting a dominant ideological myth of what feminine beauty is. It is easy to see that our ideological view of feminine beauty is not 'natural' but cultural if we look at representations of women in the past or in other cultures. In earlier historical periods, and in other parts of the world, the ideological myth of feminine beauty is not always signified by youth, slimness, tallness etc. Ideologies are specific to particular historical periods and to particular cultures.

The ideology of ads

The mythic meanings which ads generate are usually focused onto products. Ads endow products with a certain social significance so that they can function in our real social world as indexical signs connoting the buyer's good taste, trendiness, or some other ideologically valued quality. So ads give meanings to products, to buyers of products and to readers of ads, and to the social world in which we and the products exist. One central aspect of this process is the way in which ads address us as consumers of products. Critics of advertising have argued that real distinctions between people in our society are based on people's different relationships to the process of producing wealth. From this point of view, which derives from Marx's economic analysis of capitalist societies, it is economic distinctions between individuals and between classes of people that are the real basis on which society is organised. Some people are owners, and others are workers or people who service the work process. However, it has been argued that ads replace these real economic distinctions between people with a completely different way of regarding our relative status and value in society.

In ads, and in the ideology which ads reproduce, we are distinguished from others by means of the kinds of products which we consume. Social status, membership of particular social groups, and our sense of our special individuality, are all signified by the products which we choose to consume. Which beer you drink, which brand of jeans or perfume you wear, become indexical signs of your social identity. In any particular category of products, like perfumes, margarines, jeans or washing powders, there are only minimal differences between the various products available. The first function of an advertisement is 'to create a differentiation between one particular product and others in the same category' (Williamson 1978: 24). But ads not only differentiate one product from another, they also give different products different social meanings. Once products have different social meanings by virtue of the different mythic concepts they seem part of, products become signs with a certain social value. They signify something about their consumers, the people who buy and use them.

For critics influenced by this Marxist analysis, the real structure of society is based on relationships to the process of production. But far from making the real structure of society apparent, ads contribute to the myth that our identity is determined not by production but by consumption. Ads therefore mask the real structure of society, which is based on differences between those who own the means of production and those who sell their labour and earn wages in return. In a consumer society, these real economic differences between people and classes are overlaid with an alternative structure of mythic meanings oriented around buying and owning products (consumption). So according to this critical view ads have an ideological function, since they encourage us to view our consumption positively as an activity which grants us membership of lifestyle groups. But what ads are really doing is serving the interests of those who own and control the industries of consumer culture. Ideology consists of the meanings made necessary by the economic conditions of the society in which we live: a real way of looking at the world around us, which seems to be necessary and commonsense. But this ideological way of perceiving the world is there to support and perpetuate our current social organisation: a consumer society. The individual subject's need to belong and to experience the world meaningfully is shaped, channelled and temporarily satisfied by ideology. In the sense that it provides meaning in our lives, ideology is necessary and useful. But the question is what kind of meanings ideology perpetuates; whether these meanings mask and naturalise an inequitable social system. Advertising has been critiqued as one of the social institutions which perform this function of naturalising dominant ideologies in our culture, for example that it naturalises ideologies based on consumption, or ideologies which oppress women.

Problems in the ideological analysis of ads

There are some theoretical problems with the ideological critique of ads outlined above. This critical discourse claims to 'see through' the ideological myths perpetuated in advertising. The critique of ideology claims to set itself apart from what it analyses, and to investigate the way that advertising (or any other social institution) perpetuates an ideology. This notion of setting oneself apart in order to criticise advertising is parallel to the way that scientists set themselves apart from something in order to understand it objectively. Indeed, the theorist who proposed the model of ideological critique discussed here, Louis Althusser, saw his analytical method as scientific and objective (Althusser 1971). But the scientific objectivity of the critique of ideology is easy to dispute, especially if you are not a Marxist as Althusser was. There seems to be no definite reason for a Marxist analysis of ideology to be any more scientific and objective than another theoretical approach to society.

Indeed, the discourse of science can be seen to be just another ideological view. The notion of a scientific viewpoint, standing outside of experience and endowed with a special ability to see into the truth of things, gives automatic priority to this point of view over all others. Science is a discourse, a way of using language which has its own codes and a particular social meaning. The discourse of science presupposes, for instance, that what we see on the surface is less true than what we see beneath the surface. Science passes from the observation of surface effects to proposing an underlying theory which accounts for these surface effects. Semiotic analysis borrows the assumptions of the scientific discourse when it moves from the signifier to the signified: from what we perceive in the material world (signifier) to the concept which it communicates (signified). Similarly, semiotics moves from the signs on the surface to the mythic meaning which the connotations of signs signify. And again, semiotics moves from the mythic meaning of a particular set of signs in a text to the ideological way of seeing the world that the myth naturalises. In each case, looking at what is on the surface leads the semiotician to what is beneath the surface. We move from observation to knowledge, from a particular instance to a general theory. Building on the same assumptions as scientific discourse, semiotics and the theory of ideology claim to reveal what is really true by going beyond, behind or underneath what appears to be true.

Scientific discourse has a high degree of status in contemporary culture, but we can critique its coded use of signs in the same way that we can critique the coded use of signs in our perfume ad. We saw that the mythic meaning 'feminine beauty' rested on the positive connotations of youthfulness, underweightness, etc., in opposition to the connotations of elderliness or overweightness, etc. Scientific truth is a mythic meaning based on the positive connotations of objectivity and depth, in opposition to the connotations of subjectivity and surface, for instance. Scientific truth is a mythic meaning which comes from the use of signs with positively valued connotations, in the same way that the mythic meaning 'feminine beauty' works. Once we see that scientific truth is a cultural construct, a mythic meaning, its special status has to be acknowledged as cultural and not natural, not necessary but contingent on the way that our culture perceives itself and its reality. Scientific truth must be equally as mythic as feminine beauty.

If scientific discourse is not necessarily superior to the discourses which it analyses, the scientific claims made by semiotic analysis and the theory of ideology must be treated with caution. The discourse of semiotic analysis, as I stated briefly at the beginning of this chapter, requires us to adopt some 'unnatural' procedures. We have to separate an ad being studied from its context in order to study how its signs work. We have to pay more attention to the detail of how meaning is constructed in an ad than an ordinary reader probably would. We tend to come up with an underlying meaning of an ad, relating the ad to mythic meanings and ideological values which is justified only by the rigour of our analysis, rather than by any other proof which would ensure that our reading is correct. These features of semiotic analysis do not mean that it is useless, or that its results are wrong. But semioticians have to take account of the limits which the semiotic method brings with it. Semiotics is a very powerful discourse of analysis, but it always has to struggle against other discourses and argue its case. We shall be considering these issues further in later sections of this chapter, and in the other chapters of this book. Let us now examine two ads in detail, and see what a semiotic analysis might reveal.

Volkswagen Golf Estate

First we need to identify the signs in this ad. There are iconic signs here, denoting three men, and the rear half of a car. There are linguistic signs, the copy written underneath the picture. There is also a graphic sign, the logo of VW cars. Taking the three men first, we can see that their poses and facial expressions are themselves signs which belong to familiar cultural codes. Their poses and expressions are signs which connote puzzlement. The standing figure is still, looking intently at the car, with the positions of his arms and hands signifying that he is deep in thought. The two crouching men are also looking intently inside the car, with expressions which connote curiosity and mystification. For these men, there is something puzzling about this car. To decode this ad more fully, we need to examine the linguistic signs which are placed beneath the picture. The function of the linguistic signs is to 'anchor' the various meanings of the image, to selectively control the ways in which it can be decoded by a reader of the ad (Barthes 1977: 39).

The copy text begins with the syntagm of linguistic signs 'We've doctored the Golf'. Drawing on the presence of the graphic sign on the right, the VW Cars logo, and the syntagm 'The new Golf Estate', we can assume that the car denoted in the picture, and the signified of 'Golf' in the first linguistic syntagm, is a new VW car. What does the signifier 'doctored' signify? To

We've doctored the Golf. The new estate is 41% bigger on the inside than the hatchback version.' Prices start from £11,999." Telephone 0800 333666 for a brochure.

1   Magazine advertisement for VW Golf Estate

See handout

doctor something is to conduct a medical procedure, often to remove an organ, or, figuratively, to doctor is to alter something by removing a part of it. So two related meanings of the syntagm 'We've doctored the Golf' are that Volkswagen have called some doctors in to conduct a procedure on their car, or that VW have altered their car by removing something from it. This meaning of the syntagm is constructed by referring to the value of the sign 'doctored' in the code of language. Moving back to the picture, we might assume that the three men are doctors, who have just altered the car. This decoding of the picture might seem to be supported by the next linguistic syntagm in the caption, 'The new estate is 41 per cent bigger on the inside than the hatch-back version.' After being treated by the doctors, the car has been altered. But how could it become bigger if something has been removed from it? The meaning of the sign 'doctored' seems to contradict the meaning of the second syntagm in the ad.

There is a puzzle here, which can only be solved by referring to another media text. This ad can be described as 'intertextual', since it borrows from and refers to another text. The three men are iconic signs denoting actors who played fictional characters in the British TV series *Dr Who*. Each man appeared as the character Dr Who, a traveller in time and space, in separate series of the programme in the 1970s and 1980s. So the sign 'doctor' signifies Doctor Who, and the car has been 'Doctor Who-ed' rather than just 'doctored' in the usual sense. To decode the meaning of 'Doctor Who-ed' it is necessary to know something about the TV series. It involved travelling in space and time in a vehicle called the TARDIS, which appeared on the outside to be a blue police telephone box (something small) but on the inside was a very large spacecraft (something big). To do a 'Doctor Who' to the VW Golf is to make it bigger on the inside than it appears on the outside.

Once we perceive the intertextual reference in the ad to *Dr Who*, much more meaning becomes available to us. The car is blue, like the TARDIS. The car is for travelling in physical space, like the TARDIS. The Dr Whos in the picture were incarnations of Dr Who at different times, but they are together in the picture at the same time. The car seems to have acted like the TARDIS, which travelled in time, by bringing the Doctors together from their different times to the time the picture was taken. The Dr Who character solves mysteries and problems. The three Doctors are now puzzling over the apparent mystery of the VW Golf Estate's bigger internal space. These further meanings of the ad are only communicated once we decode the intertextual reference to *Dr Who* in the ad, and use this cultural knowledge to solve the puzzle set by the ad. Many of the signs in the ad function as clues to help us select the appropriate cultural knowledge, and to eliminate knowledge which is not appropriate. For instance, it does not matter whether we know the names of the actors who appear in the ad, the plots or other characters in *Dr Who*, or even whether the men in the ad are real or waxwork dummies.

The ad empties out the meanings of *Dr Who*, leaving only some of them behind. The mythic meaning of the ad, that the new VW Golf Estate is very roomy, is constructed from a few connotations of the iconic signs denoting the men looking at the car, and a few connotations of the linguistic signs 'doctored' and 'bigger on the inside'. The unexpected way that the ad communicates this message was one of the reasons that the ad was given an IPC Magazines Ads of Excellence award (*Campaign* supplement 16 December 1994), as the award judge, Tim Mellors, commented. The ad borrows signs and meanings from another media text, a process known as intertextuality. But it only borrows some meanings and not others, and the semiotic richness of the ad depends on the cultural currency of *Dr Who* among readers of the ad. Without some knowledge of *Dr Who*, the ad might seem rather mysterious. To 'doctor' the Golf might decode as to mutilate or castrate it, for instance. Perhaps the men looking at the car are working out how to steal it. Perhaps 'We've doctored the Golf' refers to the way that the photographer has cut off the front half of the car from the picture. The potential ambiguity of the visual signs and linguistic syntagms in the ad are reduced once the signs 'bigger on the inside' show us how to decode the ad. This linguistic syntagm anchors the meanings of the image and of other linguistic signs.

For someone unfamiliar with *Dr Who*, the denoted linguistic message that the Golf estate is bigger than the hatchback version would still be meaningful, but the meanings of the picture would not be anchored down by the reference to *Dr Who*. The back and forth movement of meaning between text and image, the 'relay' (Barthes 1977: 41) of meaning between the two, would also be much less clear. It is evidently important to ask who the reader of this ad is assumed to be, since the reader's cultural experience of other media texts (specifically *Dr Who*) is the condition of the ad's intertextual effectiveness.

VW Golf Estate ad's contexts and readers

The ad was placed in these magazines: *Golf Monthly, Motor Boat & Yachting, Practical Boat Owner, Horse & Hound, Country Life, Amateur Photographer, The Field*, and *Camping & Caravanning*. The readers of these magazines probably carry equipment around when they are pursuing their leisure interests, or they are people who would like to indulge in the relatively expensive leisure interests featured in the magazines. An estate car would satisfy a real need for some readers, or, for aspiring readers, to own the car could function as a sign that they belong to the group who might need an estate car like this. So there are several functions of this ad, including announcing a new VW model, associating the VW Golf Estate with relatively expensive leisure pursuits, and encouraging readers to find out about the car (the ad includes a telephone contact number). The reader of the ad is 'positioned' by the ad as someone who needs or desires a VW Golf Estate.

But all of these functions of the ad in positioning its reader do not explain why the ad is structured as a puzzle that can be solved by someone familiar with *Dr Who*. This is what Nigel Brotherton, marketing director of Volkswagen (UK) is quoted as saying:

> Estate cars are often seen as dull and boring. This is not helped by advertising which normally portrays them as the load carrying derivative of the range. We wanted the Golf Estate to be aspirational and not just a load lugger from Volkswagen. The target market was 'thirty-somethings' with young families whose lifestyle required an estate. These people were currently driving hatchbacks as the image of estate cars was not for them. By advertising the Golf Estate in a new and unusual way we hoped to convince them that the car was not like its dull and worthy rivals. (*Campaign* supplement, 16 December 1994)

Intertextuality

So the *Dr Who* puzzle, because it is 'unusual', was chosen partly to establish a correlation between unusualness and the VW Golf Estate. The mythic meaning 'unusualness' is shared by the ad, by the car, and by the potential buyers of the car. The ad stands out from other less interesting competitors, and according to the message of the ad, the car and its potential purchasers stand out too. Furthermore, *Dr Who* was a TV series which was very popular in Britain in the 1970s and early 1980s when the Doctors in the ad appeared in the programme. People who are now in their thirties are very likely to know of the programme and to remember it with nostalgic affection. Decoding the ad's puzzle is probably a pleasurable experience for thirty-something readers, because they possess the appropriate cultural memory and this memory has pleasurable connotations for them.

It should now be clear that the intertextual reference to *Dr Who* in the ad is not just amusing, not just unusual, and not just a puzzle. It is an unusual and amusing puzzle because this is a way of targeting a particular group of people. Aspiring thirty-somethings with families who are interested in certain leisure pursuits are 'ideal readers' of this ad. The ad is not simply asking these readers to buy a VW Golf Estate. It is endowing the car and these ideal readers with positive mythic meanings that can be attained only by decoding the ad appropriately. It is possible to decode the ad partially, incorrectly, or perversely. But the ad reduces the chances of these outcomes by virtue of the particular cultural knowledge it calls on, the context in which it appears, and the way that its visual and linguistic signs point the reader in the right direction, towards the correct position for understanding it.

This issue of positioning by the text is central to the way that ads (and other kinds of text) have been discussed by semiotic critics. In order to make sense of the signs in an ad, it is necessary for the reader to adopt a particular subject-position. The individual subject (the reader of the ad) positions himself or herself as a decoder of the ad's signs, and as the recipient of its meanings. The individual subject has to occupy the reading position laid out by the structure of the ad, since this reading position is the place from where the ad makes sense. The situation is like that of someone in an art gallery walking past a series of pictures. It is only possible to see a particular picture properly if you stand still, at an appropriate distance from the picture. If you walk past quickly, stand too close, too far away, or too much to one side, you can hardly see the picture. There is a particular position from which the picture 'makes sense', and to make sense of the picture you must occupy the position which it demands. Here it is a physical position in space which is important, but, returning to ads, it is not only physical position but ideological position that counts. Ads position us as consumers, and as people who have a need or desire for certain products and the social meanings which these products have. There is a subjective identity which ads require us to take on, in order to make sense of their meanings.

But this notion of positioning by the text has several drawbacks as a way of describing how people read ads. It tends to treat all ads as if they were in the end the same, since all ads are regarded as positioning the individual subject in such a way as to naturalise a dominant ideology of consumerism. It tends to treat all real individuals as the same, since the positioning of subjects by the ad's structure of signs is a general model which applies to all readers. As we have seen, a quite well-defined group of readers are positioned by the VW Golf ad to receive all of its meaning. Other readers and groups of readers might easily decode the ad perversely, 'incorrectly', in which case the ad would still make a kind of 'sense', but a very different sense from the one the advertisers intended. The theory of textual positioning assumes that there is one 'correct' reading of any ad, which is its true meaning. It de-emphasises the ambiguity of signs (like 'doctored'), since all the signs in the ad seem to lead finally to the true meaning. It assumes that the 'scientific' discourses of semiotics and the theory of ideology are more objective than other analytical techniques, and can reveal a 'true' meaning of an ad which most real readers do not perceive because these readers are in the grip of ideology. We can see in more detail how some of these problems affect the analysis of ads by looking at an ad from one of the most successful of recent campaigns, a Wonderbra ad.

Wonderbra

This ad can be read in a number of different ways, from different subject-positions, and problematises the distinction between an evident surface meaning and a concealed-depth meaning which semiotic analysis can reveal. Like the VW Golf Estate ad, it draws on cultural knowledge of other media texts. It also appeals to an awareness of the critical discourses about advertising from feminist analysts and critics of ideology. It becomes very difficult to see what the 'true' or correct meaning of this ad might be. Discussing this ad brings us face to face with the limits of semiotic analysis, and of the theoretical model of media communication which has been developed earlier in this book.

Our first step must be to identify the signs in the ad, and then to decide how they relate to mythic meanings. The picture is an iconic sign denoting a woman, who is leaning against something, perhaps an open door. She is wearing a bra, and in the original picture the bra is bright green (this is the only colour in the picture, the rest of the picture is in tones of black and white). There is a syntagm of linguistic signs, 'Terrible thing, envy', and a further syntagm 'Now available in extravert green.' There is a further iconic sign denoting the brand label which would be attached to a Wonderbra when on sale. To read this ad, we would identify the connotations of the signs present in it, seeing how the anchorage between the picture and the text directs us

2 Wonderbra poster advertisement

towards the 'correct' reading of the ad. But there are several ways of reading the connotations of the signs in this ad, and several social myths which the ad invokes.

The relay between the bra denoted iconically in the ad and the linguistic sign 'Wonderbra' makes it easy to see that this is an ad for a Wonderbra product. There is a further relay between the greenness of the bra and the linguistic sign 'envy', since green signifies envy in a cultural code (just as red signifies anger, for instance). But the iconic sign of the green bra does not anchor the meanings of 'envy' here in any obvious way. Let's assume that 'Terrible thing, envy' signifies the response of the reader of the ad to the picture. Perhaps a female reader would envy the woman because she owns this bra (the bra is signified as a desired object), but the reader's envy feels 'terrible'. Perhaps a female reader would envy the woman because of the sexual attractiveness which the bra gives the woman (the bra is a sign of desired sexual attractiveness), but the reader's envy feels 'terrible'. Perhaps a heterosexual male reader would envy the bra because it holds the breasts of the woman (the woman is signified as a desired object), but the reader's envy feels 'terrible'. Perhaps a male reader would envy the woman because she can display her sexual attractiveness by wearing this bra (female sexual display is signified as a desired mythic attribute of women but not men), but the reader's envy feels 'terrible'. Perhaps a heterosexual male reader would envy the person to whom the woman displays herself in the picture, her partner perhaps (the woman's partner is a desired subject-position), but to envy the partner is 'terrible'.

There are a range of possible meanings of the linguistic signs, and of possible relays between linguistic and iconic signs. But in each case, the relationship of the reading subject to the picture is one of desire, either a desire to have something or to be something, and in each case the reading subject feels terrible about this desire. Envy is signified in the ad as an attribute of the reader, but is at the same time acknowledged as an undesirable emotion. Another set of decodings of the ad would result if the syntagm 'Terrible thing, envy' represents the speech of the woman in the picture, but I shall not list them all here. This would affect the relay between the iconic and linguistic signs, and the way that the linguistic signs anchor the meanings of the iconic signs. Once again there would be several ways of decoding the ad, and several subject-positions available for the reader. As before, envy would be signified as an attribute of the reader, but the condemnation of envy would come from the woman rather than the reader. The ad would establish a desire to have or to be something, but also withdraw permission for the desire.

The ambiguity which I have noted briefly here is reinforced by the connotations of the model's pose. Her arms are folded. This gives greater prominence to the lifting up and pushing forward of her breasts which the bra achieves, reinforcing the decodings of the ad which focus on her sexual desirability. But her folded arms also create a kind of barrier between her and the reader, and this is a common connotation of folded arms in our culture in general. Like the linguistic syntagm 'Terrible thing, envy', the folded arms are an ambiguous sign, connoting that the woman is to be envied, but that she is unattainable or critical of the one who envies her. Similarly, the woman's sidelong glance might connote flirtatiousness, or a sardonic attitude, or both at the same time. The ad therefore exhibits a kind of give and take in the possible decodings which it allows. It offers the reader a range of possible subject-positions, but denies them to the reader at the same time. This is a feature which is very common in ads, and depends on irony. Ironic statements contain a denoted meaning, and a connoted meaning which contradicts the denoted meaning. The linguistic syntagm 'Terrible thing, envy' denotes that envy is a negative emotion, but it connotes that its speaker is envious or envied anyway, and does not really mind being envious or envied. This ironic quality of the syntagm means that envy is regretted but also enjoyed. The social meaning of envy is being made ambiguous by the ad in a very subtle way. Envy, it seems, is bad, but it is also good in the sense that it is pleasurable.

The irony of the linguistic syntagm is reinforced by a relay between it and the picture, since the double decoding of the syntagm is parallel to the doubleness in the meaning of the woman's gesture and expression. As noted above, her gesture and expression can be read in at least two ways. The mythic meaning of the ad as a whole then seems to be that the woman, the bra and

the reader, can mean several things at once. The woman, the bra
and the reader are not single and fixed identities, but sites where
several different coded social meanings overlap and oscillate back
and forth. We do not need to decide on a single social meaning
for the bra, the woman who wears it in the picture, or for ourselves as readers of the ad or buyers of the bra. The ad invites us
to enjoy the unanchoredness of its signs, and the multiplicity of
the bra's social meanings. This oscillation of meaning back and
forth, which irony makes possible, has very major consequences
for the semiotic analysis of the ad.

The outline of a critical semiotic analysis of the Wonderbra ad
would be something like this. The ad addresses women, presenting them with a sign connoting sexual attractiveness and power
(the woman wearing the bra). These social meanings, according
to the ad, can be attained by women if they buy the bra. To buy
the bra is to 'buy into' an ideological myth that women should
present themselves as objects for men's sexual gratification. To
critique the ad in this way is also to critique it as a mechanism
for perpetuating an oppressive ideology. However, as we have
seen, it is by no means certain that the ideological message of the
ad revealed by such a critique is the 'true' meaning of the ad.
There are a number of coherent alternative ways of reading the
ad, and a number of possible subject-positions from which to
understand it. The signs in the ad are too ambiguous, too 'polysemic' or multiple in their meanings, to decide on one 'true' message of the ad.

Furthermore, the ad seems to be constructed so that it can
disarm an ideological critique of its meanings. The ad signifies
(among other things) that women can choose whether or not to
become sexually desirable and to display their bras and themselves as signs of desirability, a meaning anchored by the sign
'extravert'. The irony in the ad signifies that women can both
choose to become desirable and at the same time distance themselves from being perceived as objects of desire by others. Irony
like this was used by the film star Mae West, for instance, and
the ad's irony may therefore function as an intertextual borrow-
ing, offering its readers clues about its relationship with representations of powerful and desirable women. Another
intertextual reference may be Madonna, who popularised bras as

fashion items and was also represented simultaneously as an object of desire and as the controller of her own image. To take on the identity of a desired object can be enjoyed by women, but they can also retain their power as subjects (and not just objects) by adopting an ironic attitude towards this status as a desired object. The Wonderbra ad takes on a feminist ideological critique which would see women as signs of desirability and objectification, and is ironic about this critique. The wearer of a Wonderbra has two kinds of pleasure: both the pleasure of being a desired object, and the pleasure of refusing to be perceived as a desired object while nevertheless being one. In fact, both of these pleasures can exist simultaneously. The Wonderbra product becomes a sign of a woman's power over the way she is perceived, for she is perceived as both desirable, and in control of the social meaning of her desirability, at the same time.

The Wonderbra ad's contexts and readers

The Wonderbra ad discussed here was one of a sequence, featuring the same model, similarly ironic slogans, and similarly ambiguous mythic meanings. The 'Terrible thing, envy' ad ran in a range of glossy women's magazines, and ads like it were also displayed on poster hoardings around Britain. The ad campaign began on St Valentine's Day, February 1994, a day on which romance is celebrated, so that the social meanings of St Valentine's Day clearly supported the codings of the ad. While the readers of women's magazines are mainly women, the poster versions of these ads would have been seen by a wide range of people of both sexes and of varying ages (which was one reason for offering the different reading-positions outlined above). The ad campaign was very successful. It reportedly cost £130,000 to put the first three Wonderbra posters on nine hundred hoardings around Britain for two weeks, and £200,000 to publish the same three ads in women's magazines until June (the information about the campaign was published in *Campaign*, 9 January 1995: 21). This is a relatively small cost for a national advertising campaign. The response to the ads led to the production of a total of fifteen different ads by January 1995, and by then the campaign was running in ten countries.

The effects of the campaign are difficult to assess, and the responses of real readers of the ads are even more elusive. TBWA, the agency which created the ads, won Campaign of the Year for the Wonderbra ad in 1994 (they also won silver at the 1994 Advertising Effectiveness Awards). UK sales of Wonderbras rose by 41 per cent over the preceding year and the manufacturer (Playtex) reported sales of twenty-five thousand bras per week. It seems reasonable to deduce that the multiple meanings of Wonderbra which were signified in the ads were able to prompt at least some of these sales. But in addition, the campaign was mentioned in at least four hundred stories in the local and national press, on radio and on television, supported by public relations initiatives. The woman denoted in the ads, Eva Herzigova, had previously been unknown but became both the subject of extensive journalistic interest and a minor television personality. Wonderbra ads were displayed in Times Square, New York, and during the football World Cup in Dublin, with puns and references specific to their location and occasion respectively. Kaliber beer ads were produced by another ad agency, Euro RSCG, which referred intertextually to the 'Hello Boys' Wonderbra ad by replacing Eva Herzigova with the Scottish comedian Billy Connolly pictured next to the slogan 'Hello Girls'. Giant Wonderbra ads were projected against the side of London's Battersea Power Station, with the line 'Happy Christmas from Wonderbra'.

In a situation like this, it becomes even more difficult to determine the 'correct' meaning of an ad. Even if a semiotic analysis claims to determine the 'correct' meaning which the signs and codes of a single ad construct, the ad is not a self-contained structure of signs. The meanings of the ad will be inflected and altered by the intertextual field of other ads, press stories and media events which surround the ad. Readers of the ad will bring their decodings of these related texts to their decoding of the ad. Indeed, when the Wonderbra campaign became a media event in itself, the effect of the ads may have been to advertise the campaign as much as to advertise the product. These factors, which have to do with the social context of ads and of their readers, make any reading of an ad as a self-contained system of signs with a determinable ideological effect very difficult to justify as 'true'.

This chapter has focused on the ways in which semiotic analysis helps us to decode the meanings of ads. Ads have been discussed here as relatively self-contained texts, although we have seen that the mythic meanings which ads draw on and promote are also dependent on cultural knowledge which exists for readers outside of the particular ad being read. The meanings of signs are always multiple or 'polysemic', and we have also seen how some ads narrow down this polysemic quality of signs but do not eliminate it altogether, while other ads exploit polysemy. In the next chapter, which deals with a range of glossy magazines aimed at women readers, we shall encounter polysemic signs and the importance of cultural codes again. We will be considering the importance of models of how readers are positioned again, too, drawing on some of the insights which psychoanalytic theories of subjective identity have contributed to semiotic analysis. As we have seen here in the case of theories of ideology and readership, it is always necessary to think about the limitations and assumptions behind our analytical techniques, as well as making use of the critical power they offer.

Sources and further reading

The first and still very perceptive use of semiotics to analyse advertisements is Williamson (1978), which is more theoretically dense than this chapter but illustrates its points with reference to a huge number of magazine ads that are reproduced in its pages. Later studies of advertisements include Goffman (1979), Dyer (1982), Vestergaard and Schrøeder (1985), Myers (1986), Goldman (1992), Cook (1992) and Myers (1994). There is also a useful section on advertising in Alvarado and Thompson (1990). All of these books use semiotic methods to some degree, and later books also discuss the limitations of critical semiotic studies of ads.

The advertising producers' perspective on their business can be found in *Campaign* and *Admap* magazines, and White (1988) is an example of a book by an advertising practitioner on making ads. Umiker-Sebeok (1987) contains a series of essays on advertising, some of which explicitly present the case for using semiotics to make more effective ads rather than to critique the ideologies in and of advertising.

Althusser's (1971) theory of ideology is quite difficult. There are books like Fairclough (1989) which contain explanations and discussions of ideology, but it is often better to see how this concept is deployed in relation to concrete media examples. This is done in the books listed above which use semiotics to critique advertisements (e.g. Williamson 1978), where ideology is discussed with specific reference to ads. The further reading sections of subsequent chapters in this book will also be referring to books on media which use the theory of ideology.

Suggestions for further work

1 Note the situations in which ads can be found (on bus shelters, on trains, on hoardings, in magazines, etc.). How might the situation of an ad affect its meanings and the ways it is decoded?

2 Analyse the representations of men in a group of ads. How similar or different are the codes used to represent men from those used to represent women in ads you have seen? What are the reasons for these similarities and differences?

3 Choose three ads for a similar type of product (car, training shoe, pension, or soft drink, for example). How similar and how different are the mythic meanings of the products in the three ads? Why is this?

4 Ads for some products (like cigarettes) are not allowed to recommend the product explicitly. What semiotic strategies are used to connote desirability, pleasure, or difference from competing products in these ads? Are the same strategies used in ads for other products which could be explicitly recommended?

5 Both ads discussed in this chapter contain linguistic signs as well as visual ones. How do ads with no words attempt to organise the multiple connotations of what is denoted visually in them?

6 Compare ads from earlier decades with contemporary ads for similar products (Williamson (1978) has many ads from the 1970s, and Myers (1994) has some from before World War II if you cannot find your own). What similarities and differences do you find in the semiotic strategies of each period? Why is this?

7 Analyse the connotations of the brand names and logos of five products. Why were these names and logos chosen? Could any of them be used as the name of a product of a different type?

3

Women's magazines

Introduction

This chapter focuses on glossy monthly magazines aimed at women readers. As before, it will use the techniques of semiotic analysis discussed so far, together with some of the theoretical ideas which have been allied with semiotics in academic studies of the media. This chapter deals with the signs and codes at work in a range of magazines, to consider whether women's magazines encode a coherent mythic social identity for their readers. In other words, women's magazines, it might be argued, construct social meanings for women by positioning them as readers of particular structures of signs in particular ways. To answer these questions, we will need to examine the editorial content of magazines (like their features, letters, horoscopes, interviews, etc.), and advertising material (individual ads and advertising features). As we deal with these various signifying elements of magazines, we can also evaluate the semiotic methods used here and in earlier chapters.

When investigating a whole text like a magazine, we will need to think about how the process of reading the magazines' different kinds of contents affects the meanings of the signs which are used. We will need to ask how far polysemy, the multiple meanings of signs, is limited by the context and interrelationships of signs with each other. We will need to ask how the mythic meanings in magazines relate to ideologies, and whether these meanings are being naturalised in support of an ideology. I shall argue that women's magazines do not construct a single mythic meaning for feminine identity, or promote one ideological position for their readers. Instead, the discourses of women's magazines are mixed, sometimes contradictory, and involve the reader in choices about how to decode their signs. These choices are not infinite, and the concept of conscious choice needs to be evaluated in relation to subject-positions taken up by readers which are unconsciously structured.

We saw in the previous chapter that the theory of ideology is useful for the analysis of advertising, showing how ads promote mythic ideas about the individual subject as a consumer, and about social relations and consumer society. Although there are some conceptual problems with the theory of ideology, it goes a long way to explain the function of ads in society. In this chapter, one of the issues in our analysis of women's magazines is the role of the reader in constructing meanings. In the previous chapter, it was largely assumed that the reader, though active, is engaged in putting together the connotations of ads into relatively coherent structures of meaning. This chapter will show that the reader is positioned by the discourses of women's magazines, but cannot take up a single coherent identity in relation to them because of the contradictions within and between these discourses. These issues of feminine identity will be related to a discussion of theories of subjectivity. Discussing subjectivity, subject-positions, or the construction of individual subjects, is a way to approach the question of individual identity. Theories of subjectivity stress how social forces and structures constitute us as individuals in particular ways. Language, social and family relationships, and texts in the media are all structures which lay out subject-positions from which to experience things. But like ideology, subjectivity must be seen not as a unified sense of personal identity, but as relatively fluid and contradictory.

The magazine business

Women's magazines can be divided into several categories, according to the target group of readers which they address. There are, for instance, magazines aimed at pre-teens and adolescents (like *Seventeen*), magazines for women aged between eighteen and thirty-four, which focus mainly on fashion and beauty (like *Cosmopolitan*), magazines aimed at women aged between twenty-five and forty, which focus on the world of the home (like *Good Housekeeping*), magazines focusing on specific concerns involving health and fitness (like *Slimming*), magazines for particular minorities in society, and magazines focusing on other special interests in women's lives (like *Brides*, or *Parents*). These categories, and others relating to type of employment, for instance, are used by magazine publishers and advertisers as a shorthand way of indicating the main issues discussed in the magazines' editorial material, the kind of reader the magazines are thought to have, and the kind of products advertised in the magazines. There are many more sub-categories which have been developed to give greater descriptive accuracy about magazines.

But it is misleading to think about women's magazines as divided up in such a simple way for several reasons. As publishers and advertisers know, women's magazines are read not only by their purchaser, but often by between about five and fifteen other readers as well. In general, the more expensive the magazine's cover price, the more additional readers see the magazine. Not all of the magazine's readers will belong to the group of women which the magazine targets, and some readers are men. So while a semiotic analysis might reveal that a particular magazine has an 'ideal reader' corresponding to the woman whose interests are targeted and shaped by a magazine, there will be a large number of 'non-ideal' readers of the magazine's signs and meanings. We cannot assume that a real reader corresponds to the reader we reconstruct from the ways in which a magazine's codes operate.

Publishers and advertisers divide readers into those who buy a single copy from a shop, and readers who subscribe to the magazine over a period of time. Sales of single copies to 'sample readers' are economically important to publishers and advertisers because they demonstrate an active choice to purchase the magazine, whereas subscribers might receive the magazine but not actually read it. On the other hand, subscriptions provide regular sales, and publishers can acquire information about known subscribers. This information can be used to create profiles of typical readers, to encourage advertisers to place ads in one magazine rather than another in order to target a certain market sector. Again, a profile of a magazine's typical subscriber might correspond to an 'ideal reader' or it might not, and there will be a very wide range of different sample readers for any single issue of a magazine. It is also quite common for women to buy or read more than one magazine. The magazines a woman reads may be addressed to the same category of reader, but may not. The mythic feminine identities constructed in a range of women's magazines may be related but different, just as the identities and subject-positions adopted by real women are related but different. In order to acquire a significant share of the market for these different categories of magazine, the large corporations which own women's magazines often publish several titles which target a similar readership group, and magazines which target related but different readerships. IPC magazines publish *Marie Claire* (jointly with European magazines) and *Options*, as well as *Homes and Gardens*, *Homes and Ideas*, *Country Homes* and *Ideal Home*. Condé Nast publish *Vogue* and *Vanity Fair*, as well as *House and Garden* and *World of Interiors*, for instance.

Women's magazines contain a large number of advertisements, and charges to advertisers provide about half the cost of producing a magazine. The other half comes from the purchase price of the magazine. The largest categories of products advertised are cosmetics and clothes and food, but women's magazines also include ads for cars, financial services, watches, and many other things. In her study of American women's magazines, McCracken (1993) includes editorial material recommending the purchase of products as advertising too, and she found that these concealed ads, as well as ads themselves, accounted for up to 95 per cent of the total number of items in the magazines. For McCracken, advertising is the key feature of women's magazines. Magazines contain ads, editorial material contains ads, the front covers of magazines are ads for the magazine itself, editorial material 'advertises' mythic feminine identities to their readers, and to complete the circuit, magazine publishers advertise the spending power of their typical readers to advertisers in order to attract more ads. This emphasis, as we shall see, has major implications for a semiotic analysis which investigates how women's magazines relate to ideologies of consumerism and to ideological representations of feminine identity.

Myths of femininity

We cannot assume that the representations of feminine identity
found in women's magazines accurately reflect the lives and
identities of real women. Representations are composed of signs
which are meaningful because they belong to socially accepted
codes which readers can recognise and decode. Instead of simply
criticising women's magazines for giving a false representation of
women's lives, a semiotic analysis would begin by discussing the
way that the signs and codes of women's magazines construct
mythic social meanings of femininity. One of the ways in which
this is done is for the signified concept 'femininity' to be differentiated from masculinity. Women's magazines encode the difference between masculine and feminine identities inasmuch as
they are different either from men's magazines like *Loaded* or *GQ*,
and from the greater range of 'interest' magazines, like *Golf
Monthly* or *MacUser*. This differentiation is signified by the placing of women's magazines in a specific section of newsagent
shops and magazine stands. The point is not that all readers of
women's magazines are women: about fifteen to thirty per cent
of readers of women's magazines are men (*Cosmopolitan* has the
highest proportion of male readers). But women's magazines are
signified as different from other kinds of magazine because of the
coded way in which they are presented to potential readers.
These coding systems permit the magazines to function as signifiers of a defined mythic signified of femininity.

We can begin to glimpse what this mythic femininity is by
noting the slogos (slogans which function as identifying logos for
particular magazines) which appear on the spines of a few
women's magazines. The *She* slogo is 'For women who juggle
their lives'. The *Cosmopolitan* slogo is 'Smart girls carry *Cosmo*'.
The *Company* slogo is 'For your freedom years'. The connotations
of these linguistic signs together with the titles of the magazines
include youth, sociability, worldliness, confidence, fashionableness and femaleness. With the exception of femaleness, these
connotations may not be specific to real women, but they are
specific to a mythic identity being constructed by the discourse
of women's magazines as opposed to, for instance, leisure interest magazines. Women's magazines delimit the shape of what

Winship (1987) calls a 'women's world'.

Winship argues that this world is mythic, a construct built out of signs; 'the "woman's world" which women's magazines represent is created precisely because it does not exist outside their pages' (Winship 1987: 7). From this point of view, the semiotic codes of women's magazines work to construct a mythic world of the feminine, which compensates for the lack of a satisfying social identity for real women. The function of women's magazines is to provide readers with a sense of community, comfort, and pride in this mythic feminine identity. So the magazines take up the really existing gender relations of culture, and work on them to produce a mythic femininity which supports real women and provides an identity for them. But for Winship and other critics, this mythic femininity has a negative side. It naturalises an ideological view of what being a woman means, and overlapping with this, it naturalises the consumer culture which magazines stimulate through advertising and editorial material. Women, it is argued, are positioned as consumers of products by the signs and codes of women's magazines, a role reinforced by the fact that magazines are themselves commodity products.

This critical account of the role of women's magazines considers that being feminine is a mythic identity constructed by the coded connotations of signs in society. Femininity is not a natural property of women, but a cultural construct. There is a position hollowed out by the codes of women's magazines, and real women fit themselves into this position as individual subjects. In positioning themselves as subjects in this way, women become subject to the ideologies, the social meanings encoded in women's magazines. Conscious choices, intentions and beliefs are seen as the effects of women's ideologically produced subject-position, rather than being freely chosen. But we know that it is possible for individual subjects to criticise ideology and the social order of which it is a part. After all, that is what semiotic critics and theorists of ideology do, and what feminism has done in relation to gender identity. Ideologies are not uniformly successful, and not always effective. Ideology is a site of struggle, where opposition and critique always threaten the edifice of naturalisation and conformity.

The inability of ideologies to be permanent structures, and the ability of actual individual subjects to see through some of the discourses which support them, means that we can show not only how media texts support ideology, but also how they might expose cracks and fissures in it. The ability of readers to decode texts 'against the grain', to diagnose and evade their ideological subject-positionings as readers, means that there is always a conflict of interpretations in relation to every text. The ways in which specific individual subjects read and decode signs and meanings will exhibit important differences. These oppositional possibilities must derive from somewhere, and are made available by the specific nature of an individual's place in society, perhaps a contradictory and ambiguous place. Nevertheless, as readers of codes we are always shifting between decodings which are complicit with a dominant ideology to oppositional decodings to alternative decodings of texts. In this chapter, we shall have to take account of the range of possible decodings of women's magazines, and note the fissures within and between the discourses of magazines.

The reading subject

The meanings which are decoded by readers depend in part on how a magazine is read. When you first pick up a magazine, you might leaf through it quite rapidly, stopping briefly to glance at an ad or an editorial page. In this reading pattern, which is syntagmatic (linear) and where concentration is evenly focused through the reading, visual signs and large-type linguistic signs are likely to be noticed most. Because of their size, colour and simplicity, ads may be most likely to attract your attention. Then, you might choose to read particular editorial articles closely. In this second reading pattern, which may not follow the sequential order of the magazine's pages, linguistic syntagms become the focus of attention. Next, having had the magazine for a few days, and read some of it in detail, you might leaf through it again, stopping at interesting ads or articles, reading them again or noticing them for the first time. This third reading pattern is relatively linear, evenly focused on linguistic and visual signs, and depends to some extent on a memory of the first two readings.

Each of these reading patterns will affect the decoding process, both in what is read and how it is read. The reader is controlling the speed and intensity of reading, as well as what is chosen for reading. It is difficult for semiotic analysis to take proper account of these different reading patterns, except by noting connections between the signifiers of the various ads and articles, and the various evident and more complex levels of signification in the part of the magazine under analysis. Flicking through the December 1993 issue of *Cosmopolitan*, for instance, I was struck by the odd relationship between pages fifty-eight and fifty-nine. Page fifty-eight is an illustration denoting a gold perfume bottle next to a head and shoulders black and white photograph of Elizabeth Taylor, who is denoted drawing the collar of her raincoat around her neck with both hands. Her fingers and ears are adorned with diamond jewellery. She looks wistfully towards page fifty-nine which is a white page on which ten scattered gold handbags and purses are denoted, with the linguistic syntagm 'found gilty'.

The reason for stopping my rapid reading at this point was to see what Elizabeth Taylor had done. The linguistic and iconic signs noted here at first seemed to connote a mixture of criminality, stardom and wealth. Elizabeth Taylor's pose and expression in the photograph seemed to connote guilt (as if hurrying from a courtroom in a raincoat), supported by the punning linguistic sign 'gilt' on page fifty-nine. Her look towards the handbags on page fifty-nine, together with the gold of the purse-shaped perfume bottle, seemed to be compositional signs connecting the two pages into a single text. The mythic meaning which I assembled from these connotations was that even stars could be condemned by the law despite their wealth, fame and possessions. The ideology naturalised by this myth would be the equality of all citizens before the law, despite their privilege or lack of it. But this decoding of the two pages, despite its apparent reasonableness, is 'incorrect'. Page fifty-eight is an ad and page fifty-nine is an editorial feature.

A detailed semiotic analysis of the two pages reveals that page fifty-eight is an ad for White Diamonds perfume, endorsed by Elizabeth Taylor. The White Diamonds logo appears at the top of the page, while at the bottom of the page the syntagm 'The fragrance dreams are made of' provides an anchorage for Elizabeth Taylor's pose and expression, with their connotations of 'dreaminess' which the ad attaches to the mythic meaning of the perfume, a myth concerning the unworldliness and fairytale existence of stars. The ideological message naturalised by this myth is that anyone can share in the world of Elizabeth Taylor through the purchase of the appropriate consumer products. Page fifty-nine is part of the 'stylenews' section of the magazine in which new products are recommended. The handbags and purses denoted on the page are accompanied by a listing which denotes their prices and retailers. The scattering of the handbags over the page is a compositional sign which connotes that they are part of a haul of stolen goods, a meaning anchored by the linguistic syntagm 'These are the hot accessories to the fact, used as evidence to make a style statement. You certainly won't find any of them on the black market. It's an open and shut case of gilt.' The mythic meanings of this fashion for gold are that it is new, luxurious, exclusive, and associated with an envied lifestyle (hence the joke that we might have to obtain these products criminally). The ideological message naturalised by the myth is that how we are perceived by others depends on our possessions rather than on our economic status, and we can choose how we appear in this way.

Even though the second, more complete decoding of the signs on these pages is more 'correct' and appropriate, it does not entirely displace the decoding which resulted from the first reading. The connotations of criminality, stardom, and wealth are still present in the second semiotic analysis, but they have been contained and redirected by the codes which I now recognise when looking more closely. When they are considered separately, pages fifty-eight and fifty-nine naturalise their meanings quite successfully; it is easy to receive the 'intended' meaning of each page. But since they appear together, it is much more likely that some of the 'incorrect' and 'unintended' meanings which I perceived in my first decoding will affect a more careful reading of the pages. So there are three issues here. First, the way we read (quickly, slowly, superficially, attentively, etc.) has significant effects on how signs are decoded. Second, all texts attempt to contain the multiple connotations of their signs by linking

them in coded ways. Third, every text (an ad, a magazine feature, etc.) is prone to 'contamination' of its meaning by adjacent
and related texts.

A further factor determining what is read and how it is read
will be the context in which reading takes place. My reading of
pages fifty-eight and fifty-nine of *Cosmopolitan* took place in the
context of a search for interesting ads to discuss in chapter two
of this book. I was reading the magazine as a male semiotician,
and when the two pages caught my attention, I was reading
both as a puzzled semiotician and as someone interested in Elizabeth Taylor. These contexts are not typical of how women's
magazines are read. Reading a women's magazine may be a
diversion or an escape from your surroundings, at the doctor's
or on a train, for instance, relaxing at home, or at work during
a break. Reading may be a relief from domestic work, or a way
of expressing independence from a partner or children who are
doing something else. Reading magazines always takes place in
a concrete social context, and this context (as some of the examples in this paragraph indicate) derives in part from the place of
women in society, as mothers, partners, workers, etc.

Women's magazines both represent these social contexts by
referring to them in the ads and articles they contain, and magazines also shape the meanings of these social contexts for the
women who read them. Many of the contexts in which magazines are read help to encode reading as both pleasurable (a private pleasure) and defensive (a way of holding something at
bay). McCracken sees women's magazines as constructing a
shared consensual myth about femininity which is complicit
with ideological roles that real women play out. But she draws
attention to the concrete social context of reading, which may
often be in conflict with the positive connotations which
women's magazines give to femininity.

> Readers are not force-fed a constellation of negative images that
> naturalize male dominance; rather, women's magazines exert a
> cultural leadership to shape consensus in which highly pleasur-
> able codes work to naturalize social relations of power. This
> ostensibly common agreement about what constitutes the femi-
> nine is only achieved through a discursive struggle in which
> words, photos, and sometimes olfactory signs wage a semiotic

battle against the everyday world which, by its mere presence, often fights back as an existential corrective to the magazine's ideal images. (McCracken 1993: 3)

As McCracken indicates, pleasures belonging to the 'women's world' are encoded in the contents of magazines, and also in the physical nature of magazines. They have larger pages than most books and may comprise up to 250 pages, connoting abundance and luxury. These connotations are reinforced by the frequent presence of additional free supplements which are attached to the body of the magazine itself. Magazines are glossy and colourful, connoting pleasure and relaxation rather than seriousness, just as Sunday magazine supplements and additional sections do in the newspaper medium. The smell and feel of the glossy paper connotes luxury, and the smells of perfume samples in the magazine connote femininity and its pleasures of self-adornment. The page layouts and typefaces of magazine articles, in contrast to newspapers, for instance, are often as varied, sophisticated and interesting to decode as the ads which surround them. The physical nature of women's magazines has connotations which help to encode their purchase and their reading as enjoyable private pleasures offered specifically to a woman reader.

To buy a women's magazine is itself an anticipation of pleasure and can be both regular and controlled, unlike the lack of control over pleasure in many other aspects of women's lives. A magazine is a sign which connects together the mythic meanings of femininity and pleasure. So there are ways in which buying and reading a women's magazine can function as a private resistance to the domestic and public role marked out for women. At the same time, buying and reading a magazine reinforces mythic meanings of femininity by offering subject-positions which are complicit with the ideological positioning of women as particular gendered types of consumer, nurturer, lover, or worker. For McCracken, magazines invite women to share in the pleasures of femininity, but also naturalise the ideological injunction to express one's individuality through the purchase of products. 'If women, at the magazines' urging, experience a sometimes real and sometimes utopian sense of community while reading these texts, confident of participating in normal, expected feminine culture, they are at the same time learning consumerist competitiveness and reified individualism' (McCracken 1993: 299).

Address and identity

We have already seen that semiotic features of women's magazines encode mythic meanings of femininity in their address to a woman reader, by their placement in shops, and by their slogos, for example. On the front cover of women's magazines, we often find linguistic signs which function in the same way. The March 1995 issue of *She* has these syntagms on its cover: 'The sweetest news! You *need* chocolate', 'Teaching your child right from wrong' and 'Why the modern mistress doesn't want to steal your man'. This address to 'you' is also used in ads, and in both media it invites the reader to recognise herself as the individual being spoken to, and also to recognise herself as a member of a group, 'women like you', since 'you' is both singular and plural in English. The visual space and perspective of the magazine cover (or ad) performs the same function since the reader is positioned in front of it as an individual decoder of its visual and linguistic signs, but this position can be occupied by anyone. While magazine covers and ads can address anybody, they claim to address individuals with unique desires and needs, promising that the contents of the magazine or the product in an ad will fulfil the needs of the individual and her group.

Referring to ads, Williamson argues that 'What the advertisment clearly does is thus to signify, to represent to us, the object of desire' (Williamson 1978: 60). The ad is therefore not just selling us a product with a meaning for us. The ad is also selling us a future image of ourselves as happier, more desirable, or whatever. The object being advertised stands in for the self which we desire to become. 'Since that object is the self, this means that, while ensnaring/creating the subject through his or her exchange of signs, the advertisement is actually feeding off that subject's own desire for coherence and meaning in him or her self' (Williamson 1978: 60). Women's magazines address 'you' as a woman, both an individual woman and as a member of this gender group. The linguistic syntagms on the cover position the reader as a subject who will be interested, excited, amused, or assisted by the articles in the magazine which are being advertised on the cover. The magazine cover, like an ad, is offering something and at the same time coding the reader as a particular kind of subject, a feminine subject, In one way or another, all the linguistic signs on the cover signify that the magazine will make 'you' happier or better as a woman. So as in the case of ads, women's magazines address a reader who desires to have or to be a more complete self than she has now.

This notion that individual subjects are lacking something and desire to be more perfect selves, can be clarified by a theoretical model of human subjectivity which derives from psychoanalysis and shares some of its principles with semiotics. The French psychoanalyst Jacques Lacan developed these ideas in work done in the 1950s and after (Lacan 1977), and they have since become allied to semiotic theories because they help to explain how signs, like the signs in ads, magazines or other media, latch onto fundamental forces in our inner selves. Lacan argued that the human child is born into a lack in being, a wanting-to-be. Throughout his or her life, the individual subject attempts to master this sense of lack, to come to terms with it and overcome it, but can never succeed in doing so. The subject projects back the impression that originally, in his or her union with the mother in early childhood, there was nothing lacking. This is the imaginary unity and wholeness which the subject tries to recapture throughout his or her life. The thing which would apparently restore the lost pre-lacking state, Lacan calls 'the Other'. Since there is actually no thing which could really defeat the sense of lack, the Other is always a representation, an image of totality rather than something actually graspable.

In order to explain how people come to suffer from this sense of lack, Lacan (1977) gives an account of early child development. The child begins to think of himself or herself as an individual between the ages of six and eighteen months, at a point known as the 'mirror stage'. This stage describes a moment when the child recognises himself or herself in a mirror, and sees himself or herself as just as whole and coordinated as the image which he or she sees, even though the child is in reality physically uncoordinated, and his or her experience is a mass of uncontrolled feelings and instincts. In the mirror, the child sees himself or herself as an independent entity existing in time and space, rather than as the dependent and fragmented being of his or her actual experience. The image the child sees is more whole than the child really feels, and the child's identification of himself or herself with the mirror image in this way is a misrecognition of what the child really is. The child is 'narcissistic': admiring and desiring to be the better self which he or she sees in the mirror, deluding himself or herself that he or she really is this better self. Because the child sees that he or she can become an image that can be seen, he or she can now realise that he or she appears as an image for someone else too, for an Other person, just as the mirror image was an image or Other for the child.

This rather complicated aspect of psychoanalytic theory provides a model for understanding why we identify with images of other people, like the images of beautiful models on the covers of women's magazines. These images are iconic signs which represent the better self which every woman desires to become. The desire to become the better self represented by the visual sign is a desire to overcome the lack which all human subjects experience. Since the model signified in the photograph is made to appear as she does by the various cosmetic products, hairstylists, and clothes which are detailed on the inside page of the magazine, the connotation is that the reader can become like the model by using these products. The eyes of the models signified on magazine covers always look out at the viewer, just as a reflection in a mirror looks back at us. The linguistic syntagms on the cover address the reader as 'you', offering to make 'you' happier, better. In the same way, the cover's iconic sign addresses the viewer, offering an image which signifies a better, happier self, like the image of the better self in Lacan's mirror-stage theory. Both linguistic and visual signs position the woman reader as a lacking subject, and simultaneously connote that her desire to overcome lack can be satisfied.

It is no accident that this psychoanalytic theory has the same kind of underlying structure as the theory of ideology which we have been using. In each case, the theory argues that individual subjects are positioned by a structure which they cannot control, and which precedes them. In each case, individual subjects are positioned as lacking something, and desiring to have or to be something. In fact, Althusser's theory of ideology (1971) used Lacan's psychoanalytic concept of the mirror stage to explain how ideology acts on us. Ideology calls each person to take on the image of himself or herself as a subject, to be a woman and not a man, to be 'I' and not 'you', to be a consumer and not a producer, etc. Like the mirror stage, ideology gives the individual subject a social identity. But like the image in the mirror, the subject's ideological identity is a misrecognition of what he or she really is.

The image of himself or herself which the child sees in the mirror in Lacan's theory is of course a sign. It is an iconic sign which represents the child. Lacan uses the term 'imaginary' to refer to the various signs, like the mirror image, which a subject identifies with in the quest to overcome lack and see himself or herself as a better and more complete self. So we can say that the iconic and linguistic signs in women's magazines are addressed to the imaginary of feminine subjects, because the magazines offer a better, happier self like the better self the child perceives in the mirror. The feminine imaginary coded in women's magazines is also ideological, since the connotations of the magazine's signs construct mythic pleasurable identities for real women to identify with. Despite the problems for real women in society, the mythic femininity signified in women's magazines provides an imaginary satisfaction for women. This mythic femininity is a 'women's world' which the reader of the magazine is invited to share in. Since this 'women's world' is an imaginary representation built out of signs, it can hardly be condemned for being unlike the reality which real women experience. On the other hand, since the feminine imaginary is composed of mythic feminine identities that feed off women's real sense of lack and unhappiness, the feminine imaginary in women's magazines can be criticised for offering women a form of pleasure that does little to make their real lives any better or happier. McCracken puts this point succinctly: 'within this discursive structure, to be beautiful, one must fear being non-beautiful; to be in fashion, one must fear being out of fashion; to be self-confident, one must first feel insecure'. (McCracken 1993: 136)

The 'woman's world'

The address to the reader on the cover of women's magazines, in the 'you' of linguistic syntagms, and in the look of the model in iconic signs, is common to all women's magazines. But the covers of women's magazines are not all the same. Different kinds of cover images identify the magazine's 'ideal reader' and differentiate one magazine and kind of reader from another. Although the photographed models on magazine covers are usually white, young and immaculately made-up, they vary in age, dress code, hairstyle, and the cheekiness or demureness which their facial expressions connote. The connotations of these iconic signs differentiate the magazine as either up- or down-market, focused on domestic or cosmopolitan mythic feminine identities, or traditional or trendy feminine identities, for instance.

As we have seen, the model's gaze at the buyer of the magazine is itself a sign which functions as an imaginary reflection of the buyer herself. This coincidence of the buyer's look and the model's look connotes complicity in the mythic image of femininity between the model and the reader. The imaginary and mythic feminine identity which the magazine advertises on its cover is there to be shared and enjoyed by the reader and the model, as their coinciding looks connote. But furthermore, since it is for men that attractive images of women are usually presented, there is, we could say, an absent male gaze structuring the look of the model and the corresponding look back by the buyer. While the cover image is for a woman to look at, it is constructed with reference to a wider social code in which being feminine means taking pleasure in looking at oneself, and taking pleasure in being looked at by men. The 'woman's world' of women's magazines is not a self-sufficient thing, but an imaginary world constituted by its difference from and its relationship with the world of men.

For instance, the September 1994 issue of *Cosmopolitan* includes these features: 'How can men recover their pride?', 'Is he in love with you or your money?', 'Living with the death of the man I loved', '10 ways to stop a good man turning bad', 'Why intense passion can't last', and 'Computer compatibility testing: Three couples risked it'. There are numerous other reg-

ular features and occasional articles in which the magazine's discourses addressed to women define feminine experience as a set
of possible relations to masculinity. As the titles of the features
above indicate, the myth of feminine identity does not consist of
a single way of relating to masculinity. Men and masculinity are
coded as desired, feared, pitied and a host of other positionings.
Each of these coded ways of representing masculinity requires
the reader of the article to adopt a particular subject-position in
order to decode the 'correct' meaning of the article. But the subject-positions constructed for the reader are different in different
articles. To take a simple example, some articles encode the
reader as single but seeking a partner, while others code the
reader as either married or in a long-term relationship.

But despite these differences in subject-position, the mythic
meaning of femininity is given its meaningfulness, its value as a
signified, by a distinction between the feminine and the masculine. Heterosexual sexuality is one of the key aspects of social life
which involves the distinction between femininity and masculinity as well as the interrelation of the two gender roles. Therefore
much of the mythic meaning of femininity is signified in terms of
desire and sexuality between men and women. In *Cosmopolitan*,
Winship writes: 'Sex is a means for self-discovery, sex is the
centre of a relationship; sex is a step to other things; sex is always
something that can be bettered or varied; sex is potentially
always a problem; sex is something you-never-can-forget' (Winship 1987: 112). Sex is not an activity with a fixed 'natural'
meaning. Its meaning is constructed through the ways in which
it is defined and coded as meaningful by discourses. Feminine
(and masculine) sexuality is therefore a mythic social meaning
which women's magazines work to shape. The shaping of feminine identity, achieved in part by discourses on sexuality, is pre-
occupied with men and masculinity because femininity and
masculinity are defined in relation to each other.

The notion that femininity and masculinity are defined in relation to each other is much the same as Saussure's contention
that signs acquire their capacity to mean for us because of their
position in *langue*, the system of differences which underlies language. Just as 'cat' is not 'dog', femininity is not masculinity.
Gender identity can be seen as a structure of meaning in which

each gender acquires its meaningfulness by being different from the other gender. In laying out subject-positions for the reader, women's magazines are giving specific forms to the mythic feminine identities which women take on in their imaginary. The ideological component of this process is that women's magazines encode the identities they offer to female subjects in certain ways and not others. Some feminine gender identities are coded as 'natural' while others are not. We have already seen, for example, that to be a consumer of products is a naturalised identity in the discourses of women's magazines. To be a heterosexual woman whose identity is defined to a significant extent by her relationships with men is another naturalised identity in women's magazines. Despite the plurality of subject-positions constructed by the discourses of magazines, this plurality is contained by a small number of dominant ideological myths that encode femininity in particular ways.

The naturalisation of feminine identities is accomplished by several means. In relation to the codes which structure linguistic signs, the inclusion of the reader as a friend and an equal is a significant example of naturalisation. The discourse of the articles in women's magazines connotes conversation. It is a representation of the ways that people speak when they know each other and share the same world, in this case the 'woman's world'. An article in *Company*, 'Premature infatuation', begins by referring to the conversational code immediately: 'A friend tells you she's just met the most perfect man in the world and she's going to marry him. Or she's just made the funniest new friend ever ...' (October 1994: 78). Conversation is also connoted here by, for instance, the use of contractions ('she's'), cliché ('the most perfect man in the world'), and non-literary sentence structure (beginning a sentence with 'or'). Unlike most newspapers, magazines feature a personal editorial address by the editor to the reader, often accompanied by the editor's photograph. In the same issue of *Company*, editor Mandi Norwood announces: 'In the issue, we have some spectacular revelations. For starters, we expose what women really feel about penis size. We've protected the feelings of the men in our lives for long enough ...' (October 1994: 1). As on the cover, the reader is addressed as 'you', and the editor refers to the magazine staff, its readers, and women in general as 'we'.

Women's magazines signify the mythic community of the 'women's world' in the linguistic signs and codes of their articles, which enable the discourse to overcome contradictions. For example, in the editorial quoted above, the report on penis size is a newly-discovered 'revelation', something not previously known. But at the same time the opinions of women about this issue are signified as already known, since women have apparently 'protected the feelings' of men by not telling them what women already knew to be the truth. The ideological myth which is able to contain this contradiction is the myth of the 'women's world'. Individual women may have wished men to have large penises, but this wish was both private and concealed. The *Company* survey collects the opinions of individual women and publicly shows that individuals' opinions and wishes are not unique to them, but are shared by a community of women. Reporting the results of the survey creates a mythic community in which women share the same opinions as each other. It also invites individual women to recognise themselves and their opinions as part of a 'women's world' in which the size of men's penises is significant. Furthermore, it is *Company* which creates the bridge between individual women and a community of women, and denotes the parameters of the 'women's world'. *Company* becomes a sign representing the 'women's world', a kind of mirror image reflecting women's feminine identity back to themselves. By buying *Company*, women are to 'buying into' the 'women's world' and the community it represents, although this community is a mythic construct generated by the reader's interaction with the signs, codes and myths of the magazine's discourse.

Community is also signified by surveys, letters and other interactive devices like make-overs, competitions or reader offers. Each of these features of the magazines' discourse involves an exchange between the magazine and the reader, where the reader actively responds to the magazine. In general, the higher the cover price of a magazine and the greater spending power of its typical reader, the fewer prizes, offers, and articles based on reader's experiences appear in the magazine. For instance *Marie Claire* in December 1994 (cover price £1.90) contained no reader offers except a shopping card entitling the holder to reductions in certain stores, and no make-overs. By contrast, the weekly *Take A Break* (cover price 52p) in January 1995 contained £27,500 in cash prizes, holiday prizes, car prizes etc., and numerous articles based on readers' reported experiences. The function of these interactive devices is to reinforce the mythic interchange between the real world of the reader and the imaginary 'women's world' of the magazine.

This interchange is a sign which connotes the validation of the magazine's role as part of the reader's identity. Getting readers involved with the magazine and representing readers in articles connotes that the magazine mirrors the reader's feminine identity, drawing readers into the community of the 'woman's world'. There is always a tension between mirroring the reader's identity, and offering an imaginary femininity which, as in the mirror stage, represents a future better self. Some magazines (like *Vogue*) concentrate their articles on aspects of the desired imaginary femininity to the virtual exclusion of representations which mirror their readers' experience. These magazines are aspirational: they represent a mythic femininity associated with *haute couture*, which few real women can afford to realise for themselves. Aspirational magazines very rarely include interactive devices like competitions and offers, but they contain a high proportion of advertising. The ads are for products which are quite readily affordable and available, unlike many of the products and lifestyle experiences described in the editorial. The products advertised are then able to share in the mythic meanings of exclusivity, luxuriousness and high fashion which the magazines' editorial articles encode.

Aspirational women's magazines clearly support the ideology of consumerism by linking the desirable but unattainable mythic femininity signified in their articles with the desirable but attainable mythic femininity signified in the surrounding ads. But all women's magazines associate the attainment of a desired imaginary self with products. McCracken (1993) gives a very full account of the various strategies of advertising, but only a brief list can be given here. Articles may contain recommendations of products, so that the article is in effect an ad itself. For the magazine, recommending a product may also help to secure advertising from the makers of the product, a process called 'brand reciprocity'. For the reader, a continuum is established between the codes of ads and of articles, so ads are not perceived as an interruption to the reading experience. Ads which use the linguistic and visual codes of the magazine, 'advertorials', are the clearest example of the intertextual merging of the codes of ads with the codes of articles. The credibility connoted by editorial recommendations of products helps give credibility to ads for these products, a meaning reinforced by the placing of ads in appropriate articles or sections of the magazine. Breaking an article on different pages of the magazine forces the reader of the article to pass through a series of ads to get to the conclusion of the article, setting up a relay between ads and the article. All of these relationships between ads and articles confuse the distinction between the two kinds of discourse. The effect of this confusion is for the whole magazine to encode the 'woman's world' as a world of desired mythic meanings of femininity which are attached to products.

The limits of the imaginary

In the account of Lacan's theory of the mirror stage above, the ungendered sign 'child' and the phrases 'himself or herself', 'he or she', etc. were used to explain how individual subjects come to experience a sense of lack in being or wanting-to-be. The gender of the child was not significant, because the theory applies to all human beings. The theory showed that the experience of lack gave rise to a desire to have and to be a better self, represented by an iconic sign, the reflection in a mirror. This imaginary identification with an Other promised the satisfaction of lack, and gave rise to a desire to be more and better than the self which the subject really experiences. The theory accounts for the desired images presented in women's magazines, and the better self which the magazines offer as part of their mythic 'women's world'. It was also noted that the child seeing his or her image in a mirror realises that the child can be an image seen by someone else, just as the child sees himself or herself as an image. The child is positioned in time and space as an individual subject, an Other to someone, just like the individual subjects in the world around it are also Other. The child begins to have a social existence and an identity.

It is the difference between the child's real self and the better self represented by the mirror image of the child which establishes a lack in the child's sense of himself or herself. As soon as the child recognises that he or she can be represented by a sign, something that stands in for him or her, he or she has made the first step towards the system of language. Language is of course a system in which something (a signifier) stands in for something which it represents (a signified). Just as the child's mirror image signifies the child, so the signifier 'cat' signifies the concept of a furry four-legged creature. When we use language, the signifier 'I' stands in for our individual subjective identity. Each individual subject can represent his or her identity in language by using the signifier 'I' to signify him or her. Everything we can understand and communicate about our reality has to pass through the medium of the linguistic signs we use to think, speak and write about it, and this applies also to our identity. The individual subject's identity has to be understood, represented and communicated by signs.

But the system of language, and the world which it enables us to know and speak about, are two different things. The system of language is Other to the world of the real, but we can only gain access to the real in thought and experience by apprehending it in language. We are forced to live, think and know in the realm of the Other, the realm of signs. Lacan called this realm of the Other, the realm of signs, the 'symbolic', because a symbol represents something (as a sign does) but is not the same as what it symbolises. The symbolic is the opposite of the imaginary. The imaginary is a realm where there would be no lack, where there would be no difference between a signifier and its signified. We have already seen that the imaginary for the child in the mirror stage is a realm where the child and the mirror image, the signifier and the signified, are imagined to be the same thing. But this imaginary realm where there is no lack, no difference between signifier and signified, is illusory. The child and its mirror image are not really the same. In the same way, the imaginary of magazines' 'women's world' is a world of better selves which a woman reader aspires to be part of, a world in which her real sense of lack would be abolished. Despite the pleasure of identifying with the imaginary 'women's world', the magazine cannot deliver a new and perfect identity to its reader. After all, the magazine is just a collection of signs. Women's magazines are addressed to the reader's imaginary, offering a better self in their 'women's world', but magazines have to exist in the symbolic order, the world we all exist in. Women's magazines communicate their mythic meanings by means of signs, thus their representations of the imaginary are dependent on the symbolic, the signs which do the communicating.

The discourse of women's magazines, comprising the discourses of articles and ads, constructs an imaginary for the woman reader. This imaginary consists of a 'woman's world' in which femininity is both satisfying and attainable as an identity. The discourses of magazines construct subject-positions for their readers by means of codes which address the reader as a lacking subject of the symbolic order, whose feminine identity is constructed as Other to masculinity. By constructing a mythic community for women, magazines delineate the social meaning of femininity which the reader is invited to participate in. Although the imaginary identity offered by the magazine discourse is pleasurable and secure, it can only be communicated by signs. As a structure of signs, imaginary femininity is brought into the realm of the Other, where by definition it cannot satisfy the lack which all individual subjects experience. So there is a perpetual movement back and forth for the reader between identifying with the better self which the feminine imaginary offers, and having to exist in the symbolic world of signs and social meanings. In the social world which individual subjects inhabit, there is always a difference between what we are and what we desire to be. So there are always more images of better selves which can be constructed in women's magazines, and more products which promise to lead us towards this unattainable better self.

Sources and further reading

McCracken (1993) is a long and detailed analysis of women's magazines partly based on semiotic methods, though her examples are of American magazines, and with the exception of her final chapter, the magazines discussed were published in the early 1980s. More recent magazines are discussed in essays in the collection edited by

Ballaster *et al.* (1991). Winship (1987) is a less explicitly theoretical study, emphasising the pleasure which readers (and Winship herself) derive from reading magazines, and contrasts with very critical work from a feminist point of view like Ferguson (1983). As this book was being completed Hermes (1995) was published, focusing on the pleasure of reading magazines and based on interviews with Dutch women (ethnographic research) rather than semiotics.

The psychoanalytic theory in this chapter derives mainly from Lacan (1977), but readers wishing to follow this up are advised to start with other secondary writing before tackling the original. Introductions and discussions of psychoanalytic theory include Moi (1985), Butler (1990), the introductory essays in Mitchell and Rose (1982), and part one of Macdonald (1995) which also uses these concepts in analyses of a wide range of media texts. Williamson (1978) also has discussions of the concepts explained in this chapter.

Suggestions for further work

1 Analyse the covers of three magazines which seem to be aimed at different readerships. What signs on the covers justify or contradict your assumptions about their readers? Is there a single 'ideal reader' constructed by the signs in each case?

2 Analyse some of the signs and codes in three magazines which seem to address male readers. Is there a mythic 'men's world' in the same way as this chapter has argued that there is a 'women's world' constructed in women's glossy magazines?

3 If you are already a reader of magazines, how is your usual reading pattern similar or different to that of a semiotic analyst? Can a semiotic analysis adequately explain the ways you usually read, for instance by emphasising the way of reading which seems to be invited by the magazine's format, arrangement, layout etc?

4 Select some examples of editorial discourse discussing men in women's magazines, or discussing women in men's magazines. What functions do mythic representations of the other gender perform?

5 This chapter focuses on monthly magazines. How should the analysis you have read be altered to account for the semiotics of weekly women's magazines?

6 Which aspects of the editorial discourses of women's magazines are common to other kinds of media text (like romance fiction,

self-help books, or chat shows on TV, for instance)? What are the shared myths and ideological assumptions of these discourses in the different media?

7   Look for ads in magazines where the placing of the ad in relation to editorial material seems significant to you. Analyse the relationship of ad and editorial in semiotic terms.

4

Newspapers

Introduction

This chapter discusses the ways in which semiotic analysis approaches newspapers as a medium. We shall be considering the linguistic signs used in newspapers, the iconic and other visual signs in newspapers, and the relationship between linguistic and visual signs. The front pages of two British newspapers published on the same day (18 July 1995) are reproduced in this chapter, and many of the specific examples used here are drawn from those editions.

Before considering how signs are used in newspapers, we need to define what news is. News does not consist of lists of facts or events. News is not just facts, but representations produced in language and other signs like photographs. A semiotic analysis of news discourse will therefore include discussion of the connotations of the linguistic and visual signs used in news stories. Connotation shapes the meanings of a news story, and connotations can only be perceived when they belong to coded ways of using signs which the reader can recognise. So codes have a social dimension, they are ways of using signs which are more or less familiar to groups of people in society. As we shall see, some codes are specific to newspapers and others are more widely used in society. One of the most common codes in the media and social life generally is the narrative code. News in newspapers is presented in stories, and stories are narratives about people and events. How something is narrated using the narrative code will be just as significant as what is narrated by a news story.

Codes more specific to the newspaper medium are found in

newspaper photographs, which commonly connote actuality and evidence. One of the issues this chapter deals with is the relationship between linguistic signs, photographic signs and graphic signs in the pages of newspapers. Each of these kinds of sign and their coded connotations play a role in establishing the mythic meanings of what is reported in the news. As we have seen with the media discussed so far in this book, mythic meanings have a relationship to ideology. We shall need to consider how the mythic meanings of the news are related to ideologies, and the ideological status of news as a specific set of ways of communicating. Newspapers and other news media shape what can be thought of as news, by reporting some events and excluding others. So news discourse is an ideological representation of the world because it selects what will be reported, and sets the terms of what is significant. A semiotic analysis of newspapers will need to consider what kinds of message are communicated by the codes of news discourse, the contexts in which these messages are produced by news professionals and decoded by newspaper readers, and the ideological significance of news discourse.

The newspaper business

News is a commercial product in that newspapers are businesses controlled by corporations whose aim is to generate profit for their shareholders. Of the twenty-one British national daily newspapers and Sunday newspapers, eleven are owned by two corporations, News International and the Mirror Group. The two corporations between them control about two-thirds of the national newspaper market. This situation is even more marked in the United States, where in 1995 there are only two major national newspapers: *USA Today* and the *New York Times*. There are very prestigious newspapers based in regional areas, including the *Washington Post*, the *Chicago Tribune*, and the *Los Angeles Times*, but these newspapers do not compete for a share of national readership in the same way as the multitude of titles in the British market. Despite the regional nature of the American newspaper market, only New York has more than two daily newspapers.

Newspapers make money through sales, and need to maintain

large circulation figures to stay profitable. In January 1995, Roy Greenslade in the *Guardian* reported on the economic factors which affected British newspapers in 1994 (Media Section, 2 January 1995: 12). There has recently been a price war between the 'quality' broadsheet newspapers the *Daily Telegraph*, *The Times* and *The Independent*, which all reduced their cover prices. The recorded sales of both 'quality' and 'popular' newspapers were boosted by 'sampling exercises' where free copies were provided on trains and aeroplanes, and bulk sales were made at a discounted price to restaurants and hotels. Some newspapers reduced their cover price even further on particular days to increase opportunist sales. As a result of these changes sales have increased, but the underlying trend in the British newspaper market is down. In April 1994 the *Daily Telegraph*'s daily sales dropped below one million for the first time since 1953. Many newspapers reduced their journalistic staff and/or employed staff on a freelance and short-contract basis. Market pressures led to the copying by competing titles of sales-boosting techniques like new formats, extra sections, or prize quizzes.

Greenslade compared editions of two newspapers on 10 December 1994 and the same day ten years earlier, to see whether these economic factors had affected the contents of newspapers. He found that the 'quality' papers had become more like the mass-market 'popular' newspapers. The *Daily Telegraph* had fourteen stories on its front page, a relatively small photograph and small headlines in 1984. On the same day in 1994 there were eight stories on the front page, a big photograph, big headlines and four 'blurbs' advertising the features on inside pages which included a contest, a celebrity interview and fashion advice. *The Times* had nine stories on its front page in 1984, a small photograph, eight brief trailers for stories on inside pages and an article on the winners of Portfolio, the first money-winning game in a 'quality' newspaper. In 1994 *The Times* had six front-page stories, three brief items announcing stories on inside pages, three 'blurbs' and a bigger photograph, in colour. In recent years, the sport sections of British 'quality' newspapers have increased in size significantly, and 'lifestyle' sections have been added to attract a wider range of advertising.

It is dangerous to speculate too much about the reasons for

these changes in the appearance and contents of newspapers. But, for Greenslade, this diachronic analysis showed that the traditionally sober style of 'quality' newspapers was giving way to the forms of self-advertisement which have been common in 'popular' newspapers for many years, caused by the increased competitiveness and falling profitability of the newspaper industry. We shall be returning to the meanings of front pages, and comparing 'quality' and 'popular' newspapers synchronically later in this chapter. In another article, Greenslade reported that about fourteen million newspapers were sold in Britain every day in the first half of 1995 (the *Guardian* Media Section, 12 June 1995: 15). Figures provided by the Audit Bureau of Circulations showed an average daily sale between December 1994 and May 1995 for these 'popular' daily newspapers of: the *Sun*: 4,069,928; the *Daily Mirror*: 2,478,109; the *Daily Mail*: 1,780,155; the *Daily Express*: 1,280,904; the *Daily Star*: 738,759; *Today*: 565,731. The 'quality' newspapers averaged: the *Daily Telegraph*: 1,062,775; *The Times*: 471,847; the *Guardian*: 400,813; the *Financial Times*: 294,766; *The Independent*: 289,057. As these figures show, the terms 'quality' and 'popular' are signs which do not always denote the relative size of the recorded circulations of newspapers. They are used to separate broadsheet-size 'qualities' from smaller tabloid-size 'popular' newspapers, and to distinguish between the kinds of reader addressed by the newspapers' discourses.

As in the case of women's magazines, small newspaper circulations can be viable if the readership is an attractive market for advertisers. Large circulation figures mean that ads reach large numbers of consumers, but a small and significant readership group (like businesspeople who control their companies' purchasing decisions) may be enough to attract advertising income. Just as newspapers are commercial products which gather income from sales, the purchasing power of their readers is also a kind of product, which is offered to advertisers. As an industry producing newspapers and readerships, newspapers are part of consumer culture. This context is reflected in the ideologies which are naturalised in newspaper discourse, as a semiotic analysis can reveal.

This chapter deals mainly with the items which are presented in the news stories on the front pages of newspapers. The material discussed here is what we commonly mean by the term 'news' in ordinary discourse. But it is clear from a look at figures 3 and 4, the front pages of *The Times* and the *Daily Mirror*, that 'news' is not the only kind of material on the front pages. The *Daily Mirror* has a large box on the upper right of its front page, advertising a lottery game inside the newspaper. *The Times* has three boxes at the top of its front page, advertising feature articles inside the newspaper, and an ad placed by Direct Line Insurance. These signifying elements of the front pages are not 'news' in the conventional denotative meaning of the term. They will not be discussed in detail in this chapter, because they have more in common with ads and with magazine features, topics which are discussed elsewhere in this book. But these 'non-news' items are significant to the role of newspapers in culture, and to the mythic meanings and ideological role of newspapers. The ads are clearly important because they either advertise products and services, connecting the newspaper to commercial discourses which address the reader as a consumer, or the ads advertise the newspaper itself as consumer item, as something which will inform, entertain or amuse. We shall see later in this chapter how 'news' can itself be entertaining and amusing as well as informative, so that the divorce between news as a kind of serious and impartial discourse, and news as a kind of entertainment or advertisement is not in the end a useful distinction. But first we need to consider what kinds of events are coded as news in the discourse of newspapers.

News value

Newspapers are produced by professional workers who select some events for reporting as news, and exclude others. The pattern of inclusion–exclusion differs from one paper to another and from one news cycle (usually one day's news) to another. 'Qualities' have more foreign news for instance, 'popular' tabloids have more crime-based or personality-based news. So clearly, news is not a fixed category which arises naturally. News is neither found nor gathered, as if it were already there. It is the product of professional ways of thinking, writing and composing

which are all codes of behaviour learned by news workers. These
general points about what news is and how it is produced need
to be substantiated by a closer examination of what can become
news and the codes which structure news discourse. Then we
can see how these structures of news encoded the meanings of

3   *The Times*, front page on 18 July 1995

news in some news stories, and consider how the readers of newspapers might make sense of the news.

There are an infinite number of possible facts about the world which could be reported, but news discourse reports only a selection of facts. What is reported is the selection of facts assumed to

4 The *Daily Mirror*, front page on 18 July 1995

be significant. But it is obvious when looking at a group of news-papers that what counts as most significant for one newspaper is often quite different from what counts as significant for another newspaper. As you can see from figures 3 and 4, both *The Times* and the *Daily Mirror* reported accusations about an alleged affair between the Dean of Lincoln and a verger on Tuesday 18 July 1995. The other front-page items are all different. The *Sun*, the *Guardian* and *Today* did not report that story on their front pages that day at all. So one of the first questions we need to ask about news discourse is how news is constructed by the use of criteria for selection. This selection process depends on criteria which give greater 'news value' to some facts and events than others. Galtung and Ruge (1973) described the criteria used informally and unconsciously by journalists and editors to decide which events are newsworthy, and which are more newsworthy than others. In other words, these criteria form a code shared con-sensually by news workers which enables them to determine the degree of news value which any event has. Events which can be narrated by news discourse in terms of these criteria are likely to become printed news stories, and the more criteria which an event satisfies, the greater news value it possesses. Below are out-lines of the main criteria for encoding news which Galtung and Ruge discovered.

1 Frequency: short-duration events (like a conference on ozone depletion in the atmosphere) are close to the daily frequency of newspaper publication and are more likely to be reported than long processes (like the progressive depletion itself).

2 Threshold: the volume of an event (like a multi-car pile-up) or degree of increased intensity (like an escalation in deaths from AIDS) must be high to be reported.

3 Unambiguity: the event must be clearly interpretable by news codes (like the Queen suddenly goes into hospital – a 'royal story'), even if its meaning is itself ambiguous (no one knows what is wrong with her).

4 Meaningfulness: to the assumed reader (an event occuring in or close to Britain, or which is relevant to current preoccu-pations in the British news).

5 Consonance: the expectedness of an event (like more soccer

violence at an international match), or assumed reader demand for news about it (like a royal marriage).

6 Unexpectedness: the surprising unpredictability of an event (the Foreign Secretary suddenly resigns, for instance), or the scarcity of such events (major floods in London).

7 Continuity: the persistence in the news of a story deemed newsworthy in the past (like the persistence of stories about the royal family).

8 Composition: a full newspaper will exclude other stories due to lack of space, whereas an empty newspaper will pull in stories to fill it.

9 Reference to élite nations: news relating to nations of world importance (like the United States, Germany, Russia, etc.).

10 Reference to élite persons: news relating to important or very well-known figures (like the President of the United States, the Queen, Michael Jackson, etc.).

11 Reference to persons: the simplification of processes by reference to a person who is used as a sign of something abstract (Miners' leader Arthur Scargill, for instance, appeared in the 1980s as a sign of the negative value of union militancy).

12 Reference to something negative: disasters are more newsworthy than successes, for instance.

It is obvious from reading this list of criteria for news value that events in the world do not 'naturally' exist as news. What is selected as news depends on the usually daily rhythm of a newspaper office and the shared professional codes of journalists. News is dependent on the organisation of news institutions, and the construction of a mythic reading subject whose interest newspapers aim to engage. On the front page of *The Times*, the story 'French UN rescue force is "too small"' exhibits unambiguity (its dominant code is that of international diplomacy); meaningfulness (our British representatives are rejecting French proposals); consonance (there is perceived demand for updates on the Bosnian situation); continuity (part of the ongoing news discourses about Bosnia); reference to élite nations (Britain, France); and reference to élite persons (British Government ministers, the Chairman of the US Joint Chiefs of Staff).

The apparently quite different story in the *Daily Mirror*,

'Robbie quits Take That', can be accounted for by many of the same criteria. The story exhibits unambiguity ('exclusive' news in the code of showbusiness gossip); meaningfulness (the Take That pop group is a familiar name to young people and their parents); consonance (assumed demand for news of the band); unexpectedness (Robbie was not expected to quit the band); continuity (Take That have been featured in 'popular' newspapers for some time); and reference to élite persons (Robbie is a pop star).

The criteria of news value are useful in showing that despite the different referents of news stories, news stories exhibit a number of consistent and repeated features. So the news value criteria can be regarded as a coding system which is knowingly or unknowingly used by journalists in order to structure and shape the meanings of events as news. One of the consequences of this must be that journalistic 'objectivity' is a mythic meaning for news discourse which is created by the assumptions about news that underpin the professional activities of newspaper workers. Since journalists narrate news using the codes of news value in general and of their newspaper in particular, the news discourse which they produce cannot be the 'natural' way of understanding news or an 'objective' account of facts. For over twenty years, critical analysis of news by, among others, the Glasgow Media Group (1976, 1980, 1986), has shown that news is shaped by the commercial, ideological and semiotic structures through which it is produced. This is not at all to accuse journalists of 'bias' or distortion, since that accusation implicitly assumes that there is such a thing as an 'unbiased' news story. As we have seen in previous chapters of this book, signs never simply denote a reality 'objectively'. They always encode connoted meanings, drawing on mythic social meanings which support a particular ideological point of view.

So news value criteria are a code which can be usefully tested against the stories which have appeared in particular newspapers, to see which news stories have more news value than others in journalistic professional codes. But there are also a number of drawbacks to the use of the news value criteria. As the two examples of news stories above indicate, they do not discriminate between the kinds of news story in different kinds of newspapers. They tell us little about the linguistic and visual signs, the codes of newspaper discourses, in which news stories are represented. They tell us even less about how newspaper readers make sense of the news, although the criteria are based on assumptions held by journalists about what readers are interested in.

In representing newsworthy events in news stories, newspapers make use of familiar narrative codes, ways of narrating stories with different contents in similar terms. For instance, the stories 'Cedric snubs curbs' in the *Daily Mirror*; 'French UN rescue force is "too small"', 'Bottomley rules out new laws to curb the media', and 'Greenbury fails to stop "fat cat" attacks' in *The Times* are all narratives concerning a conflict over the appropriate institutional response to a political problem. The connotations of the narrative code being used are significant in shaping and containing the meanings of news in particular ways. Although, by definition, the content of each news story must be different to all others, the contents of stories are given meaning by invoking narrative codes which define, order and shape the contents. An event attains news value not simply because of what it is, but also because it can be narrated in the terms of an existing narrative code. News events, when narrated as news stories, reinforce existing narrative codes, and familiar narrative codes attract stories which exemplify them. So selecting events for the news cannot be thought of as neutral, nor can it be prior to the representation of the event in a narrative code. The activity of selection already involves an awareness of the narrative codes in news discourse.

As well as noting what news discourse represents, and how it represents by means of connotation, we need to consider the coding systems used by different newspapers. Just by glancing at a few newspapers in a newsagent's shop, it is easy to see that newspapers do not all look the same, because they use page layout, photographs or headlines differently. A closer look will reveal that their linguistic registers and 'tones of voice' are different. Although there are some mythic meanings which are common to news discourse in general (news is immediate, relevant and significant, for instance), there are varied ways that news is encoded by linguistic and visual signs. These differences affect not only the meanings of news stories, but also affect the ways in which the newspapers can be read. Later in this chapter, we shall need to consider the reading patterns which real readers adopt, and the contexts in which reading newspapers takes place.

News discourse

Because newspapers are organised institutions with habitual ways of doing their job, and because they have to generate news stories quickly, efficiently and almost continuously, they rely on information relayed to them by existing and accessible news sources or by news agencies which produce news information. The news sources, as Whitaker lists them (1981: 31–2) include Parliament, local councils, the police and emergency services, law courts, Royal press offices, 'diary' events which happen each year (like sporting events or party conferences), and other news media. Newspapers also receive news from organisations which issue press releases and give press conferences, including government departments and local authorities, companies, trades unions, charities and lobby groups, and the armed forces. Some individuals (like people in newsworthy court cases) also make public statements and news might then be acquired from them.

These bodies are organised, established by status, and maintained by funding. They are 'accessed voices', to whom the media have access, and who expect access to the media. The discourses of these groups therefore become the raw material for the language of news stories, since news language is parasitic on their discursive codes and ideological assumptions. News is intertextually related to, and permeated by, the discourse of these news sources' press releases and public statements. Organisations usually train their press officers (who produce news information for newspapers) to write press releases in the style and language of news discourse, so that the distinction between newspaper discourse and public relations discourse can be difficult to draw. But the linguistic codes used in newspapers are not all the same. Particular linguistic signs, narrative forms and mythic meanings deriving from a news source must be assimilated into the habitual discourse of an individual newspaper.

One of the most interesting aspects of newspaper discourses is the way that they address their readers. Particular linguistic signs and ways of combining them according to socially-accepted codes connote that newspaper discourse is a sign of the reader's discourse, a representation of the reader's own discursive idiom. Newspaper discourse cannot be the same as the reader's real discourse, since the newspaper does not know who the reader is, and newspaper language is written, not spoken. But newspaper discourse takes the form of a coded discourse which stands in the place of the reader, asking the reader to identify with the subject-position implied by the code. 'Popular' tabloids use an orally-based, restricted set of vocabulary and sentence structures, while 'quality' newspapers use a more elaborated and complex set of codes which have more in common with written communication than spoken communication. This does not mean that 'popular' newspaper readers cannot write, or that they do not understand long words. The orally-based discourses of 'popular' newspapers connote familiarity, camaraderie, and entertainment value as opposed to the connotations of authority, formality and seriousness which are present in the discourses of 'quality' newspapers.

Orality is connoted by: the use of deliberate misspelling; contrastive stress (like italics or bold letters in contrast to the standard typeface as in '**FIRST**' and '**SECOND**' in the *Daily Mirror*'s 'My affair with dirty Dean'); paralanguage (features of spoken discourse, like writing words in ways that connote slurred or hesitant speech, for instance); information structure (the use of short or incomplete sentences); slang words ('romps' in the 'My affair' story); idioms ('Fat Cats' in the *Daily Mirror*'s 'Cedric snubs curbs' story); clichés, first names and nicknames; contractions (for example 'don't'); deixis (words like 'here', 'now', 'you', 'we', 'this', which make reference to the situation of a speaker); modality (implying a speaker's subjective judgement with words like 'correct', 'should', 'might', 'regrettable', 'certainly', etc.); and the use of words which constitute speech acts (questions, commands, accusations, demands, where the word is also performing an action in itself). Alliteration is very common ('dirty Dean', 'cheating churchman' in the 'My affair' story), as are puns. It is not just particular linguistic signs which connote speech, but also typography and layout. Typographic devices break up the linear appearance of print, and such devices include variation of type-face, and dots or dashes connoting unfinished sentences or shifts of thought in the same sentence. Fowler (1991), from which this analysis derives, has a much fuller discussion of these linguistic features.

On the other hand, 'quality' newspapers use longer sentences (the eight-line first paragraph of *The Times*'s 'French UN' story is a single sentence), no misspelling or contrastive stress within stories, no signifiers of paralanguage, no incomplete sentences, and fewer of the other devices mentioned above. This may not mean that 'quality' newspapers are better because they appear more 'authoritative' than 'popular' tabloids. Authority is a mythic meaning connoted by the discourse of the 'quality' press, and is no less a mythic meaning than the 'entertainment value' connoted by the discourse of 'popular' newspapers. To make a value judgement about the two kinds of discourse would be to assume that there is a discourse which is 'transparent' and uncoded. This assumption is itself a mythic meaning of news 'objectivity' which is constructed in discourse.

The mythic equivalence between a reader's speech codes and the newspaper's written discursive codes enables the newspaper to seem to engage in dialogue with the reader. This establishes an imaginary community of readers, reader loyalty to the paper's identity as manifested in its discourse, and a familiar environment in which ideological values circulate between newspaper and reader. Dialogic modes of discourse have the effect of presupposing an ongoing, comprehensible reality which is the referent of a conversation between newspaper and reader. Both parties, it seems, know what they are referring to, and do not need to analyse or define the subject of their 'conversation'. The ideological function of this way of using linguistic signs and their connotations of speech is to make the referent of the news story (the news event) seem naturally given. When consensual agreement between newspaper and reader is established by the news discourse, there is no apparent need for an analysis of how the meaning of the news event has been constructed, coded by the signs used to represent it.

The desire for items of high news value will militate against the presentation of consensus, of a smoothly-running and coherent reality, because news stories are so often about events which seem to threaten stability. In the context of this contradiction in news discourse, the maintenance of the ideology of stability is displaced onto the linguistic structuring of the discourse. Stability is evident in the consistent use of the same news discourse for all the stories and in every issue of the newspaper. 'Quality' newspapers demonstrate discursive stability by the relatively formal language and considered tone of their stories, connoting the measured assessment and objective reporting of the mythic 'responsible' journalist, and the supposed good sense of their readers. Tabloid newspapers demonstrate stability in the maintenance of the orally-based language used, connoting a consistent 'tone of voice' which stands in for their reader's assumed discourse. There is also consistency in the repeated use of the same narrative forms in newspaper stories, despite the perpetually different events which are being reported.

News stories use a lot of personalisation (reference to individuals) in stories where the individual is a representative of some larger news issue relating to an ideological meaning. If we recall Barthes's example of a black soldier saluting the flag on the cover of *Paris-Match*, a particular person was pictured because he became the instance of the myth of French imperialism. In news stories, personalisation techniques include the use of linguistic signs like names, ages, job descriptions and gender roles. However, as in the case of the black soldier, this personalisation is not only connoting the uniqueness of the person, but relating him or her to a category of person (like popstar, mother, spokesman, premier, etc.) with a mythic meaning. Both *The Times* and the *Daily Mirror* use personalisation in their discursive treatment of the alleged affair between Dr Brandon Jackson and Verity Freestone, mentioning names, ages and the job descriptions 'Dean' and 'verger', for instance. But the personalisation here signifies membership of particular social groups with mythic meanings, rather than uniqueness.

Church officials are coded as non-sexual and morally upstanding, and the signs 'Dean' and 'verger' invoke this connoted meaning. The alleged affair between the two people would clearly threaten their socially coded meaning, so that the 'scandal' attains news value by being unexpected and controversial.

It also exhibits unambiguity, since it can be narrated in terms of existing narrative codes. News stories about the sexual misadventures of church officials have been common for decades, and this variant of the 'sex scandal' narrative makes the Dean and verger story readily encodable and decodable in ideological terms. Ideologically, extra-marital affairs are coded as sinful, immoral and socially disruptive, but also pleasurable. All of these naturalised meanings of affairs are invoked in the news stories, which can be seen as an extreme example of a current contradiction in the dominant ideology. While individual identity is constructed as sexualised and gendered, there is considerable pressure to regulate individual sexual identity by legal, economic and political means. The individuals in the 'sex scandal' stories become the bearers of mythic meanings, since stories about individuals are always in newspapers because they are examples of some larger issue which has ideological importance (if this were not the case, the individual's story would have no news value). Whether or not Dr Jackson and Verity Freestone had an affair (they were later judged not to have had one), the accusation that they did have an affair was an occasion for a narrative that encoded a current ideological conflict.

Headlines and graphics

The function of the linguistic syntagms of headlines is to draw the attention of the reader to the topic of each news story, and through the connotations of the linguistic signs to propose some of the social codes appropriate for understanding it. The five main headlines on the front page of *The Times* are all almost complete sentences whose connotations refer us to our existing knowledge about particular news stories. 'French UN rescue force is "too small"' connotes disagreement between nations in the field of global politics, and the attribution of the quote '"too small"' is relayed and substantiated by the smaller headline 'Britain favours 4,000 troops'. The headline does not mention the Bosnian conflict, and could be decoded by reference to mythic meanings of the UN as weak, or France as militarily ineffective, although the first paragraph of the news story closes down these connotations. The relatively polysemic headlines and relatively unequivocal text work together to both open out and close down decodings of the story. 'Verger tells of sordid affair with the dean' activates several narrative codes. As discussed above, it invokes 'sex scandal' narratives involving church officials. The sign 'tells' in conjunction with 'affair' connotes the public confession of supposed private misdeeds which are given their coded significance as both exciting and sinful by the sign 'sordid'.

The three headlines on the *Daily Mirror*'s front page also denote the news topic concerned, and connote the mythic social meanings to be brought to the story. 'My affair with dirty Dean' connotes the confessional in 'my affair', and sordidness in 'dirty Dean' activating the same narrative codes and mythic meanings as in *The Times*. But since the sign 'Dean' is unaccompanied by the definite article 'the' it could also denote a person named Dean. This polysemic value of the sign is relayed and contained by the smaller headline 'Ex-verger tells of steamy romps' and the text of the news story accompanying it. Unlike the mainly denotative 'Robbie quits Take That', the headline 'Cedric snubs curbs' is difficult to decode except in relation to the accompanying photograph, text, graphic sign and photograph caption. The photograph denotes Cedric Brown, head of British Gas, whose occupation is connoted by the blue flame-shaped graphic sign. This sign of a flame is an intertextual reference to British Gas advertising in several media, which uses the flame as a logo. The linguistic slogo in these ads, 'Don't you just love being in control', which connotes the efficiency and controllability of gas fuel and appliances, adds to the mythic meanings of the headline.

Cedric Brown is 'in control' of British Gas, but his 'control' over the pay levels of his company's executives is threatened by 'Government-backed moves' to impose pay guidelines. There is a contradiction between two ideological positions here. Either free enterprise justifies companies in paying top businesspeople whatever they deem appropriate, or social harmony should be supported by political intervention in pay deals so that the difference between top businesspeople's and ordinary workers' pay is reduced. Each of these ideological positions seems like 'natural common sense', and yet they are incompatible. The story exhibits the news values of meaningfulness, continuity, unambiguity and reference to an élite person. The intertextual reference to an ad campaign in the gas-flame graphic triggers the mythic meaning 'control' which this story both naturalises and also debates.

Photographs in the news

This section is a discussion of the signs and codes of news photographs, based on an essay by Roland Barthes called 'The photographic message' (1977) which deals with newspaper photographs in semiotic terms. Some of the issues considered here have already been touched on in earlier chapters of this book, for instance the fundamental argument that photographs always denote something, but that what is of more interest in decoding their meanings are the connotations which photographs generate. The connoted message of these iconic signs depends on what is denoted, but goes much further in providing a mythic significance which contains and shapes the decoding of a photograph's connotations.

Press photographs will have been carefully selected from a number of possible choices, and may have been 'cropped' (cut down to emphasise particular parts of the image), or technically processed to alter contrast, colour or some other aspect of the photograph. So the photograph 'is an object that has been worked on, chosen, composed, constructed, treated according to professional, aesthetic or ideological norms which are so many factors of connotation' (Barthes 1977: 19). Each photograph will not be a 'pure' 'natural' image, but one which has been selected and processed in order to generate particular connotations. This recalls the status of photographic signs in advertising, where obviously the picture is used because its connotations support particular mythic meanings. The photographs denoting Dr Jackson and Verity Freestone on the front page of the *Daily Mirror*, for instance, have been cropped into oval shapes and overlapped. This cropping and framing connotes 'romance' by referring to the cultural code in which lovers' photographs are conventionally framed together in this way.

Photographs must gain some of their meaningfulness from the newspaper context in which they appear. This context is the channel through which their messages are transmitted, which shapes their significance for us. The newspaper is a message too,

or more accurately a collection of various messages which surround the photograph. The newspaper in which the photograph
appears will give rise to certain expectations about the kinds of
picture we expect to see (pictures of royalty, criminals, popstars,
or politicians, foreign wars, diplomats, etc.). One kind of photograph may seem 'out of place' in a particular newspaper, but be
routinely used in another paper. For instance, it would be
unusual for a photograph of Robbie from Take That to appear on
the front page of *The Times*, but not unusual in the *Daily Mirror*.
In the same way, different pages and sections of newspapers deal
with different kinds of news. So a photograph may connote different meanings when used on a 'hard news' page than when it
is used on a page dealing with personality stories.

Photographs usually appear with a news story, and the text of
the story will anchor the meanings of the photograph, supporting some readings of the photograph while discounting others.
From the point of view of our analysis of the photograph, the text
will provide connotations from its linguistic signs that set limits
to the meanings of the picture, and direct us to construct its
mythic significance in a certain way; 'the text loads the image,
burdening it with a culture, a moral, an imagination' (Barthes
1977: 26). The caption underneath it similarly provides a set of
linguistic meanings which shape our reading of the picture. The
role of the linguistic message is to load down the image with particular cultural meanings. But since photographs bring with
them the assumption that they simply record something which
'naturally' happened, the meanings which the text loads onto
the photograph are themselves 'naturalised', rendered innocent
and apparently self-evident. The photograph functions as the
'proof' that the text's message is true.

Moving to a more detailed analysis of the meanings of photographs, Barthes proposes six procedures through which connotations are generated. The first three procedures relate to the
particular choices about what is in the photograph, and the
ways in which the photograph was produced condition the
ways in which the photo is decoded. These three procedures
therefore affect what the photograph denotes, and thus how we
read the connotations of what it shows. The final three connotation procedures relate to the context of the picture, and

depend on the relationship between the signs in the photograph and other signs outside it.

The first connotation procedure which Barthes identifies is what he calls 'trick effects'. Here the photograph has been altered specifically to produce a particular mythic meaning. Perhaps parts of two photographs have been combined, so that two people who never actually met appear to be present in the same place, or the facial expression of the subject of the picture has been altered to give the person a guilty, evil or dangerous look. The use of trick effects in such a blatant manner is rare, but is sometimes discovered in the sensationalising coverage of crimes, for instance. This kind of trick effect is now much easier because of the widespread use of computer technology to 'brush out' unwanted details in pictures, or to enhance the colour or definition of the picture. Trick effects then, 'intervene without warning in the plane of denotation' (Barthes 1977: 21), using our assumption that photographs simply denote what was really there to load the image with connotations, to code it in a particular way.

The second coding system in Barthes's list of connotation procedures is pose (1977: 22). In photographs of people, their physical pose very often provides connotations which affect our reading of the picture, and thus the mythic meanings attached to the person. These gestures and facial expressions mean something to us because they belong to a code or language of gesture and expression which is recognised in our culture. Denoting someone's hands clasped together connotes 'praying' for us, and might generate the mythic meaning 'piety' for the person in the picture. The photographs of Dr Jackson and Verity Freestone on the front page of *The Times* denote the two people looking in each other's direction. Ms Freestone is frowning, and pursing her lips together, an expression which connotes disapproval and anger. Dr Jackson is looking upward, with his mouth open, an expression which connotes surprise and naïvety. Clearly, these connoted meanings support and relay the connotations of the linguistic signs in the caption of the picture and the headline of the story. The choice of which pose to photograph someone in is a choice of what to denote in the picture, but also a choice about which cultural codes are brought to bear when constructing the connoted meaning of the photograph.

The third connotation procedure Barthes proposes is 'objects' (1977: 22), the denotation of particular objects in the photograph. The presence of certain denoted objects which already possess cultural connotations can enable the transfer of these connotations from the objects to the news story. There are no objects in the front-page photographs of the newspapers reproduced here. But on page eight of *The Times* there is a photograph denoting five cameras with long-range lenses pointing towards a house. Because these cameras are used to obtain photographs of reclusive stars, they are objects which can connote 'intrusiveness'. The photograph accompanies a story concerning government regulation of the press, in which the main issue discussed is the right of people to privacy. The connotations of the cameras relay the connotations of the headline 'Victims of intrusion may be given compensation', in which the linguistic sign 'victims' naturalises the mythic social meaning of the right to a private life.

The three connotation procedures so far discussed relate to what is denoted in the photograph, and the connotations of what is denoted. The next three connotation procedures refer to the manner of the photograph and its context. The first of these Barthes calls '*photogénie*' (translated as 'photogenia'), which denotes the quality of photographing well, or looking good in photographs. The connoted message of *photogénie*, Barthes suggests is 'the image itself, "embellished" ... by techniques of lighting, exposure and printing' (1977: 23). Because of the hurried nature of much press photography, *photogénie* is not often seen in newspaper pictures. It is sometimes seen in non-news sections of newspapers, where photogenic models are photographed simply because they look attractive in photographs. There were some photographs of the model Elle Macpherson in the *Daily Star* on 18 July 1995, with the caption 'The ultimate pictures of the ultimate girl', connoting both her own *photogénie* and the attractiveness of the pictures.

The next connotation procedure Barthes outlines is 'aestheticism', where photographs borrow the coding systems of another art form, giving the picture an aesthetic, or self-consciously artistic quality (1977: 24). News photographs rarely use aesthetic codes in this self-conscious way, since they would conflict with mythic meanings of objectivity and immediacy. Aestheticism is a connotation procedure used in other media like advertising, and the 'lifestyle' sections of newspapers use 'aesthetic' photographs when the articles concern fashion or holidays, for instance, where the aesthetic codes of advertising images can be intertextually referred to.

Finally, Barthes discusses 'syntax', a connotation procedure relating to the placing of one photograph next to another, like the placing of words next to each other according to the syntax of a language (1977: 24). Sequences of photographs are sometimes found in newspapers when they record a dramatic event, like an earthquake or a sports event. Each photograph may well contain a multiplicity of coded connotations individually, but clearly the meaning of the sequence of pictures depends on the differences of one from the next as the event unfolds in time. The repetition and variation of the signs in the pictures 'add up' to produce particular connotations for the sequence as a whole, which become the signifiers of the mythic meaning of the event, like 'tragedy' or 'triumph' for instance.

Barthes returns at the end of his essay on press photographs to the thrust of Saussure's analysis of language; that language shapes thought and experience by providing the signs and codes which give form and meaning to our social reality. Language, Saussure argued, cuts up the world and its meaning into specific shapes. Language 'cuts out' the signifieds and signifiers which are available to us for thinking and experiencing. Therefore, even though photographs appear to denote the things they show, and simply record what is in front of the camera without the intervention of language and culture, there can be no such thing as a purely denotative photograph. Once we perceive what the photograph denotes – man, tree, the Houses of Parliament, etc. – we perceive it through the linguistic code which gives us the signs 'man', 'tree', 'the Houses of Parliament' and so on. Since thought and perception are enabled by the language system, the meanings of every photographic image depend on the system of language despite the fact that they are made up of iconic and not linguistic signs. Photographs, because they mechanically reproduce what was in front of the camera, claim to denote reality.

But as we have seen, this denotative aspect of photographs is a mythic foundation on which connotations are built. The cultural significance of photography as a medium rests on this 'double message' of photographs. They appear to denote their subject without coding it, but when subjected to a semiotic analysis, they reveal the cultural codes of connotation at work to produce mythic meanings.

Newspaper readers

At the beginning of this chapter, I quoted some figures showing the circulations of a number of British daily newspapers. This numerical data is helpful in getting an idea of the various titles currently available, and their relative popularity. But the figures tell us nothing about what kinds of people read which newspapers, and nothing about how newspapers are read in concrete social contexts. It is startling to discover, for instance, that in 1990 the most popular British newspaper, the *Sun*, was read by a quarter of all adult males and one fifth of all adult females (not all of these people will have actually bought the newspaper themselves). This statistic seems to show that the *Sun* has a huge influence on the news people perceive, and how they perceive it. Critics of the news media have often bemoaned these apparent influences, and have also attacked the legal framework which allows a few corporations to own several mass-market newspapers and therefore perhaps to exert significant political influence.

However, when we can gather some further information (although still of a statistical nature), blanket critiques of newspapers' influence become more difficult to sustain. A National Readership Survey conducted by the Audit Bureau of Circulation, detailing who read what over the period from January to June 1993, tells us a little about readership groups. Among managerial, professional, and skilled workers (known as social groups A, B, and C1), 61.5 per cent of people read newspapers. The *Daily Mail* was read by 13.9 per cent of this group, the *Sun* by 12.7 per cent, the *Daily Telegraph* by 11.4 per cent, the *Daily Mirror* by 10.5 per cent, the *Guardian* by 5.7 per cent, and *The Times* by 5.1 per cent. It would clearly be incorrect to say that only 'quality' broadsheet newspapers are read by the most wealthy and

high-status people in society. Among manual or unskilled workers and people with very low incomes (known as social groups
C2, D and E), 62.1 per cent of people read newspapers. The *Sun*
was read by 28.6 per cent of this group, the *Daily Mirror* by 22.2
per cent, the *Daily Mail* by 7.5 per cent, the *Daily Telegraph* by
1.7 per cent, the *Guardian* by 1.4 per cent, and *The Times* by 0.6
per cent. We can see from these figures that no 'quality' broad-
sheets had significant penetration of the less wealthy market sectors. But one of the striking features of all these statistics is the
fragmentation of readerships which they imply. A wide variety
of different groups of people (even in the restricted economic
sense of 'group') are reading different newspapers. Once we go
beyond this raw statistical information, and think about the
ways in which newspapers fit into people's life experiences, the
picture becomes even more fragmented.

Some individuals and households buy more than one newspaper, or buy different newspapers on different days in the week, so
that at least some of the time more than one narrative encoding
of a news item can be compared, contrasted and intertextually
mixed. News is now consumed by many people from television
news programmes, or radio, teletext, or even on-line news services, as well as or instead of newspapers, adding another
medium to the intertextual mix. Newspapers are often read at
work, and on journeys to work or elsewhere. In these work and
domestic situations, news items are discussed, extracts are read
out and commented on, so that the meanings of news are negotiated between a reader and the newspaper, and between several
readers and the newspaper, and between several readers and several encodings of the same item in different newspapers. Aside
from the ways in which these contexts affect the meanings of
news items, talking about the news and about newspapers is
itself a medium of social communication. Conversations relating
to news items become a medium in which the news is not foregrounded as 'content', and the form of the conversation as a
medium of social exchange is what is significant. In this social
situation and in others, neither newspapers nor news may be
'taken seriously', so that reading and discussing news involves
recoding news discourse in a quite different way to its original
presentation in the newspaper.

Even in the most close reading of news discourse, the reader is an active participant in constructing the meanings of the text, not only by decoding signs and meanings, but also by anticipating the codes needed to make sense of the discourse, and checking the mythic meanings constructed by the text's connotations against the reader's own ideological assumptions. The reader is not only a consumer of already-encoded meanings, but also a producer of the meanings of the text. Readers of 'popular' tabloids may become expert in the discursive codes used in the paper, where language is often used in foregrounded ways including puns, metaphors, alliteration, etc. On one level, these features work against the reader's consumption of the 'content' of the discourse, since the linguistic signs through which news is conveyed are being self-consciously displayed as artifice. The reader can actively enjoy decoding the text and its almost 'literary' discourse. However, this pleasure reinforces the paper's 'brand identity', and allows the reader pleasure in the newspaper as an entertainment medium as well as an information medium. The pleasure of reading might either reinforce or work against the newspaper's ideological coding of news events.

As we have seen, news discourse frames events as significant by a variety of semiotic processes, but the practices of reading newspapers in concrete social contexts will always be a significant factor which semiotic analysis cannot deal with adequately. By conducting a detailed analysis of newspaper stories, much can be discovered about how newspaper discourse is structured and how it constructs news and the meanings of news. But there are some limitations to the certainty with which we can discover the meanings of news stories by using semiotic methods, since semiotics cannot reproduce the ways newspapers are read in real social contexts. One quite successful response to this problem is a sociological approach known as the encoding–decoding model (Hall *et al.* 1980). It concerns the ways in which messages are encoded by a sender (like a newspaper journalist) and decoded by a receiver (like a newspaper reader). First, both senders and receivers probably share a number of common codes, like language, gesture and occasion (certain signs carry meanings dependent on their situation in time and place) as long as they live in the same culture. But because the fit between the sender's and the receiver's knowledge and familiarity with codes can never in principle be exact, it is not possible to argue that an encoder's 'preferred meaning' will always be understood by the decoder.

This way of understanding communication acknowledges that all signs are polysemic, or open to a range of different interpretations. Preferred meanings are more likely to be encoded and decoded with the same result when both parties in the communication share common codes and ideological positions. Decoders who take up different codes and ideological positions will probably construct 'oppositional' or 'aberrant' decodings, which may be far from identical to the sender's encoded meanings. Indeed, much of the academic writing about newspapers has discussed news stories and photographs to try to reconstruct what the preferred meanings of news stories might be, whether the journalists who wrote the stories knew that they were encoding these meanings or not. The meanings uncovered by academic studies of news have often been very much oppositional decodings, which have critiqued news discourse for its ideological naturalisation of particular social meanings. But preferred meanings have a very uncertain usefulness as knowledge, since it is unclear whether they are meanings necessarily produced by the signs within a text, or the meanings most commonly perceived by real readers, or whether preferred meanings are only evident to academic analysts looking below the surface meanings of signs to the mythic social meanings they support.

Over the years that semiotic analysis has developed, it has shifted its emphasis as far as this problem of decoding and preferred readings is concerned. The earlier phase of semiotic analysis, known as 'structuralism', assumed that there are 'correct' meanings of signs which can be discovered by looking at the relationships between signs and codes in particular texts. Structuralist semiotics would claim to reveal the preferred meaning of a text. But later, in a variant known as 'social semiotics', semiotic analysis acknowledged that it is only one of many ways of investigating the meanings of signs. As only one discourse among many competing discourses, the results of a semiotic analysis may not reveal the 'correct' meaning of signs, but merely the meaning which the discourse of semiotic analysis allows it to reveal. Here, the preferred reading is simply the one which the discourse of semiotics is likely to discover. Once it was accepted that real readers, with their own discourses, are likely to decode meanings in a wide variety of ways, research on the responses of real readers seemed to be necessary.

One way to draw together these different approaches to meaning is to acknowledge that each way of analysing meaning is likely to produce a different preferred reading of what the meaning of a text is. The only way to decide which account of the meaning of a text is better than another is to see how effective it is. The discussion of newspapers in this chapter shows how semiotic analysis can determine the meanings produced within a text made up of linguistic and visual signs, by looking at the structural relationships of signs to each other, and of signs to wider social codes. The limitation of this approach is that it can only partially take account of how real readers construct meanings for themselves in concrete social contexts. But on the other hand, the advantage of this approach is that it shows how news discourse attempts to close down the range of possible decodings of its signs, by relaying together the connotations of, for instance, photographs and captions, or headlines and news stories. This book argues here and in the other chapters that semiotic analysis is highly effective in revealing how meanings are communicated by signs, read in relation to social codes, and related to wider ideological positions in society. But although this kind of semiotic analysis is effective in these terms, it must always be acknowledged as one kind of discourse among a range of other competing ways of dealing with the media.

Sources and further reading

Earlier studies of news focused on its ideological assumptions and economic and institutional organisation. Cohen and Young (1973), the Glasgow Media Group (1976, 1980, 1986) and Hall *et al.* (1978) are examples of this approach. The discussion of news discourse from a semiotic point of view in this chapter is indebted to the still persuasive Hartley (1982) and the rather different form of semiotic analysis used by Fowler (1991). Part one of McNair (1994) discusses the evolution and various methodologies of academic research on news in print and on television, though the book does not contain semiotic analyses and focuses instead on the political, institutional and professional organisation of news in Britain.

Some of the books listed in the Sources and further reading section of the next chapter are also relevant to the study of newspapers, and some of the books listed above also contain sections on TV news.

Suggestions for further work

1 Compare the treatment of the same news event in two different newspapers published on the same day. How similar or different are the relationships between headlines, text, picture, layout, etc? What effects do the connotations of different coded ways of presenting the story have on its meanings?

2 Compare an edition of a local newspaper with an edition of a national newspaper. How do news values appear to differ between the two papers? Why is this?

3 Choose a news photograph which is interesting to analyse in terms of the codes and conventions outlined in this chapter. How do these relate to the accompanying story, caption and headline?

4 Cut out three photographs from a newspaper. Try to devise three captions for each photograph which anchor their connotations in quite different ways from each other and from the original caption. How resistant were the photographs to your re-encoding of them, and why?

5 Analyse the advertisements in a 'quality' broadsheet and a 'popular' tabloid newspaper. How much similarity is there in the products or services advertised in each paper, and how much difference is there between the semiotic codes of the ads in the two papers? Why is this?

6 Compare a current newspaper with a newspaper from decades ago (Hartley 1982 reproduces pages of past newspapers if you cannot obtain your own). What changes are evident in the codes of language, layout, photographs, etc? How much change do you find in the naturalised ideologies of then and now?

7 Analyse the signs in a newspaper of 'you' the reader, your demands, pleasures, linguistic codes and ways of reading. How coherent or contradictory are these representations of 'you'? Is there an 'ideal reader' of the newspaper?

5

Television news

Introduction

This chapter is primarily about evening news programmes on British television. It follows on from the chapter on newspapers by discussing the semiotic analysis of the linguistic and visual signs which communicate news, and the mythic social meanings and ideological significance of news discourse. The detailed analysis of TV news draws on some of the items in two news programmes on different TV channels, the BBC *Nine O'Clock News* and the ITN *News at Ten* broadcast on the same day, Tuesday 18 July 1995. This was the same day on which the two newspapers whose front pages are reproduced in the last chapter were published. So one of the issues considered in this chapter is how the news items on TV news relate to the news items in the newspapers which some viewers will have read on the same day. This is also the first chapter in this book in which moving images are discussed in detail. It will be necessary to start discussing how semiotic analysis approaches the mix of spoken and written linguistic signs, still and moving images, music and graphics which are all present in TV news and in the television medium in general.

Some conceptual issues relating to the television medium are introduced here, and are followed up more fully in the next chapter, which is about a range of mainly fictional television programmes. In particular, this chapter begins to address the facts that television is a broadcast medium received by a mass audience, and that television is not exclusively national, but also transnational or global in its reach. Because of the wide variation in audience groups which this situation produces, the issues

of polysemy and audience decoding are given further discussion
in this chapter. A related issue is the fact that TV news is not
often watched in isolation from the other kinds of programmes
on TV. While this chapter primarily explains a semiotic approach
to TV news in particular, it sometimes becomes essential to see
how the meanings of TV news interrelate with the meanings of
other TV programmes. This way of writing the chapter is
designed to allow for a clear discussion of TV news as a specific
genre or category of television programme. But my aim is also to
begin to introduce the idea that much can be learned by thinking of television not as a set of self-contained programmes, but
as an intertextual field in which programmes interrelate and
affect each other.

So first the role of news as part of the heterogeneous television
output will be discussed, to see what role news plays in the total
TV schedule. Then we move on to the coding systems which
organise the signs and meanings of TV news. News is a specific
genre of TV discourse which is highly coded as we shall see, and
it is easy to recognise a news programme when we switch on the
TV because of this restricted repertoire of codes. A reminder of
the discussion of codes of news value in the previous chapter will
show that news value works rather differently in TV news and
newspapers, and this issue will lead into some preliminary
remarks about the semiotics of television as a medium. As the
word 'medium' itself connotes, TV news is a mediator between
the viewer and a reality constructed by signs. A semiotic analysis of TV news will show how particular mythic meanings of reality are shaped by signs and codes, and how watching TV news
also shapes the subjective identity of viewers in different ways.
As we consider the role of the viewer as a decoder of signs, we
shall again encounter questions about the power of semiotics to
discover the 'correct' meanings of signs in real social contexts.

News in the TV schedule

News has a significant role in the broadcast output of television
channels. Satellite and cable offer all-day news channels, and all
terrestrial television stations in Britain broadcast news several
times each day. The longest news bulletins are in the early

evening, the time when people return from work, and at the end
of the 'prime-time' mid-evening period when family entertainment programmes give way to programmes aimed at a more
adult audience. From the point of view of television stations,
news not only serves to fulfil the requirement that they inform
their audience about contemporary events, but is also used to
manage the TV audience's patterns of viewing. A popular early-
evening news programme may encourage viewers to remain
watching that channel for subsequent entertainment programmes in the prime-time which follows the news. Later news
bulletins occur at times when adult-oriented programmes begin
to be shown after the 9.00 p.m. 'watershed', when children are
presumed not to be watching. Watching the long late-evening
news bulletin may encourage viewers to remain on that channel
for subsequent programmes. BBC1's evening news at 9.00 p.m.
falls at exactly this watershed point, and on 18 July 1995 there
were trailers for the three programmes to follow the news, which
were a documentary on the charity Barnardo's, a programme on
health issues presented by comedienne Ruby Wax, and *You
Decide*, a current affairs debate (discussed in chapter six). ITV's
10.00 p.m. news bulletin occurs at a less convenient time for the
change in audience composition, and ITV executives campaigned
in 1994 (unsuccessfully) to shift their news timeslot for this
reason.

TV news is usually regarded as authoritative, with most people
in Britain gaining their knowledge of news through TV rather
than newspapers. The dominance of TV as a news medium
comes in part from the perceived impartiality of news broadcasting. There are rules of 'balance' and 'objectivity' in the regulations governing television broadcasting, and we shall consider
what balance and objectivity connote later in this chapter. Newspapers are not subject to these rules. The increasing dominance
of TV as the news medium has been reinforced by a shift in
newspaper coverage to other kinds of material, like lifestyle features or sensational stories, or to greater coverage of areas not
extensively covered by TV news, like sport. The dominance of TV
news derives also from its immediacy, since newspapers must be
produced several hours before being distributed, while TV news
can incorporate new reports even during the programme broad-

cast. On Tuesday 18 July 1995, almost all national newspapers carried stories on the continuing Bosnian conflict which was featured in the main stories of ITV's and BBC's news programmes. Several national newspapers contained feature stories on Lisa Leeson, wife of a banker whose dealings caused the collapse of his employer, Barings bank. This continuing news story was featured in both TV news programmes since an official report on the bank's collapse was published on 18 July, but no newspaper had the opportunity to present a story about the official report on the day of its publication. The TV news coverage of these two stories form the main examples discussed in this chapter.

The newspapers published on the following day, 19 July, almost all carried a front-page story on the report into the collapse of Barings bank, and all 'quality' broadsheet newspapers also reported the threat to UN peacekeeping troops in Bosnia. So while there are evident parallels between the news values of newspaper journalists and television journalists, there are constraints imposed by the different timing of news production in the two media which determine the degree of immediacy which can be connoted in each. The different stories on the front pages of 'quality' and 'popular' newspapers also show that the news values of television news programmes are more similar to those of 'quality' newspapers than to 'popular' ones. This sharing of news values by 'quality' newspapers and TV news is also paralleled by the authoritativeness, objectivity and balance which are connoted in TV news discourses and in 'quality' newspapers' discourses. These mythic meanings are discussed later in this chapter. Like newspapers, television channels compete to attract audiences and advertisers, but the differences in funding arrangements for British television channels make a direct comparison between them, and between television news and newspapers, much less straightforward.

In Britain, the BBC's two terrestrial channels are funded by a licence fee which must be paid by all owners of television sets. The regional TV companies broadcasting on the ITV channel, and the fourth terrestrial channel, Channel Four, gain their income from advertisements. There are TV commercials before and after ITV's *News at Ten*, and half-way through the news. TV broadcasting companies funded by commercial advertising need to attract audiences for advertisers, and TV broadcasters funded by licence fee need to justify the compulsory payment of the licence fee by attracting large audiences. So broadcasters continually compete against each other to achieve large audiences for their programmes ('ratings'), and to encourage viewing of their own programmes rather than the competing programmes from other channels which are shown at the same time ('audience share'). On 18 July 1995 the *News at Ten* was preceded by a trailer for the film *Beaches* to be shown the next day from 8.00 p.m. until the *News at Ten*, thus advertising both the film and the news. So the trailer can be regarded as an advertisement for the ITV channel (and the Carlton television company which broadcasts on this channel), attempting to attract audience share for the following day's TV. About six million people watched each of the two late evening news programmes broadcast on Tuesday 18 July 1995, but since they were broadcast at different times they were not competing for audience share. News on TV is not only significant in itself, but also has an important role in the daily schedule and in the attraction and control of audiences.

Defining TV news

As we have seen in the discussion of newspaper discourse, news is a mediator of events, defining, shaping and representing the real by the use of linguistic and visual codes. The discourse of TV news is composed of language and visual images, organised by codes and conventions which the news viewer has to perceive and recognise in order for the viewer to construct sense. This competence in decoding news derives in part from the viewer's competence in the discourses which the news borrows from society at large. For instance, the presenters of TV news programmes adopt a formal dress code. Men wear suits and women wear business clothes (blouses, jackets, unobtrusive jewellery). On 18 July 1995 both Michael Buerk, presenting the *Nine O'Clock News*, and Trevor Macdonald, presenting the *News at Ten*, wore ties and jackets. News presenters are thus coded as professional, serious, and authoritative. These connoted meanings are supported by the impersonal linguistic codes used in news presenters' speech (they hardly ever say 'I'), and the lack of gestural signs which might connote emotion or involvement in the news stories they present. The mythic meaning that news presenters are neutral and authoritative is constructed from these connotations, which viewers recognise from other aspects of social life and not only from the codes of television.

Viewers of TV news will also make use of their knowledge of codes specific to the medium in which the news is broadcast. Here are some examples of television codes. Like all other TV programmes, TV news is separated from other programmes and commercials by title sequences. Title sequences are syntagms of signs which signify boundaries between one part of the continual flow of TV material and the rest of it. News programmes contain interviews which are visually coded in similar ways to current affairs programmes and some sports programmes. Camera shots alternate back and forth between speakers, signifying the to and fro of conversation, or unseen speakers put questions to people denoted in studio or outside locations. The news presenter's head-on address to the camera is also found in current affairs, sports and quiz programmes, signifying the presenter's role in mediating between the viewer and the other components of the programme. News programmes feature actuality film with voice-over, which is also found in documentary programmes and signifies 'observed reality'. These examples show that TV news is not a unique television form, but rather a genre of television whose codes draw on the viewer's knowledge of the codes of other genres of programme. The meanings of TV news derive from some codes which are borrowed from social life in general, and from codes used in the TV medium.

As in the case of newspaper discourse, TV news does not consist of lists of facts, but of narrative reports of events. Like newspapers, TV news makes use of criteria of news value, where the set of priorities and assumptions shared by news broadcasters determines which news reports are given greatest significance within the news bulletin. In general, reports with high news value are those which appear near the beginning of the bulletin, just as the front pages of newspapers present stories with high perceived news value to readers. Two of the first three news reports on the 18 July 1995 *News at Ten* and *Nine O'Clock News* relate to the same news stories (developments in the Bosnian conflict, and the publication of a report on the collapse of Barings bank). But some news bulletins are segmented by being interspersed with commercials, so that each segment of the news programme will contain a hierarchy of news items, with the first item in each segment having greater news value than the items which follow it. The first news story following the commercial break in the 18 July 1995 *News at Ten* (concerning an imminent rail workers' strike) was the third news story in BBC's *Nine O'Clock News*. As in newspapers, the ranking of reports according to their perceived news value gives us an insight into the ideology of TV news, and the ideology of society in general.

The representation of reality offered by TV news is not reality itself, but reality mediated by the signs, codes, myths and ideologies of news. News both shapes and reflects the dominant common-sense notion of what is significant (because what is significant is what is in the news), and also therefore contributes to the ongoing process of constructing a dominant ideology through which we perceive our reality. One obvious example of this ideological function of TV news is to naturalise the myth that what is significant is what happens from day to day in the public arenas of politics, business and international affairs. Eight of the thirteen news stories in the 18 July 1995 *News at Ten*, and eight of the twelve stories in the *Nine O'Clock News* concerned politics, business or international affairs. This encoding of events as of high news value in TV news is much closer to the discourse of 'quality' newspapers than to 'popular' tabloid newspapers.

Mythic meanings in TV news

Immediacy is a key mythic meaning of TV news. While newspapers have to be printed and distributed several hours before they can be read, electronic news gathering (ENG) techniques like the use of satellite links allow images and sound to be almost instantaneously incorporated into TV news programmes. Immediacy is connoted by the use of signs like the on-screen caption 'live' denoting the simultaneous occurrence and broadcast of an event, or by a spoken linguistic syntagm from the news presenter like 'Joining me now from Sarajevo is our correspondent there, Jeremy Bowen' (*Nine O'Clock News*, 18 July 1995). However, the organi-

sational chaos potentially caused by this incorporation of immediately occurring events makes broadcasters use it sparingly.
News programmes have to be meticulously planned and operate
under powerful constraints of timing, so that there must always
be a conflict between the desire to connote immediacy and the
desire to connote orderliness and authority. Compromises
between these two impulses include the use of 'packages', where
distant reporters beam pre-made sequences of pictures with voice-
over reports to the news organisation just in time for broadcasting in a prearranged timeslot, and live interviews in which a
certain time is allowed for live discussion of a news story.

The mythic meaning 'authority' in TV news is connoted by a
variety of means. One of these is the structuring of news stories,
which is discussed in the next section of this chapter. Another
coded use of signs connoting authority is the title sequence of the
news programme itself. TV news programmes tend to use music
featuring loud major chords, often played on brass instruments,
with connotations of importance, dignity and drama. Visually,
title sequences often use computer graphics in fast-moving syntagms which connote technological sophistication and contemporaneity. Each news programme's title sequence establishes the
mythic status of news as significant and authoritative, while
simultaneously giving each channel's news programmes a recognisable 'brand image' which differentiates it from its competitors.
The BBC *Nine O'Clock News* begins as a clock graphic's second
hand reaches 9.00 p.m. precisely. First, Michael Buerk is shown
at his desk with the BBC logo on the screen to his right. He outlines three main news stories, each anchored by brief actuality
footage. At the end of this syntagm, the viewer sees the edge of
a revolving globe, and as the camera pulls back and pans to the
right the globe is revealed as the centrepiece of a huge shield set
in a coat of arms. In the distance Michael Buerk can be seen,
behind a very long curved desk, with three large screens behind
him showing the edge of the globe as before, and a large cinema-
screen-shaped image to be used in the programme's first news
story. The lighting rig above the studio floor can be seen. Brass
and percussion music accompany the sequence.

This title sequence signifies the authority of BBC news through
the connotations of, for example, the coat of arms (tradition and

dignity), the revolving globe (global coverage of news), and the studio (large, technological, professional). The title sequence of the *News at Ten* also has brass and percussion music, with a voice-over announcing 'Now, from ITN, *News at Ten*, with Trevor Macdonald'. ITN, Independent Television News, is the company which produces news for the ITV channel, funded jointly by the regional companies like Carlton television which broadcast on the ITV channel. The ITN logo is superimposed over an airborne shot of the top of the Westminster clock tower in London known as Big Ben. The camera tilts down to its large clock showing 10.00 p.m., and pans over the Houses of Parliament before mixing to a closer shot of the clock again. Then the image cuts to the news studio in which Macdonald is at his desk. Behind him are a bank of TV screens showing the Big Ben clock, and to his left is a large screen also showing the clock. Macdonald announces four news stories, each accompanied by stills or brief visual sequences, and divided by the sound of the Big Ben bell chiming the hour. Like the title sequence of the *Nine O'Clock News*, the *News at Ten* sequence connotes authority. Iconic signs denote the Big Ben tower (in London, our capital city, Big Ben the name of the clock's bell is commonly used to refer to this

5   Martyn Lewis reading BBC News

building in the Houses of Parliament complex, thus connoting national political affairs, its gothic architectural style connoting tradition and dignity), aural signs denoting the clock chiming 10.00 p.m. connote contemporaneity and immediacy, the TV studio with its bank of screens connote technological effectiveness and professionalism. The title sequences of news programmes share many of the functions of ads, in differentiating similar products and providing them with a consistent identity. As this brief look at the title sequences of the two main evening news programmes shows, each sequence constructs similar mythic meanings, through the connotations of different sets of signs.

Balance and objectivity are shared mythic meanings which are also connoted in several different ways. The neutral vocal delivery of news presenters has already been mentioned, a sign connoting the mythic objectivity of the presenter and the news institution he or she represents. News programmes seek to connote balance by quoting or describing the responses of conflicting parties and interested groups to the news events narrated in news stories. For instance, in both Mark Webster's report on the Barings bank news story for ITN, and Greg Wood's report on the story for BBC, the Government's Chancellor of the Exchequer and the Opposition's Shadow Chancellor are each shown presenting their opposing views of the situation to Parliament. The mythic meanings 'balance' and 'objectivity' are constructed by the codes which organise the structure of news programmes and also of individual news stories, as outlined in the following section. The ideological significance of these mythic meanings is that balance and objectivity can only be defined in relation to a 'common-sense' view held consensually in society. A common-sense view is of course a naturalised ideological position, rather than an opinion which is necessarily true.

The structure of TV news

Events in the world are always potentially interpretable in different ways because events only become meaningful when they are represented by signs, and signs are organised by codes which establish the framework of meanings that are brought to bear in decoding signs. TV news discourse always attempts to deal with the ambiguity of reality by containing events within the codes of conventional subject categories, and conventional codes of narrative. News programmes very often divide news reports into categories like 'foreign news' or 'business news', reflecting the institutional divisions of their reporters into specialist staffs. Both BBC and ITN programmes on 18 July 1995 denote their news stories partly by captions like 'Bosnia', 'Report', or 'Immigrants' which appear next to the news presenter on the TV screen, connoting the specificity and uniqueness of each news story. But the majority of the stories are narrated by correspondents in terms of their specialist area of knowledge, like 'business', 'diplomatic' or 'economic' news. One important effect of this categorisation is to restrict the discursive codes through which news is represented. Even though news events often have very wide-ranging effects in different places and on different groups of people, the placing of news reports in coded discursive categories produces the mythic meaning that news events are unique but are significant in the terms of only one discursive code. For instance, a 'foreign news' story about an African famine may omit issues like the structural causes of the disaster (deforestation, debt crisis, trade barriers, etc.) because these causes 'belong' in other news categories like 'environment news' or 'business news'. The containment of news reports in categories of news discourse gives mythic meanings to news stories, and has ideological effects, since it naturalises the mythic meanings proposed and precludes decoding of the news story from alternative points of view.

By definition, all news events are new and different to what has gone before, but TV news discourse represents events by means of narrative functions which are established by convention. As Hartley shows (1982: 118–19) TV news stories make use of four main narrative functions. These are 'framing', 'focusing', 'realising' and 'closing'. By means of framing, the topic is established by a 'mediator', usually the news presenter, in the discursive code which will contain the story (for instance political news is usually coded as adversarial). The neutral language of the mediator encodes the mediator and the news organisation as neutral, with the effect of naturalising or rendering invisible the ideological significance of the mediator's framing or closing of the news story. The news stories about the report on the collapse of Barings bank in both the *Nine O'Clock News* and *News at Ten* are framed by the news presenters in the 'headlines' at the start of the programmes and again by the news presenters when the news stories are more fully narrated in the main body of the news.

Michael Buerk frames the Barings story by the syntagm 'The official report into the collapse of Barings bank says Nick Leeson destroyed it, but the bank let him' in the 'headline', and by this syntagm in the main body of the *Nine O'Clock News* :

> Here, the official report into the collapse of Barings bank has found that their trader, Nick Leeson had been running up massive losses since nineteen ninety-two. The Chancellor of the Exchequer said that serious failures of control and managerial confusion at Barings meant Mr Leeson's trading in derivatives went undetected. Labour said that the report gave a damning indictment of the Bank of England's approach to regulation.

So the discursive frame of this story encodes its meaning as both a sensational story about Leeson's errors and an example of institutional ineffectiveness. On *News at Ten*, Trevor Macdonald frames the story by the syntagm 'Official report attacks Barings' deceit and confusion' in the 'headline' sequence, and by this syntagm in the main body of *News at Ten*:

> The official report today on the dramatic collapse of Barings bank pins most of the blame on Nick Leeson, the trader who ran up losses of eight hundred and twenty-seven million pounds on the Singapore futures market. It says he deliberately concealed what was happening. But the report also criticises a confused Barings management for not detecting it. It's critical too of Barings' auditors, and blames the Bank of England for an error of judgement and a lack of rigour in its supervision.

The framing of the story here is very similar to that in the *Nine O'Clock News*, proposing that the story is about an individual's wrongdoing, and about inefficient public and private institutions.

The topic is 'focused' by contributions from a reporter or correspondent, who functions as an 'institutional voice' (Hartley 1982: 110–11) speaking with the authority of the news institution. The reporter's institutional voice explains the significance of the news event in detail, and draws out issues in the news story which are coded as significant by the discursive frame. Greg Wood, BBC News's Business Correspondent, presents a report which includes the syntagms 'the report presents a picture of deception and confusion on a grand scale', and 'As for the Bank of England, its reputation has again been damaged by a banking collapse. It'll need more than today's report to restore confidence.' The reporter's institutional voice confirms the framing of the story as sensational, centred on an individual, and an instance of inadequate bureaucracy. Similarly, Mark Webster, ITN's Business Correspondent, describes the report on Barings as 'hot property' which is 'damning in its conclusions' and 'spares no one'. He concludes 'But however the blame is apportioned, and whoever is ultimately held responsible, the reputation of the City of London has undoubtedly been tarnished.'

'Realising' is the process of lending authenticity to the story and confirming it as real by the use of actuality footage, interviews and 'accessed voices' (Hartley 1982: 111), the contributions of individuals invited to put their views on the story. These realising techniques tend to confirm the frame and focus which have already been established. The two versions of the Barings story on 18 July 1995 use a very wide range of realising techniques, including shots of the exterior of institutional headquarters (the Bank of England, Coopers & Lybrand auditors), parliamentary debate, interviews with Mr Leeson's lawyer, his wife, a former director of the defunct bank, a press conference given by the Governor of the Bank of England, and library footage of Leeson. These linguistic and visual syntagms anchor and relay each other's meanings, wrapping the news story up in a consistent narrative.

Finally, 'closing' refers to the movement throughout the news story towards one discursive construction of the story, a preferred meaning. This closure can be achieved by discounting alternative points of view on the news story, or by repeating and insisting on the point of view already connoted by the frame or focus, if there is a marked absence of competing discursive positions in the story itself. Closing will occur not only at the end of the story, but will be ongoing throughout it. As you can probably see from the necessarily brief extracts given here, the focusing and realising functions in the Barings story confirm the mythic meanings proposed by the frame in each news programme. Despite the various points of view on the story accessed linguistically and visually, the coverage of the Barings report represents the actions of an individual (Nick Leeson) as an instance of a larger failure of bureaucratic controls on financial affairs. Ideologically, this mythic meaning of the news story relies on a series of naturalised assumptions. It takes for granted the importance and value of financial dealing to the British economy, the propensity of individuals to wilfully deceive others if they can get away with it, and the necessity for institutional regulation of private companies despite the recurrent failure of these regulations.

Visual signs in TV news

TV news stories are almost always dependent on the use of different kinds of visual syntagm, and the use of a variety of denoted speakers. Because the 'talking head' of the news presenter is coded as boring, the maximum possible number of stories in a TV news bulletin will be constructed as a visual syntagm, a sequence of pictures, as well as a linguistic syntagm. The dominance of iconic visual signs (part of the realising function discussed above) has a significant effect on the news value of TV news stories. News stories which are lacking in pictures will be less likely to be included in a news bulletin than stories which can be illustrated by actuality footage which connotes drama. While actuality pictures could be regarded as the dominant type of sign in TV news, it is extremely rare for pictures to be shown without accompanying voice-over by an institutional voice (like a reporter). As we have seen in relation to news photographs in newspapers, iconic photographic signs like these are potentially ambiguous in their meaning because of their denotative dimension.

In the BBC's 'Bosnia' story, images denote, for example, armoured cars firing, bullet-marked buildings, tanks on a road, soldiers carrying wounded men, and littered roads and paths. The visual syntagm connotes war, destruction and chaos, but its meaning for the news story narrative has to be anchored by Tom Carver's voice-over. The linguistic signs in the 'Bosnia' story include the phrases 'rows of bodies', 'the Serb soldiers move in', 'within days of this film being taken, most of the evidence of what happened was cleaned up, making it almost impossible for human rights investigators'. The parties to the conflict are given value-laden mythic identities, usually that Serb soldiers are the aggressors against Bosnian forces. The story is framed and closed by these interacting linguistic and iconic signs, with the meanings that UN peacekeeping efforts have collapsed, war and barbarity are continuing, and the situation of the Eastern Bosnian populations has become desperate. So the connotations which support the framing and closing narratives of a news story have to be provided by anchoring and relaying the meanings of iconic signs by the use of linguistic signs. Captions perform these anchoring and relaying functions in newspapers, and voice-over has the same functions in TV news.

Interviews in news programmes are visual as well as linguistic. In his or her mythic role as the representative of the viewer, interviews are conducted by the mediator with accessed voices who are either 'live' in the studio or via satellite link with a reporter functioning as an accessed institutional voice in another location. Here the mediator puts questions which represent the questions which may be asked by an informed viewer. The mediator him or herself must not appear to hold any opinion, but will reflect the assumed concerns of the audience. In a 'live' interview of the BBC's reporter in Sarajevo, Jeremy Bowen, conducted by the news presenter Michael Buerk, Buerk asks 'The situation of the UN peacekeepers in Zepa is sounding increasingly desperate, isn't it?', closing the story and completing the framing of its meanings already undertaken. The question reinforces the mythic meaning of the UN as weak, and the Bosnian conflict as 'a terrible, terrible mess' in Jeremy Bowen's final words. These mythic meanings of the 'Bosnia' news story, centring on its barbarity and complexity and producing reactions of sympathy and helplessness, have already been encoded by the connotations given to the 'evidence' of the images described in the previous paragraph above.

As the last chapter described in relation to newspaper photographs, the meanings of particular shots in TV news sequences will be generated by the connotations of composition within the shot, framing, colour and lighting. Movement of the subject in the shot, pose, objects shown, and movement by the camera are also coded signs with connotations. TV news pictures are often heavily coded, constructed according to recognisable conventions. There are conventional, coded ways of representing press conferences, the arrival of the accused at a sensational court case, starving children in developing countries, etc. Each conventional code will trigger the mythic meanings, of authority, victimisation, the sensational, etc. which are regularly signified in each case. In the studio, similarly familiar and repeated visual codes are used in TV news. The news presenter is shot in medium close-up, full face, and is neutrally lit. Through these coded signs, the news presenter is endowed with the mythic role of mediator of events, addressing us as viewers but also making the link between the news organisation, its reporters in the field and the personalities in the news. The mediator is a link between the domestic world of the viewer and the public worlds of news events.

The context and surroundings in interviews with accessed voices often have significant connotations, connotations which are likely to support the framing and closing of the news story in the studio by the mediator. In a story where there are interviews with three different accessed voices, the connotations deriving from the situation of the interview could significantly affect the viewer's assessment of their authority. For instance, prominent people like politicians or businesspeople may be in plush offices, spokespeople for protesters may be in a rainy street surrounded by noise and commotion, and an independent expert may be sitting next to the newsreader in the TV studio. Accessed voices in TV news can be either empowered or disempowered by the connotations produced by the signs of situation which are present in the shots. In the BBC's 'Bosnia' story, refugees (whose comments are translated in an English voice-over) are denoted standing in the open air, with tents and other refugees behind them. They are untidily dressed, and some of the men and women are crying. These visual signs connote helplessness and despair.

In the same story, the coding of the denoted UN peacekeeping troops is ambiguous. They are denoted driving their military vehicles, which like them are tidy and ordered. Some of the shots are taken from inside or on top of UN vehicles, which are slowly moving around the refugee camp's airstrip. On the one hand, these images connote disciplined military effectiveness, and align the news camera with the point of view of the UN troops. But on the other hand, the lack of purpose and action connoted by the physical positioning and low speed of movement of the vehicles, and the blank expressions of the peacekeepers' faces, all connote passivity and ineffectiveness. In this news story, the Bosnian civilians are coded as weak and desperate, while the UN is coded as potentially effective but disempowered and passive, mythic meanings of the two groups which confirm the framing of the story as discussed above.

Myth and ideology in TV news

In conducting a semiotic analysis of TV news, it is important to bear in mind not only the mythic and ideological meanings produced in individual news programmes, but also the intertextual context of TV news. TV news programmes are part of the daily television schedule, and part of their meaning must derive from the way in which they work as TV, as well as the way they work as news. Television literally means 'seeing at a distance', and the TV medium has always been used to bring distant events and uncommon sights into the private arena of the home. TV news participates in this mythic identity of the television medium. Most people have very little direct experience of the political decision-making, wars, disasters and business affairs which TV news reports narrate. TV proclaims its ability to bring what is different, strange and interesting into the viewer's familiar and domestic world. The TV medium has a mythic identity as a technology which bridges this gap between public and private, and TV news is one component of it. This mythic identity of TV has ideological significance, since, for instance, it naturalises the idea that the TV viewer can be informed and aware of affairs outside the private sphere, but can have no direct effect on the wider public world. TV (and TV news in particular) involves the viewer, but disempowers the viewer, positions him or her as passive, at the same time.

News programmes have to be entertaining and interesting to

watch, like any other programme. The newsreader's address to the viewer and direct look at the camera are ways of demanding our attention, while the rapid alternation of studio settings with filmed reports and interviews encourages the viewer to actively assemble these segments for himself or herself. News programmes also use increasingly sophisticated graphics, montage and image manipulation for visual interest and to connote sophistication. The title sequence of the *Nine O'Clock News*, for instance, denoting a large shield and the open space of the news studio, is created by computer-controlled graphic design and image manipulation. Only the small area of the image denoting Michael Buerk (or Martyn Lewis in figure 5) is 'real'.

Some of the structuring of news programmes is interestingly similar to that of fictional programmes, thus invoking known codes used in other kinds of TV. News programmes feature a quite consistent set of characters from one day to the next, the news presenters and reporters who give continuity to TV news in the way that the protagonists of TV fiction programmes do. While news is perpetually different, the cast and format of news programmes are consistent. This pattern of repetition and difference is part of TV news programmes' mythic identity, their 'brand image'. The news programme's mythic meaning of 'newsness' is personalised, in the way that advertised products are personalised by the use of recurring models, TV stars, etc. in advertisements, or like the personalisation of the law in police fiction series, where Inspector Morse, for example, becomes the mythic representative of justice.

TV police fiction sets up the narrative opposition of law versus crime, where the audience is aligned with the law and the protagonist, and crime and criminals are 'other' to us, different, and negatively presented. TV news sets up the narrative opposition between 'us', including the viewer, the general public, the news presenter and news organisation, versus 'them', including other nations, bureaucratic institutions, criminals, and fate, which are all 'other' entities which appear to cause the mainly negative news events to happen. As we have seen, the 18 July 1995 news programmes report events which are either caused or exacerbated by 'others' which include the UN, Nick Leeson, the Bank of England, and further 'others' are found in the news stories not discussed in this chapter. Clearly, this mythic narrative structure has ideological significance, since it naturalises 'us' and presents 'the other' as the source of disruption and disorder. But the requirement to connote objectivity and balance in news narratives reduces the potential for the viewer to intervene with his or her own discourse about the events reported in the news, and instead passively aligns the viewer with the news institution presenting the news.

News generally constructs the mythic identity of life in our society as something which is fragmented into different spheres (like business, sport, politics, or family life). Society is also represented as naturally hierarchical, since some events, people, places or issues, are coded as more important than others. News discourse regards society as consensual, or operating by the informal agreement and cooperation of its members. The nation is unified but it is seen as diverse, plural, and fragmented. It is assumed in news discourse that the democratic system provides for equality before the law, shared interests among the population, equality of opportunity, and a common heritage and culture, which are the bases of a consensual model of society. But this mythic consensual model cannot therefore explain dissent within the culture, except by coding it as irrational or criminal. Dissident actions (by Animal Rights protesters, strikers, terrorists, criminals, etc.) are often framed in relation to actual or potential violence, which is a concrete way of encoding these groups' perceived threat to the consensual and democratic process. News constructs a mythic norm, against which disorder and disruption are measured.

The ideological role of news, then, is to construct a mythic 'climate of opinion' about life in our society, and this mythic reality is produced by the structure and form of news discourse, as well as its language and images. News's mythic definition of normality, since it is a cultural construct and is not natural, will therefore shift and change according to the current balance of power. In the 1970s for instance, the nationalisation of major British industries was a tenable political position which reporters and interviewers could discuss pragmatically with politicians. This is far from true today, after the introduction and normalisation of competitiveness and the free market into previously publicly owned industries. News discourse, even in the apparently 'balanced' and 'objective' context of TV news, will use the currently dominant ideological myths about society as its 'neutral' way of perceiving news events. What is perceived to be factual and neutral is a mythic construction determined by the dominant ideology.

Making sense of TV news

The ideological myths of TV news cannot always succeed in imposing themselves on the viewer of TV news, however. For the viewer of TV news, the meanings of news stories will always be negotiated with reference to the connotations and myths proposed by the news discourse, since whatever other meanings are brought to bear on the TV news story by the viewer, the viewer will decode at least some of the meanings which TV news discourse constructs. But negotiation can take a very wide range of forms. One form of negotiation of meaning relates to the way in which viewing takes place. Tunstall (1983) distinguished between primary, secondary, and tertiary involvement with media sources. Primary involvement is where watching the TV news is done attentively and with concentration. The analysis of TV news in this chapter has been done by a special kind of primary involvement, watching attentively and critically. Secondary involvement denotes ways of watching where something else is going on, like doing your ironing or flicking through a magazine. All kinds of TV programme are very commonly watched in this way. Tertiary involvement denotes a very inattentive way of watching, where for instance you are deeply engaged in a conversation while the news is switched on, or even half-listening to the TV news switched on in your living-room while you are making a cup of tea in the kitchen. The degree of attention given to the TV news programme will obviously affect the sense made of the news.

TV news programmes are constructed in order to attract and reward primary involvement with them. The loud and dramatic music of their title sequences is a sign which calls for your attention because it connotes the importance of the programme, and the dramatic connotations of news. The news presenter's address to the viewer as 'you', which is even implied by the opening remark 'good evening' which most news presenters begin with, also calls to the viewer as an individual. Indeed, this address calls the viewer to adopt a subject-position in which he or she plays the role of the addressee of the news discourse, and is invited to accept its naturalised ideological framework. As the news programme proceeds, primary involvement is rewarded by the fuller decoding of news discourse which will result. News stories assume at least some primary involvement with past news programmes and with earlier moments in the news programme. This is particularly evident in the case of the 'Bosnia' items in TV news at the time of writing this book. A tertiary involvement with the TV news might enable the viewer to decode only the mythic meaning 'chaos' or 'war' with reference to 'Bosnia', or a secondary involvement might enable the decoding of the additional mythic meanings 'disempowerment of international peace-keeping forces' and 'continuing Serb military success'. Primary involvement in the TV news discourse might enable the decoding of a much greater range of meanings from the various sequences and accessed voices presented in the news. But primary, secondary and tertiary involvements in this news story share the same ideological subtext. The 'Bosnia' story is encoded as a concrete instance of the ineffectiveness of political institutions, the regrettable but inevitable tendency toward violence in 'human nature', and the ability of news institutions to bring the viewer an 'objective' account of a distant reality.

Most of the time, the framing, focusing, realising and closing in news narratives probably succeed at least partially in delimiting news stories, and offering mythic connotations for news events. But it is difficult to know how much of this ideological coding of the news is consciously retained by viewers, and how much is unconsciously retained in a muddled and partial form. Because of the density of news discourse, which contains a very large number of short syntagms comprising written and spoken linguistic signs, still and moving iconic images, and graphic signs, it is very unlikely that the TV news could be remembered and described in detail after it has been broadcast, even by the most attentive viewer. On 18 July 1995 the *Nine O'Clock News* comprised twelve news stories, and *News at Ten* comprised thirteen stories. Each news story contained linguistic and visual signs, and many stories used maps, still images, on-screen quotations, the voices of interviewees, reporters and the news presenter, or several short sequences of actuality film. Each news story is a highly complex and rapidly-changing text.

Many viewers of TV news probably decode a mythic 'newsness', made up of fragments of narrative, and individual linguistic and visual signs. The 'newsness' of TV news, in combination with newspaper encodings of news and other kinds of discourse like conversations, becomes the basis of a cultural knowledge of events. Some of this cultural knowledge of newsness must be widely shared, but some of it must be specific to the media involvements of individuals. It is this mix of shared and specific news knowledge which enables TV news quizzes, for instance, like *Have I Got News for You* (a satirical programme based on current news stories), or current affairs phone-in radio programmes, to be both comprehensible and entertaining. Despite the various negotiations with TV news discourse made by viewers in making sense of it, the meanings proposed by TV news discourse evidently become part of a naturalised 'newsness' which pervades social life.

Global news

This chapter has concentrated so far on evening TV news programmes in a British cultural context. Many of the semiotic structures outlined here are similar to those in the news programmes broadcast in other nations, despite differences in the particular news stories which are broadcast. The structure of news programmes is shared in other cultures because the professional codes of news broadcasters which determine news value are now largely shared by the news journalists of many national and international TV institutions. We can investigate this phenomenon further by a brief discussion of the globalisation of news. Gurevitch (1991) outlines the relationship between the institutions of news broadcasting and the social meanings of global news, and this section discusses some of his ideas from a more semiotically-based perspective.

Gurevitch notes that globalisation has been seen from two

dominant but opposed points of view; either positively or negatively. The availability of new technologies like satellite broadcasting allows very large and diverse groups to have access to
'sophisticated' media products. News and other current events,
like moon landings or the Olympic Games, can be broadcast globally and might appear to provide unprecedented 'open' and
'democratic' access to information. This is the positive view. But
clearly, there must be a code of news value operating here which
assumes that some news stories exhibit sufficient consonance,
threshold, reference to élite persons or nations, etc., for them to
be worthy of global dissemination. On the other hand, globalisation can be negatively evaluated as the monopoly control over
information and broadcasting networks by a few multinational
media owners. From this point of view, global news produces the
imposition of Western cultural values across the world so that
local cultures are drowned out by the dominant ideologies naturalised in the codes of news value which determine what is
broadcast. This is the negative view. However, even if ownership
and control of news networks is concentrated in the hands of a
few corporations, it does not follow that audiences simply consume the ideological meanings encoded in news programmes.
Both the positive and negative evaluations of global news need
to be analysed more closely by looking in detail at the forms of
global and international news broadcasting, since these forms
and the institutions which control them are different and varied.

International news agencies like Reuters have been distributing news around the world mainly in linguistic forms since the
mid-nineteenth century, but the use of satellite technology has
altered the nature of this distribution process. The international
agencies which provide news material for television are Visnews
and Worldwide Television Network. They operate twenty-four
hours a day, sending both raw footage and complete news packages to national and regional TV stations. Because the international news agencies deal mainly in pictures rather than words,
it is common for their news material to be perceived by the news
editors of broadcasting companies as denotative and 'objective'.
This impression is reinforced by the written material which the
agencies provide, which explains and describes what is denoted
in their pictures. The language of these texts is encoded as 'objec-

tive' because it must not conflict with the ideological norms of the hundred or so subscribing nations' broadcasters whose ideo-logical norms are likely to be very different. There are no uses of linguistic signs like 'terrorist' or 'tragedy', which all connote a particular ideological perspective on the news which the images anchor and relay. The visual rather than verbal satellite news material now being used is more open to polysemic interpreta-tion and thus to different uses by the broadcasters who include it in their news story syntagms.

Since the visual material provided by the agency does not arrive with an obvious mythic meaning, it is easy to impose a range of different mythic meanings on it by, for instance, the connotations of linguistic signs in an accompanying voice-over. Gurevitch (1991: 181) reports this anecdote from one of World-wide Television News's staff in Tel Aviv, Israel: a WTN camera-man shot some footage of people enjoying the local seaside resort, which it was thought would appeal to European broadcasters since Europe was suffering an unusually cold winter. However, the footage was used by Jordanian television to anchor the mythic meaning in their news story narrative that the Israeli tourist industry was in decline, since the beach was not very crowded. This anecdote illustrates that the denotative iconic signs of news film do not contain 'natural' and 'objective' mean-ings. The connotations of the linguistic signs in an accompany-ing voice-over can be used to construct the mythic meaning that Mediterranean beaches are hot when Western Europe is cold, or that the Israeli tourist industry is collapsing. The denotation of people on the beach becomes a 'proof' anchored by the linguis-tic signs of voice-over with either of these very different mean-ings. Although the beach footage was provided to many broadcasters in different countries, the footage itself did not deter-mine the mythic meanings of news stories. News stories were made possible by the footage, but the stories were dependent on the mythic social meanings deemed significant and interesting to a particular TV audience group by broadcasters in particular countries.

News services which broadcast complete news programmes by satellite include Cable News Network (the largest, broadcast to about 130 countries) and Britain's SuperChannel, Sky News and

BBC World Service Television. CNN provides news from an American ideological viewpoint, covering domestic American news and foreign news. Because its programmes are complete, CNN news is not subject to the recoding by national broadcasters which occurred in the case of WTN's beach footage. There are several issues here. Because CNN broadcasts the same news globally, its criteria of news value influence the professional codes of news value used by broadcasters in particular nations. If a news story is broadcast by CNN news, it carries the mythic meaning of global significance simply because CNN broadcast the story. Thus the Gulf War, the Tiananmen Square uprising in China, the revolutions in former Eastern Bloc countries, and the O. J. Simpson trial, have all been given high news value in a global, as well as in a national or regional sense. In addition, the fact that CNN news coverage is broadcast virtually 'live' back into the countries in which these events are occurring can also have the effect of 'making' news events happen, by alerting viewers to a news event (like a political demonstration) and encouraging them to participate in it.

CNN news coverage also shapes the responses of politicians and institutions inside the country to what is being reported, as well as shaping the mythic meanings of news for other distant nations. For this reason, politicians and interested groups either impose restrictions on CNN reporters, or invite them to film particular events for CNN news stories which will provide support for one or another political strategy. The management of news by political organisations has always happened at national level, but global news gives news management greater significance in shaping the mythic meanings of broadcast news. In terms of the codes of news value and the structure of TV news programmes, CNN's representation of American news professionals might affect the professional codes of broadcasters in other nations. However, since CNN is usually an alternative news service to national broadcast news programmes, it does not necessarily dominate the perception of news where it is broadcast, and since it is in English, it is probably watched most by a small group of well-educated people in many of the countries which can receive its transmissions. While global news is significant, it is easy to overestimate the extent to which it eradicates national and cultural differences in favour of the global dominance of American ideology.

In several regions of the world, news is exchanged between nations under the auspices of broadcasting organisations which service the national broadcasters in the region, like the European Broadcasting Union (EBU) or the Asian Broadcasting Union. The EBU, for instance, is staffed by news coordinators from various national member broadcasting organisations, who liaise with the member national broadcasters to see what news material (usually raw film footage) is available and what might be provided to each national broadcaster. The news coordinators decide which news items are available for sending by satellite to member countries, and which broadcaster's version of a story is made available in this way. Gurevitch reports that, perhaps surprisingly, there is usually a consensus about which news items and which versions of news coverage are put into the selection which is made available on the satellite link (1991: 182). This consensus occurs because the news coordinators from different member countries share professional codes, the same codes of news value which their customers in other nations of the region use. As far as national news broadcasters are concerned, they have greater access to a wide range of footage from distant places which they could not afford to send their own reporters or crews to. The availability of news material from a number of sources reduces the control over the news agenda which has been exercised by national broadcasters. For the audience, there is more news, and more broadcast packages of news from different sources. But as news from a greater number of places and social contexts is made available, the importance of the news broadcasters in making sense of the news through their professional coding systems becomes more significant, since viewers have little knowledge about news which is not delivered through these news organisations.

Sources and further reading

Hartley (1982) discusses both TV news and newspapers using a semiotic approach, but many analyses of TV news are in chapters of books covering a range of genres of TV programme. Examples of

these which make use of semiotics are Fiske (1987), Fiske and Hartley (1978), and Lewis (1985). Corner (1995) discusses British TV
news coverage with some implicit use of semiotics. Very influential
but also controversial work on news was done by the sociologists of
the Glasgow University Media Group (1976, 1980, 1986), who
mapped out the content of British TV news, aiming to show political bias, but who also used some semiotic methods to discuss the textual forms of news discourse. The contribution made by their work
is assessed by Harrison (1985) and Philo (1987).

From other analytical points of view, Dahlgren (1985) involves
research on viewers' decodings of news as academics and 'ordinary
viewers', both Schlesinger (1978) and McNair (1994) discuss the
professional practices, ideologies and economics of TV news, and van
Dijk (1988) discusses the discursive structures of news communication. The globalisation of the media is discussed by Gurevitch (1991)
in relation to news and by Lorimer with Scannell (1994), though
with little reference to semiotics. There is a bibliography on news,
focusing on American sources and broadcasting, in Jacobson (1995).

Suggestions for further work

1 Watch an evening TV news bulletin. An hour or so after you
   have done this, how much of the news and the way it was
   encoded can you remember? Are there any shared characteristics of the signs and meanings which you remember?
2 Obtain a newspaper on two successive days, and watch the
   evening news on the evening of the first day, analysing the news
   stories which appear in more than one of these three texts. Are
   the stories treated differently in the two media? Why is this?
3 Analyse the news bulletins on as many TV channels as you can.
   How are the mythic meanings of news programmes signified in
   their title sequences? How much similarity is there in the signs
   and codes of the title sequences?
4 Select a TV news story which is presented by several linguistic
   and visual sequences (newsreader, filmed report, interview, etc.).
   How do framing, focusing, realising and closing operate? What
   ideological viewpoints emerge from your analysis?
5 Which of the semiotic codes of TV news outlined in this chapter
   are common to other genres of TV programme? How and why
   are their connoted meanings the same or different in these different contexts?
6 Compare a local TV news bulletin and a national TV news bul-

letin. What similarities and differences in their semiotic codes and their assumptions about the viewer do you find? Why is this?

7 If you have access to TV news programmes from satellite or cable as well as terrestrial channels, compare and contrast the stories covered and the discourses used to make sense of the news. What conclusions do you draw from your analysis?

6

More on television

Introduction

This chapter continues the semiotic analysis of television, but will be structured differently from the previous one, for three main reasons. First, the television medium broadcasts a very wide range of different kinds of programme. Rather than trying to cover all TV genres in this chapter, I have limited myself here to a few critical issues in the semiotic analysis of television, and exemplified them with short discussions of a few programmes and references to a larger number of programmes and TV ads which are not discussed in detail. The Sources and further reading section at the end of this chapter names several books devoted solely to the TV medium which supplement the discussion here and address issues which cannot be covered. Second, the chapter on TV news considered only one kind of programme, and treated news as a relatively discrete form of text. In this chapter, the range of different kinds or genres of programme is acknowledged much more fully, and relationships between programmes are considered. To do this, this chapter has to focus less on individual examples and more on ways of grouping programmes together. Third, there is a relatively large and growing body of research on TV which shifts the emphasis of academic work away from the detailed semiotic analysis of programmes and towards the study of how viewers of TV construct meanings in different ways. Some of this research, known as audience studies or ethnography, provides us with useful information about the role of TV in people's actual lives, and shows that different viewers construct different meanings in their decoding of the signs and codes of TV. While this research is not strictly part of semiotics, it both supports and challenges semiotic analysis and therefore it is discussed quite extensively later in this chapter.

The main focus of this chapter is on TV viewers and audiences. We begin with some statistical information about how much television is watched in Britain, and the audiences for the different TV channels and genres of programme. Then there is a short section on the signs and codes of TV which extends the discussion of TV signs and codes in the previous chapter. This leads on to the question of how TV programmes address the viewer, and how positions are laid out for the viewer from which TV programmes make sense. As this chapter continues, the viewer is seen less as a destination to which meanings are directed, and more as a specific person in a social context. As this stress on 'real' viewers becomes more marked, we shall see that while the discourse of semiotic analysis is a powerful way of analysing television texts, it needs to be extended and problematised by research done on the reception of texts. Many of the sections in this chapter give brief accounts of studies of television by other writers, aiming to show how various critical discourses develop and challenge semiotic methods.

Watching television

In Britain, the average person spends between twenty-one and twenty-seven hours per week watching television, depending on the time of year. A survey of what was watched in 1990 (*Social Trends 22*, HMSO 1992) gives an indication of the kinds of programme which occupied people's TV-watching time. Drama was watched 22 per cent of the time, news 21 per cent, light entertainment 17 per cent, films on TV 11 per cent and sport 11 per cent, documentaries and feature programmes 8 per cent, children's programmes 7 per cent, and other kinds of programme 1 per cent of the time. We have already considered news programmes in the previous chapter, and here most of the programmes referred to are drama and light entertainment. For the moment, it is interesting to note that watching TV is a very significant activity for most people, and that fictional programmes are the predominant type of programme watched. In Britain, 99 per cent of all households possess a television, and more than half of all households have more than one TV set. Nearly two-thirds of households also have a video cassette recorder, and in 1990 7.3 million videotapes per week were hired in Britain, the great majority of these being feature films. So while watching broadcast television is the main subject of this chapter, there are also some brief references to video viewing using domestic TV equipment, though video is also addressed in the next chapter of this book.

At the beginning of chapter five, the distinction was made between the measurement of the total audience for a particular programme (ratings), and the measurement of the proportion of the audience watching one TV channel's output rather than another's (audience share). As the number of broadcast channels has grown, and the new technologies of satellite and cable tele-vision have offered even more channels, the measurement of audiences and the competition for audiences has become even more important to broadcasting organisations. In 1994, the Broadcasters' Audience Research Board (BARB), which collects information from a representative sample of British households about what they watch, reported that in all homes ITV was watched 40 per cent of the time, BBC1 34 per cent, Channel 4 10 per cent, BBC2 9 per cent, and other non-terrestrial (satellite) channels 7 per cent of the time. In homes with access to satellite television in 1994, ITV was watched 31 per cent of the time, BBC1 25 per cent, BSkyB's satellite programmes 19 per cent, pro-grammes broadcast on the Astra satellite channels 9 per cent, Channel 4 7 per cent, BBC2 5 per cent, and other non-terrestrial channels 4 per cent. As more channels become available, the audience becomes more fragmented although the time spent watching TV remains about the same. Broadcasting organisa-tions are therefore very concerned to capture a significant share of the audience for their own programmes, particularly if they rely on advertising for funding. Only the BBC is not funded by advertising, but the BBC has to justify its compulsory licence fee by demonstrating that a significant share of the population is watching its programmes.

Broadcasters funded by advertising are especially concerned to capture desirable sectors of the TV audience, like employed people aged between eighteen and thirty-five for instance who

have relatively high dis‍‍‍‍‍‍‍‍‍‍‍‍‍‍‍‍‍‍‍‍‍‍ich they could spend
on the consumer ‍‍‍‍‍‍‍‍‍‍‍‍‍‍‍‍‍‍‍‍‍‍‍‍‍‍‍‍vision. For example,
Channel 4 pu‍‍‍‍‍‍‍‍‍‍‍‍‍‍‍‍‍‍‍‍‍‍‍‍ programmes one
after the o‍‍‍‍‍‍‍‍‍‍‍‍‍‍‍‍‍‍ke *Ellen, Friends,
Frasier,* and ‍‍‍‍‍‍‍‍‍‍‍‍‍‍‍‍‍‍ttracted a high
proportion o‍‍‍‍‍‍‍‍‍‍‍‍‍‍‍‍and C1 social
classes with th‍‍‍‍‍‍‍‍‍‍‍‍‍‍‍‍ass audience but
it is a desirabl‍‍‍‍‍‍‍‍‍‍‍‍‍‍no are charged about
£55,000 per min‍‍‍‍‍‍‍‍‍‍‍‍between 9 p.m. and 11 p.m.
on Fridays. The ‍‍‍‍‍‍‍‍‍‍ported American programmes like
those listed above a‍‍‍in general cheaper for Channel 4 to buy
than original British programmes, and the Friday evening 'strip'
is expected to make the channel about £42 million in 1995
(*Broadcast* 1 Sept 1995: 17).

While film audiences pay directly for a cinema experience, TV
viewers pay indirectly by buying a TV licence or by buying
advertised products. TV companies sell the mathematical proba-
bility of a certain size and type of audience to advertisers, an economic exchange in which the audience is itself a product. So this
economic structure positions the TV viewer as active. Switching
on the TV set is a conscious choice, and despite the accusation
that watching television is a passive and pacifying experience TV
programmes and commercials demand active decoding. But perhaps more significantly, the form of commercial TV itself is predicated on the economic activity of the viewer, since the
naturalised ideological assumption is that the viewer is active in
making purchasing decisions and consuming products and services. While it might appear that watching television is a release
or respite from the economic processes of earning money or
spending it, the TV viewer is addressed as someone who earns
and spends 'by nature'. Furthermore, it is generally supposed by
advertisers that the greater the degree of primary involvement in
a particular programme, the more likely that the viewer will pay
attention to and remember TV ads. Channel 4's Friday night
comedy strip is praised by advertising agencies because it
amounts to a 'brand' (a product with a known identity and
image like Coca-Cola or Levi jeans) which viewers deliberately
choose to watch and which encourages primary involvement in
the programmes and the ads between them.

Although there are statistical methods for measuring viewers' interest and involvement in programmes and ads, one of the problems with statistical information is the difficulty of evaluating how people watch television, why they watch it, whether they enjoy it, and whether they retain any of the meanings they have constructed in relation to it. Ien Ang (1991) has analysed the discourse of audience measurement, showing that in the fragmented marketplace of contemporary television there is an insistent desire to find ways of measuring audience figures and kinds of involvement in programmes and ads. Audience measurement is a discourse whose methodology and assumptions set limits to the kind of conclusions which can be drawn from it. The ethnographic research on particular viewers and groups of viewers is another discourse about television viewers which we shall encounter later in this chapter. Its limitation is that it relies on what people say about what they watch; it is a discourse based on viewers' discourses, and on very small samples of viewers. On the other hand, the discourse of semiotic analysis is limited by its focus on texts and a tendency to forget the social context of media involvement. Each discourse about television competes with others, asking and answering a different kind of question, and this chapter discusses and gives examples of several different discourses about TV and its audience. This section has adopted aspects of the discourse of institutional and economic analysis, which is mainly descriptive and statistical. Next we shall return to the discourse of semiotic analysis.

Television signs and codes

Semiotic discourse begins the analysis of any medium by identifying the kinds of sign which it uses. The television medium makes use of visual and aural signs. Some of the visual signs are iconic and apparently denotative, like the images of people and places in both fictional and non-fictional programmes which resemble their referent. But the photographic realism of these denotative signs is itself coded and mythic, relying on the codes of composition, perspective, and framing which are so conventional and naturalised in our culture that the two-dimensional image seems simply to mirror three-dimensional reality. Similarly, television's aural signs are denotative, like the speech or sounds which accompany images of people speaking or moving. But this speech and sound is also coded, since technical codes of recording, editing and processing intervene between 'real' sound and the sound which comes out of the TV set's loudspeaker. Much of what is on television is presented as denotative, but achieves this meaning by the use of technical and professional codes either specific to television or shared by other audiovisual media like cinema. The connotations of music, for instance, are largely shared by the cinema medium (in uses of romantic or dramatic music for example), and derive from the social meanings of the kinds of music in the wider culture.

The technical codes of television images include framing, lens type, composition, camera angle, focus and colour. Framing varies from extreme long shot (ELS), often used to establish a setting, to extreme close-up (ECU), often used to present emotion signified by actors' facial expressions (as in *Dallas* and other TV melodramas, or documentary programmes). Lens type varies from wide angle, used to accentuate perspective and connote drama, to telephoto, to connote voyeuristic concentration on a small part of the camera's field of vision. Composition varies from static composition, connoting order and calm (as in shots of the presenter in news programmes) to dynamic composition, connoting disorientation and disorder (as in *NYPD Blue*'s ever-changing shot composition). Camera angle varies from high-angle, connoting dominance and authority, to low-angle, connoting powerlessness. Focus may be selective, connoting the importance of the part of the shot which is in focus, or soft focus, connoting romance or nostalgia, or deep focus, connoting the importance of all the elements in the shot (as in street scenes, for instance). Some colours are coded as warm and comfortable, like yellow, red and brown (as in *Cheers* and shipboard scenes in *Star Trek: The Next Generation*), while others like blue, green and grey are coded as cold and uncomfortable (as in police drama and some documentary programmes). Black and white (monochrome) has traditionally connoted actuality (via newsreel film) but now often connotes artiness (these two coded meanings were brought together in 'arty' black and white Levi's jeans commercials set in the past, for instance). It is important to note that the connotations of each of these sets of coded signs do not arise 'by nature'. They are meaningful in these ways because of their use in particular kinds of TV programme or in texts in other media, at particular times and in particular cultures.

Television's graphic signs are very varied. Some of these graphic signs are used to present linguistic signs like the names of programmes. The graphic sign which introduces *Roseanne* is a denotation of the linguistic sign 'Roseanne', for instance. But it is not only denotative, since its position in the centre of the TV screen connotes that it is a programme title, while its shape and colour are connotative too. The graphic sign 'Roseanne' is yellow, rounded and has few sharp edges. Its connotations might therefore include informality and friendliness (yellow), and its roundedness might correspond to Roseanne Arnold's round body-shape (she is denoted in the title sequence where the caption appears) to begin to construct the mythic identity of the Roseanne character and the world of the programme. The connotative meanings of this graphic sign are clearly coded, and could be contrasted with the coded connotations of the title graphic signs of different programmes, like *The X Files* or *Homicide: Life on the Street*, where very different connotations would be discovered. Some of television's graphic signs do not denote words at all. The title sequences of breakfast television programmes, for instance, include coded representations of the sun rising, while sports programmes often include graphic signs representing stopwatches or tables of statistics. Each of these graphic signs has connotations which support a coded mythic meaning for the programme, like 'cosy start to the day' or 'expert evaluation of performance' in the two examples given here.

So far this section has concentrated on individual images and uses of sound. In actual TV programmes and most advertisements, these linguistic and visual signs are part of a narrative. TV programmes do not only narrate fictional stories (news discourse is also narrative), but in all TV narratives the aim is to keep the viewer watching by assembling verbal and visual signs in ways which are entertaining or informative. So for instance camera shots change more rapidly than in cinema, and moments of silence are rare. The semiotic analysis of television has tended to concentrate until recently on image more than on sound, but

sound is particularly important to TV's narratives and mode of
address to the viewer. It was pointed out in the previous chapter
that the loud brass music of news programmes was used to draw
the attention of the viewer as well as to connote authority. Music
and other sound in TV programmes is not only a use of signs to
relay the meanings of images in narratives, but has a vital role
in TV's address to the viewer. Because the TV image is small, and
television competes with other activities for the viewer's attention, sound is used to call the viewer to look at the screen. Whatever the denotative meanings of sound, or its connotative
relationship to images, TV sound is a set of signs which share the
function of announcing that something interesting or entertaining is being broadcast. This issue of the ways that TV is watched
leads on to the question of the ideological role of TV as a medium
in everyday life, in a cultural context.

Television narrative and ideology

Television is still mainly a domestic technology, where the TV set
is a piece of furniture in the home, and one of a number of different kinds of technological device (like the radio, microwave or
stereo system) which are integrated into everyday life. There are
some developments of television towards more public uses, like
the huge TV screens in sports stadia, and some developments of
TV towards more private uses, like miniature 'wristwatch' television. But in each context the television apparatus is socially
coded as something which gives us access to a privileged vision,
a new and different point of view. Television invites us to take
the position of an individual subject with the same point of view,
and at the same time to join in with an imaginary community
of viewers who are all watching the same thing. We have
already encountered this structure before in each of the preceding chapters of this book, since it is the structure which
Althusser (1971) described as the way that ideology works.
People become individual subjects, subject to ideology and constituted as subjects by ideology as the unique destination to
which signs are addressed. As in Althusser's conception of dominant ideology, the TV viewer is a consumer of meanings, while
appearing to be their producer because it is the viewer who actu-

alises meanings by watching television and decoding them.

Television programmes call for the recognition and identification of the television medium as a delegate of the viewer. There is always the sense that someone or something is doing the storytelling or the observing for us, on our behalf. *Star Trek: The Next Generation* begins with the famous syntagm 'Space, the final frontier ...' which narrates the scenario of the series, followed by the 'Captain's log' that narrates the scenario for each episode, like a storyteller. Scenarios are also narrated by the title songs of programmes, as in *One Foot in the Grave*. Series like *LA Law* may begin by reminding us of the previous programme with a short narrative syntagm of extracts introduced by a narrating voice, 'Previously, on *LA Law* ...'. Some drama programmes include a narrator in the discourse of the plot, as in *The Wonder Years*. Some non-fiction programmes like nature documentaries, quiz shows, commercials, cooking shows, and 'reality' shows (like *Rescue 911, 999, Crimewatch UK*), use a narrator who addresses the viewer directly, constructing a subject-position for the viewer through codes of vocabulary, tone of voice, gesture and expression. In each of these cases, the narrator or narrating function makes a link between the viewer and the programme's or ad's narrative, inviting the viewer to recognise and identify with the represented scenario.

While some programmes specifically foreground a narrator, many commercials and the majority of TV fiction consist of a narrative made up of camera shots in a narrative progression, with an implied rather than evident narrator. The alternation of camera shots in drama is very similar to the cinema's use of a mobile point of view, in which the viewer is aligned with the point of view of particular characters in a scene, or with a 'neutral' point of view which observes the whole acting area. The performers in TV drama behave as if the viewer is absent, connoting that the drama is happening in a life-like world to which we are given access via the power of television. In situation comedy, a 'three-camera live tape' recording practice is used, where the actors perform complete scenes in the TV studio (though further shots like close-ups and reaction shots may be added later) in a set with a missing 'fourth wall', with three cameras recording simultaneously and the director cutting between their different points of view. So there are a range of positionings of the viewer in different genres of TV programme. Some sitcoms like *Roseanne* remind the TV audience that they were 'live' three-camera performances by showing mistakes and 'out-takes'. Unlike drama with its connotations of life-likeness, sitcoms fracture the illusion of denoted reality. A similar display of TV's codes of performance occurs in programmes which show amusing mistakes and disasters in TV programmes (like *Auntie's Bloomers* and *It'll Be Alright on the Night* on British TV).

There is a wide range of foregrounded or implied narrators, but even in programmes like gameshows and chatshows which are not structured like fictional narratives, there is still a sense that something 'tells' the programme. Here the narrator is not a voice or a character or even solely the camera. As in other programmes with more foregrounded narrators, this 'super-narrator' (Kozloff 1992: 94) is the TV institution, which connotes this role through identifying logos, voice-over and graphic captions. These signs connote that it is the TV institution which brings the programme and the commercials to us. In mythic terms, the TV institution is our representative, a meaning anchored by the announcer's voice-over address to 'you' the viewer, on whose behalf the TV channel is broadcasting. Britain's Carlton Television announcers speak over shots of people from the local TV area exhibiting their professional, sporting, or leisure interests. These people are signified as both 'like us' (they live in the Carlton TV area) and not 'like us' (they do things we do not do), and all of them are represented by Carlton just as we are. The mythic meaning of these signs is that Carlton represents a community made up of diverse individuals, so that Carlton Television is itself a sign connoting a 'community' to which we belong. The mythic 'viewer's delegate' role of the TV institution is particularly evident on commercial channels when programmes are interspersed with ads. The evening's TV is not coded as a series of discrete units (the programmes) but a flow of diverse images and sounds. The TV institution is mythically encoded as providing a space in which a flow of segments narrated by the TV institution is delivered like a gift to the viewer.

Ideologically, television is coded as a provider of very diverse offerings to the individual subject, who is continually asked to shift subject-position in relation to the rapidly-changing semiotic fragments which he or she is asked to decode. The mythic meaning here is that TV is a gift rather than a commodity, as Allen (1992) argues. Allen finds this mythic gift-giving in TV in general, but also notes the prevalence of gift-giving in TV ads in particular (1992: 119–120). In many ads a viewer's representative in the ad, someone 'like us', is addressed by a narrator about a problem and presented with a product as a gift which solves this problem (many washing-powder and household cleaner ads use this narrative structure). In the ad, the viewer's representative can have a face-to-face relationship with the narrator–provider, where this is not possible for the viewer in reality. Here the viewer has a mythic representative on TV, and there are many other variants of viewers' representatives, some of which will be discussed later in this chapter. In chapter five, it was argued that TV news presenters and institutional voices like interviewers also function as mythic intermediaries representing the viewers' supposed interests and concerns. Other mythic representatives include studio audiences, talkshow hosts, and any other figure who mediates between the TV viewer and the world of a programme or an ad. By means of this aspect of TV's coded discourses, the viewer is invited to identify with the mythic representative, as well as to take up a subject-position appropriate to the 'preferred' decoding of the programme or ad, and appropriate to the position of receiver or consumer of the TV institution's gift-like offering of mythic meanings. By means of these signs and the codes of TV narratives, the viewer is invited to actualise the meanings of programmes and ads for himself or herself, becoming the 'you' to whom they are addressed.

Viewer involvement

This section is a discussion of the ways in which viewer involvement is invited by the discursive codes of non-fictional programmes, with a fairly detailed look at one British TV programme. Primary involvement by the viewer in TV can be stimulated by discourses which allow for interaction with programmes and ads. In chapter two, it was noted that some print ads in magazines and newspapers provide opportunities for interaction, like puzzles which the reader of the ad is invited to decode, or jokes and puns where the meanings of linguistic signs can be completed by the interpretive action of the reader. Ads also include telephone numbers to ring for further information, or special offers where presenting an ad in a shop will give the consumer a discount or a prize. TV ads also use some of these discursive devices, especially jokes and puns, but also telephone numbers, Internet addresses, or 'data bursts' where the viewer has to record the ad on videotape and play it back at slow speed to read product information. These discursive structures directly address the viewer with an invitation to do something. A special case here are the shopping channels on American cable TV, where the viewer is explicitly addressed as a buyer as well as an audience member. There is a direct address to the viewer by the narrator who describes and recommends products, and direct invitations to act through on-screen displays of price, reminders about the amount of time remaining for placing orders, tele-phone number, number of units so far sold of this item, and sometimes one of the phoning viewers is talked to live about why he or she liked and ordered this product.

The primary involvement invited by shopping channels has a clear economic and ideological function oriented around buying. But many other genres of programme invite viewer activity. TV sport is mythically coded as professional, dramatic and open to the viewer's involvement through the discursive codes of evalu-ation provided by the 'expert' institutional voices of commenta-tors. Live sports programmes use a mixture of codes. Shots of the sport in progress provide a much closer view of events than a spectator in the arena can get, and alternate between close shots of the competitors, offering identification with their efforts and emotions, and long shots of the arena which connote television's special power to observe a denoted reality. The sound in sports programmes denotes the sounds of the spectating crowds, as rep-resentative of the viewers' reactions, and sometimes also use music over replays and slow-motion sequences adding dramatic connotations to the event. Voice-over commentary uses discur-sive codes which foreground achievement, drama, and profes-sional evaluation of the competitors' performance. Intervals in the event are often taken up with discussion between 'experts' who also evaluate performance, and whose discourse the viewer is invited to share by judging the strengths, weaknesses and tactics of the competitors for himself or herself. TV sports programmes invite viewer involvement by alternately positioning him or her as a spectator of drama and as an expert evaluator of performance.

The Oprah Winfrey Show and other 'chat' and 'problem' TV programmes also include 'expert' evaluation by invited professionals who are separated from the studio audience. The host mediates between these professionals, members of the public who have 'problems' relevant to the programme's topic, the studio audience, and the TV audience. The TV viewer is invited by the programme's discourse to take up a range of subject-positions in which the viewer can identify with any or all of these various participants and evaluate their discourses. Live *Oprah* programmes not only include a studio audience who are invited to speak as 'members of the public' and viewer representatives, but also the voices of viewers who phone in to the programme. In programmes like this, viewer involvement can take a variety of forms. At one extreme, the viewer can become a participant in the programme by phoning in, adopting a confessional subject-position and describing their own experiences, or adopting an 'expert' subject-position and questioning or evaluating the discourse of someone denoted in the programme. At the other extreme, the viewer is a participant only as a voyeur, looking in at the fascinating or squalid mythic world which the programme represents. From this subject-position, involvement in the programme alternates between repudiation of the denoted speakers as not 'like us' and identification with the 'exterior' observing camera and the TV institution which offers the opportunity to glimpse a world with which the viewer does not identify.

Even when viewers are denoted in programmes by phoning in, the viewer's role is constrained by the presenter's and the programme format's control over how long to speak, what kind of discourse is legitimate, and by being represented through a semiotically impoverished technological medium like the telephone. As in all TV programmes, the codes of the programme 'hollow out' at least one subject-position for the viewer, but the possible positionings and involvements of the viewer are not infinite. A

particularly interesting case of this management of viewer positioning occurs in the BBC's *You Decide – with Paxman*. This programme is a weekly series of fifty-minute studio debates about
issues currently 'in the news'. There is a mix of several different
TV genres and their codes in the programme. It is news-related
and includes statistics, élite persons, accessed voices, graphics
packages and an expert mediator like news programmes. Like
Oprah it features a panel of members of the public, experts who
give opinion and advice, and a studio audience representing the
TV audience. It is a live programme, but is structured to contain
this liveness by Jeremy Paxman as mediator and by the inclusion
of packages of prerecorded information. A brief look at the codes
of this programme will show how codes deriving from TV news
can be mixed with codes deriving from other TV genres, and how
viewers and viewer representatives are invited to interact with
the programme.

Jeremy Paxman is himself a sign, known for his confronta-
tional style of interviewing on BBC2's *Newsnight* programme.
Paxman is coded as an authoritative, knowledgeable and con-
frontational mediator representing the TV institution in the news
genre. Each edition of *You Decide* is focused on a single question,
asking, for instance, whether British troops should be withdrawn
from Bosnia, or whether single mothers should have their state
welfare benefits reduced. So the questions derive from the categories of news in TV news programmes. In trailers before the programme, viewers are asked to telephone to record a 'yes' or a 'no'
vote in response to the programme question. As the title of the
programme connotes, 'you' the individual viewer and 'you' the
viewing public are simultaneously addressed and given an opportunity to 'decide' about an issue which is naturalised as significant by its relationship to the codes of TV news. Trailers for the
programme denote Paxman in shirt-sleeves and a middle-aged
man in a suit. Paxman advertises the programme as 'your'
opportunity to consider current issues 'without *him*' (indicating
the man, who is an actor playing the role of a stereotypical politician). Paxman invites the viewer to identify with him and the
programme's mythic meanings, in contrast to the politician and
the institutional discourses he represents.

At the start of each programme, Paxman announces the 'yes'

and 'no' votes received as a percentage of the telephone calls (which have sometimes totalled more than forty thousand). The programme mostly consists of a presentation of the 'main arguments' which oppose the majority response by telephone callers. The studio audience are accessed voices who are coded as experts, but their expertise takes different forms. Some people speak about their own experience rather than as representatives of an institution, and appeal to a code of personal involvement. Other accessed audience members present statistical information, coded as 'objective' and neutral, while yet others present political argument, coded as partial and ideological. The programme consists of the confrontations between these different discourses, each legitimated by an appeal to a different rhetorical code.

6   Jeremy Paxman on the set of *You Decide – with Paxman*

Three people who oppose the telephone callers' majority opinion are selected from the studio audience to sit on a panel which will put and respond to arguments about the programme's question, and three members of the public who have not made up their minds form another panel who are asked at the end of the programme whether what they have heard has changed their minds. At the beginning of the programme and at several points within it, graphics packages containing statistics, summaries of rhetorical points, and actuality footage are presented on a large screen above Paxman in the centre of the studio and on the viewer's TV screen, with an unidentified woman's voice-over calmly presenting information. Paxman is coded as a *provocateur*, mediator, and interviewer, speaking directly to the TV audience, putting points raised by the studio audience to the panels, asking for contributions, and questioning studio contributors. At the end of the programme, viewers are given telephone numbers to vote again on the programme issue, and these votes are totalled after a few minutes to produce another percentage division of 'yes' and 'no' votes as at the beginning of the programme. The votes recorded sometimes reverse the dominant view recorded at the start.

The aim of the programme, as Paxman describes to the camera, is to promote public debate about current news issues and to make viewers think, even if they do not make up their minds. *You Decide* focuses on issues from the TV news agenda which are already naturalised as significant because they are in the news. There is therefore a mythic position already laid out for the viewer in which the programme's question is both relevant and yet to be decided. By using the discursive codes of television debate, the programme invites the viewer to take up a subject-position aligned with one or more of the contributors to the programme, as well as to align himself or herself with the format of the programme and with Paxman as mediator. The programme's phone-in element both invites the viewer to interact with the debate (if only as a statistic) and to debate with other viewers in the household about the question and the terms in which it is encoded in TV discourse. Voting either before or after the programme invites the viewer to participate in a mythic community of 'deciders' which is constructed only by the programme itself, and which limits the viewer's interactivity. The involvement offered by *You Decide* is much more 'real' and active than that normally offered by TV's use of viewer representatives and other strategies for viewer identification in linguistic codes and codes of camera position and editing. But it relies on the conventional mythic role of the TV medium as a broadcast to a mass audience which is mythically encoded as an interaction with the individual viewer. Apart from the coded discursive representation of the programme question, which is itself necessarily ideological, the programme format's ideological role is to hail the viewer as an individual subject and simultaneously to invite the viewer to participate in an imaginary democratic community constructed by TV discourse.

Viewer positionings: TV comedy

Studio debates and phone-in programmes clearly involve the viewer by both opening up and controlling the ways in which responses to the programmes' discourses can occur, but this process is also evident in quite different genres of programme. This section discusses the codes of TV comedy, in situation comedy and in sketch shows, focusing on audience representatives, identification with characters and scenarios, and narrative codes. There are prominent visual and aural signs in TV comedy which invite the viewer to take up particular subject-positions in relation to a programme's discourse. The denoted laughter which frequently breaks into programmes' soundtracks marks the points at which the mythic meaning 'comedy' is constructed. This mythic meaning can derive from a range of different signs and relationships between signs. These include a point of conflict between the discourses of characters, a conflict between the connotations of the image and the connotations of sound or denoted dialogue, or an absurd extension of a particular discursive code or gestural code. The function of laughter is to relay the mythic meaning 'comedy' between viewer and TV discourse, and to confirm the subject-position of the viewer by representing an audience which shares this position. While TV viewers are watching individually or in small groups, the collective laughter of the denoted audience makes the link between the viewer at home and the mythic community of viewers to which the programme is broadcast. At moments of laughter, any uncertainty and ambiguity about the decoding of the signs of the programme is closed off by offering the viewer one kind of relationship with the TV discourse, by offering one way of decoding those moments of the text. The patterning of laughter which momentarily stops the TV discourse enables the viewer to become 'you', the one who is addressed by the discourse and who is expected to share in the imaginary community's laughter.

Moments of laughter interrupt any narrative progression in the programme's discourse, but narrative is a secondary coding

7   Victor (Richard Wilson) and Margaret Meldrew
(Annette Crosbie) in *One Foot in the Grave*

system in TV comedy. The code which primarily structures TV comedy is 'excess'. In terms of characterisation, Roseanne in *Roseanne* is excessively candid, cynical and apparently heartless. Frasier Crane in *Frasier* is excessively snobbish and proper. Victor Meldrew in *One Foot in the Grave* is excessively irritable, vindictive and moody. These situation comedies exaggerate characters' social codes of behaviour so that they become excessive, inappropriate, and therefore comic. Close up shots of the exaggerated facial expressions of the characters are signs which cue audience laughter and where the viewer is invited to decode the character's identity from a single 'overcoded' image. Figure 7 is a publicity still from *One Foot in the Grave* showing Victor Meldrew (Richard Wilson) with a characteristically exaggerated facial expression connoting moodiness, irritability and discontent. The character's clothes and body stance support the connotations of his expression, and the mythic meaning of the character as a testy old man. By contrast, his wife's (Annette Crosbie's) expression and stance connote pleasantness and long-suffering. The comedy of *One Foot in the Grave* derives not only from Victor Meldrew's excess in itself, but from the contrast between his behaviour and the behaviour of the other characters.

Comedy depends on a shifting pattern of identification between the viewer and the programme. When a character is comic, the viewer must identify with the character but also distance himself or herself from the character in order to find him or her funny. The viewer must also identify with the studio audience denoted by laughter on the soundtrack, taking up a shared position in relation to the comic moment in the programme. The viewer must also identify with the scenario presented by the various camera shots and sounds which make up the programme, so that the programme seems to be 'for us' and addressed to us as viewers. Finally then, the audience must identify with itself in the role of audience for the programme. Comedy relies on this shifting of the viewer's subject-position, and a rhythm of identification and disavowal of identification. The semiotic effect of comedy as a genre is to move and reposition the viewer, as this section has so far described in rather abstract terms. But of course the positioning and repositioning of the viewer might succeed or fail for different real viewers in different programmes or parts of the same programme. While the discourse of TV comedy lays out a position for the viewer in relation to its signs and codes, whether or not the viewer actually occupies this subject-position depends on the huge range of variables which determine each viewer's social identity.

As an example of how social identities affect viewers' decoding of situation comedy, here is an outline of some research on viewers of *The Cosby Show*. The results do not tell us about whether the viewers found the programme funny, but instead about how viewers identified with characters and narrative. Lewis (1991) interviewed a sample of both black and white viewers of an episode of *The Cosby Show* from all social classes. He found that white viewers perceived the characters in a 'colour blind' way, seeing them as ordinary and middle class, like the many other families with children who appear on American situation comedy programmes. For these white viewers, the characters were naturalised as 'like us'. The programme was decoded by the white viewers as being consonant with the American dream of upward mobility unaffected by colour, and was not identified with what the white viewers perceived as 'black humour' which they saw as loud and dominated by physical comedy. *The Cosby Show* was funny in the same way as many other situation comedies. But the black viewers approved of the show partly because of their awareness that it was a positive portrayal of black people, in contrast to what they perceived as a lack of positive images of black people on TV. They were very aware of the show's references to a specifically black culture (represented by the Huxtable family's ownership of paintings featuring black figures, anti-apartheid posters, etc.). Black viewers were far from 'colour blind' in their reading of the programme, and while they noted the lack of 'realism' in the Huxtables' freedom from racism and prejudice in the programme, this was more than compensated for by their approval of its representation of a cultural group which they identified with. *The Cosby Show* was both funny and favourably encoded an 'alternative' ideological position.

For Lewis, this analysis did not show that TV viewers are free either to accept a dominant reading or to construct an alternative or oppositional one. Instead it showed how *The Cosby Show* addresses different audiences in different ways. The identification

with characters and with the narrative structures of the programme which a particular viewer experiences may be determined by the social and cultural position of each viewer, but the
semiotic structure of the programme as a text has to be open
enough to allow for these variations in decoding. The same kind
of multiple address can be seen in the reception of comic characters created in sketch shows rather than situation comedy. The
comedian Harry Enfield created a character known as Loadsamoney in the late 1980s, who appeared in a British late-night
satire and music programme. Enfield's Loadsamoney was a working-class man who had the characteristics of excessive masculine
bravado and excessive pride in the high wages he earned as a
plasterer. These characteristics were signified by signs like a
swaggering walk and waving a large wad of twenty-pound notes
in the faces of the studio audience. In the context of a late-night
satire programme, the character was a critique of the get-rich-
quick selfishness encouraged by the policies of the Conservative
government. But the name Loadsamoney and some of Enfield's
catchphrases were taken up by the popular press and became
idioms in conversation, where they began to connote approval of
free enterprise culture as well as criticism of it. As the audience
group for the character changed and Enfield's inflection of the
signs in his performance was removed, since the television context of the signs was no longer shaping their decoding, the
mythic meanings of Loadsamoney were reversed. The decoding
of the Loadsamoney character depended on the discursive codes
brought to bear on him by viewers and readers, and these viewers and readers were different in different contexts of reception.

In the case of another of Harry Enfield's comic characters,
known as The Alien, comedy derives in part from intertextually
mixing codes from different genres and different media, which
are foregrounded by the signs in the character's physical appearance. As figure 8 shows, The Alien is wearing a white shirt and
tie which are signs in a dress code of conventional male formal
dress. His nose, ears and pointed head with its antenna are coded
as unconventional and non-human. The contradiction between
the two codes is itself comic, and they are brought together and
contrasted further by the spectacles which The Alien is wearing.
He is not human, but he is wearing humans' spectacles. Fur-

thermore, the signs of alienness in the character's appearance draw on the viewer's intertextual knowledge of representations of aliens in various media. Aliens in contemporary film and TV do not look anything like this, although aliens in low-budget 1950s films sometimes did, as did aliens in cartoons. The viewer is not asked to decode The Alien as first believable, then realise that he is a comic character. Instead, the viewer is asked to recognise the unbelievability of The Alien's aliennness by referring to his or her cultural knowledge of unbelievable aliens in media representations of decades ago. The Alien is a parody of previous unbelievable aliens, a self-conscious performance of ali-

8   The Alien (Harry Enfield) in *Harry Enfield's
Television Programme*

enness which is connoted by the 'H' shape (for Harry Enfield the performer) of The Alien's antenna.

Parody and excessive representation like this in TV comedy rely on the viewer's 'media literacy', so that intertextual references can be recognised and their connotations made part of the comic character's or scenario's comic excess. This issue of audience knowledge, and the ability of television programmes to target different audience groups by targeting viewers' different cultural knowledge, can be explored further by a discussion of the TV serial *Twin Peaks*. The viewer of a sketch featuring The Alien is asked to hold together several different codes to decode it; the coded ways of representing aliens in contemporary media texts, including the coded ways of representing aliens in previous media texts, the codes of TV sketch-show comedy, and the coded ways in which Harry Enfield is represented as a comic performer. In *Twin Peaks*, the discursive codes which structure the meanings of the programme both in the TV text and in other texts demonstrate the highly complex way in which contemporary television positions groups of viewers and kinds of cultural knowledge.

Polysemic television and multiaccentuality

On the day that *Twin Peaks*'s first pilot episode was shown in the United States (6 April 1990), the *New York Times* carried a full-page ad for the programme. The ad quoted other newspapers and magazines declaring that the serial was going to change the face of television, that it was original, the work of an acknowledged *auteur*, that it was stylistically complex and well made. These codings of *Twin Peaks*'s mythic meanings rely on cinematic codes of value, where some directors are given the cultural status of literary authors (*auteurs*), and where films can be described as avant-garde and seem to push at the boundaries of form. The pilot episode was the length of a film, and its director David Lynch had already made several films including *Eraserhead* and *Blue Velvet* which were critically acclaimed as avant-garde and original. The ad and other secondary texts like those quoted in the ad were therefore proposing a particular set of codes to be brought to the viewing of the programme, and endowed it with a mythic meaning. However, once *Twin Peaks* had attracted a relatively sizeable audience and a regular following, the discursive codes used in coverage of the programme changed. It began to be described in terms of viewer mania and addiction, as if it were a prime-time soap opera like *Dallas*. Articles on *Twin Peaks* appeared in the United States at the same time (October 1990) in both *Newsweek* and *Soap Opera Weekly*. Collins, whose essay on *Twin Peaks* discusses this context in more detail, therefore describes the programme as 'polysemic' (1992: 345), meaning that its signs and codes were open to a range of decodings. He calls *Twin Peaks* 'multiaccentual' as well (a term discussed in Fiske's (1992) essay in the same book), meaning that it was being understood in different ways by different audiences.

Collins calls the *Twin Peaks* phenomenon 'postmodern', and this is a critical term with several different meanings (1992: 341). Postmodern can denote a distinctive style, a self-aware playfulness with the codes of a form or a medium, such as is found in TV programmes like *Twin Peaks* or *Dream On* and in many TV ads which play on other ads or advertising conventions. For instance Harry Enfield, who we encountered in the previous section, has appeared in TV ads for Mercury telephone services which play on both public information films of the 1940s and on characters developed for his comedy sketch programmes. What is postmodern about programmes and ads like these is their ambivalence towards the original texts which they parody, where the codes of the original are recognised and used but their ideological and stylistic limitations are also foregrounded, as Hutcheon (1987) has described. *Twin Peaks* made intertextual references to the codes of science fiction, the police series, soap opera and Gothic fiction. These textual codes exist within and between scenes, and are sometimes taken seriously and sometimes not (for a more detailed discussion see Collins 1992: 345–7). So the viewer of a *Twin Peaks* episode is always being shifted around from one code and relationship to the text to another code and relationship. Making sense of *Twin Peaks* demands an active, mobile and TV-literate viewer.

The term 'postmodern' can also denote a socio-economic condition, emphasising the decay of industrial culture and the rise of 'post-industrial' media culture. There is a philosophical discourse based on this assumption (see Baudrillard 1983, for instance) that questions the assumptions of previous philosophy, and includes a focus on the perpetual alienation from 'reality' which a radical version of semiotics proposes. Postmodernist thought claims that all 'real meaning' is vanishing because experience and reality are now shaped or 'simulated' by the discourses of the media. According to this view, we might experience a love affair through the codes for presenting love affairs in films or TV programmes, or our perceptions of policemen would be determined by the mythic meanings of the police in *The Bill* (a popular police drama taking its name from the British slang term for the police force) or *Homicide: Life on the Street*. In a culture where people's experience is shaped by media representations, TV programmes are regarded as not denoting 'reality' in the usual sense, but denoting the realities represented through the codes of other TV programmes and in other media texts. Collins argues that postmodern texts like *Twin Peaks* are aware of the conditions of their own production, reception, and circulation in this media-saturated culture, and are enjoyable because they require the viewer to assemble, contrast and move between the codes he or she recognises from his or her experience of media involvement.

Collins reports that Mark Frost, the producer of *Twin Peaks*, said he wanted the series to appeal to people who liked 'quality' drama like *Hill Street Blues*, *St Elsewhere*, or *Moonlighting*, and to viewers of evening soap operas (1992: 342) as well. Frost was evidently thinking of a discerning and TV-literate audience, in fact exactly the audience which American TV networks were most interested in attracting. In the 1980s, cable TV had been eroding the three major American networks' audience share. In 1979, 91 per cent of viewers watched network TV in the evening prime-time. In 1989, the network share had fallen to 67 per cent. Among this mass audience video recorder owners and cable subscribers were attractive to advertisers because they included 'yuppie' viewers, who had sufficient disposable incomes to buy expensive consumer goods. Rather than considering the audience as a mass, the networks had to consider them as a collection of diverse but interconnected market sectors. This unstable and diverse marketplace gave rise to marketing strategies like those used to promote *Batman: The Movie*; its source was a comic-book read mainly by male children and teenagers, while Prince's theme music was especially popular among female teenagers. By combining these elements, there was some likelihood of encouraging related but different audience groups to see the film (Collins 1992: 342). As we have seen, *Twin Peaks* was promoted as both 'art' and 'soap', addressed both to 'yuppie' viewers and to the more differentiated (and mainly female) soap audience. At an institutional level, *Twin Peaks* was designed to be multi-accentual, appealing to different audience groups. At a textual level, its postmodern polysemy coming from the shifting codes and multiply-connoting signs of its images and sound allowed multiaccentuality to succeed economically. The programme's cultural visibility was both supported and extended by spin-off products including the books *The Secret Diary of Laura Palmer* and *Dale Cooper: My Life, My Tapes*, and a soundtrack album.

Earlier in this chapter we saw that TV programmes encode subject-positions for the viewer by linking their signs together in particular ways. But it has also emerged that not all viewers read the signs of television in the same way, and are therefore taking up rather different subject-positions in relation to the same TV text. The case of *Twin Peaks* shows that one of the responses to this situation by the makers of television is to produce TV which either allows or invites these different ways of decoding meanings. This can be done either by foregrounding the polysemic nature of signs in the programme, or encouraging multiaccentuality by framing the programme with different publicity discourses addressed to different groups of viewers. Collins argues that *Twin Peaks* is postmodern in its self-aware style, and in the deliberate cultivation of multiple subject-positions for the viewer in the programme and in secondary publicity discourses so that the viewer is always suspended between several different codes while watching it.

> What distinguishes *Twin Peaks* from, say, *Dallas* or *Knots Landing* is not that it encourages this alternation in viewing positions but that it explicitly acknowledges this oscillation and the suspended nature of television viewing. In other words, *Twin Peaks* doesn't just acknowledge the multiple subject positions that television generates; it recognises that one of the great pleasures of the televisual text is that very suspension and exploits it for its own ends. (1992: 348)

The intertextuality of *Twin Peaks* is in itself nothing new in TV. Some TV programmes refer to TV as constituting our knowledge of the past (comically in *Dream On* for instance). TV from the past is particularly prone to reappropriation in contemporary television programmes because TV's past is still being broadcast in the present. On any day there will be repeated programmes, 'television classics', and references to past programmes in comedy sketch shows and elsewhere. The semiotic significance of these past materials is different according to their different contexts. They are either taken seriously as great TV from the 'golden age', or coded as comic camp programmes for a youth audience (the *Batman* TV series, for instance), or their content may be seen as of historical interest, or as a look back at a simpler more innocent age, or as ideological myth which was never really true. An evening's TV viewing requires us both to shift subject-positions frequently, and also to decode programmes in relation to their position in the TV schedule and their intertextual relationship to other programmes. Some programmes include intertextual references to contemporary programmes to position themselves and their characters in this intertextual field. Characters in both *thirtysomething* and *LA Law* have referred to each other's programmes, while characters in *Knots Landing* refer to their attraction to TV presenters or characters (Collins 1992: 334–45). TV literacy is naturalised in programmes because it exists among viewers, and because it is a sign connoting the mythic identity of the programme in relation to the mythic identities of its competitors or companions in the schedule. As Collins argues, some TV programmes and ads make this fluid relationship between media texts one of the chief pleasures offered to the viewer. The next section concentrates more closely on viewers' pleasure, and outlines some research on the specific example of *Dallas*.

TV viewers: the case of *Dallas*

In 1985, Ien Ang's study of Dutch women's reactions to the American soap opera *Dallas* was published in English (revised in 1989). Ang set out to understand how women viewers experienced and enjoyed the programme, which was watched by half the population of the Netherlands in spring 1982, and has been broadcast in over ninety countries, including Turkey, Hong Kong, Australia, and Morocco. *Dallas* is still being shown in Britain even now, some ten years after the peak of its popularity. After outlining Ang's study of *Dallas*'s reception by women viewers in the Netherlands in this section, the next section of this chapter compares her findings with those of a study of non-western *Dallas* viewers to further discuss the decoding of programmes by particular groups of viewers. *Dallas* is set among fictional oil barons living in Dallas, Texas, and focuses mainly on the Ewing family, their business colleagues and extended family. Its plot is characterised by sudden reversals of fortune, emotional crises and interactions between business deals and family allegiances. Ang wanted to find out what made watching *Dallas* pleasurable for its audience, nearly three-quarters of whom were women. She placed an ad in the Dutch women's magazine *Viva*, asking people to write to her about their reactions to the programme. She got forty-two replies, and her book is an analysis of both the discourses of the programme and the discourses of the women who wrote to her about the programme. So although she uses semiotic methods in analysing these discourses, Ang is also an ethnographer studying the place of television in the life experience of particular viewers.

Because the narrative of *Dallas* is mostly concerned with the emotional problems of the characters, Ang describes *Dallas* as having a tragic structure of feeling. In other words, the programme presents a naturalised mythic world in which any resolution of the characters' problems leads on to further complication and suffering. In order to decode the programme in this way, Ang argues that viewers must be equipped with a cultural competence or orientation that she calls a 'melodramatic imagination' (1989: 78). This consists of a disposition to be vaguely dissatisfied with the everyday world and its restrictions, in which the viewer's imagination dignifies everyday life with the grand emotional significance and moral weight of theatrical melodrama or tragedy, making life much more meaningful by understanding it in this way. *Dallas* both fits in with this way of experiencing and supports it because the programme is itself melodramatic. Melodrama is characterised by emotional heightening and moralism, and uses archetypal characters and situations as signs to communicate meanings. In *Dallas*, Sue Ellen's alcoholism, for instance, is a sign of her emotional turmoil and her lack of control over her husband J.R. Ewing's selfish and aggressive actions.

For Ang, women have decoded and enjoyed *Dallas* through a melodramatic imagination because ideological factors position them as particular kinds of social subject. Women in western culture are positioned as emotional, psychologising, caring, community-forming (as opposed to adventuring, aggressive, money-making and individualist), so that the mythic moral and emotional world of melodrama corresponds to a dominant subject-position for women viewers:

> the pleasure of *Dallas* consists in the recognition of ideas that fit in with the viewers' imaginative world. They can 'lose' themselves in *Dallas* because the programme symbolises a structure of feeling which connects up with one of the ways in which they encounter life. And in so far as the imagination is an essential component of our psychological world, the pleasure of *Dallas* – as a historically specific symbolising of that imagination – is not a *compensation* for the presumed drabness of daily life, nor a *flight* from it, but a *dimension* of it. For only through the imagination, which is always subjective, is the 'objective reality' assimilated: a life without imagination does not exist. (1989: 82–83)

Pleasure in *Dallas* comes from the close relationship between the social and ideological ways in which viewers' experience is structured, and the ways in which the mythic world of the programme is structured. Beyond the text itself, pleasure comes from the fact that it is an entertainment, a reward and a relaxation. So enjoying the programme has a social as well as a textual dimension, and viewer involvement in *Dallas* was fuelled by tabloid headlines, spin-off merchandise, and the social value of awareness of the programme among friends, workmates and family members. Watching *Dallas* and knowing about the programme connected individual viewers to a mythic community with shared knowledge and experiences.

Ang analysed the semiotic codes of the programme to see how its structure and mythic meanings contributed to its appeal to a very large and diverse group of viewers. She found that episodes of *Dallas* contain few story cliffhangers, connoting that action is not especially significant to the programme's meanings. There is very little action in the programme and it is almost all dialogue. Episodes usually end on a close-up and the cliffhanger is an emotional and psychological one. Close-ups invite the viewer to identify with a character's predicament, and to predict what its effects will be on other characters. Characters' personalities and significance are constructed through each character's interrelations with the others. As in other soap operas, 'identification with a character only becomes possible within the framework of the whole structure of the narrative' (1989: 29). There is a 'community' of characters in *Dallas*, each of whom lives in a 'realistically' denoted setting, in which 'lifelike' accidental events and interactions occur. The denotative level of the programme is seen by some of Ang's letter writers as unrealistic, but this is excused at the connotative level where the mythic world of *Dallas* is consistent and makes sense. The expensiveness of the lifestyle and *mise en scène* in *Dallas* makes viewers acknowledge that it is a fictional world, but its distance from everyday 'reality' also allows them to indulge in emotional excess in relation to the narrative and characters. So the realism of *Dallas* is not a cognitive realism (providing knowledge about the concrete facts of the real world), it is an emotional realism, 'the realism experience of the *Dallas* fans quoted bears no relation to this cognitive level – it is situated at the emotional level: what is recognised as real is not knowledge of the world, but a subjective experience of the world' (1989: 45).

This 'realistic' world, and the naturalistic acting style of the performers gives the world of *Dallas* a unity and comprehensibility. Ang's letter writers talk about the characters as if they are real people with real personalities (as does the publicity discourse and popular-press coverage of the programme), so that even though all letter writers are aware that the characters really are actors, the characters are discussed in the ways that real people are. So in *Dallas*'s melodramatic world, the viewer is unlikely to identify with just one character in the narrative. We are informed about the secret pasts, hidden desires and emotional crises of all of the characters, so when they say what they do not mean, and mean what they do not say, we are able to read them, often through close-ups, and understand and identify with the psychological make-up of each contending party. Also, characters quite often change their personality, becoming suddenly 'good' or 'bad', so there are no consistent personality types which can be coded as role models or heroes for long. By combining 'realism' with melodrama, *Dallas* allows for a wide range of identifications with characters and identification with the mythic *Dallas* world.

There are various genre elements in the show, like western, soap and murder mystery, which allow for multiaccentuality or decoding in different ways by different audience constituencies. Ang refers to a survey in which most women questioned said that they enjoyed family problems and romantic entanglements in the show, while most men said they enjoyed the business problems, cowboy elements and power–wealth themes. It seems that *Dallas* was watched and enjoyed in different ways by each gender of viewers. Ang's study was written from a feminist point of view, and while she stressed the value of *Dallas* in the lives of real women, she was critical of its ideological role. Since the women in the programme can never attain a happy resolution (or any resolution) to their problems, it is not a feminist utopia despite the significance and number of major female characters. The women in *Dallas* are either trapped in a subordinate relationship to a man (as the Sue Ellen character is to her husband, for instance) or they wish for an equal relationship with a man that cannot be achieved (as the Pam character does). They also assume that marriage and children is their automatic lot in life, despite sometimes being independent and powerful businesswomen. Ang argued that pleasure in the show is not itself necessarily positive for women viewers, since it does not lead to action or to political consciousness of their gender roles.

Among Ang's letter writers there are some women who do not like *Dallas*. They justify their dislike by a critique of American mass culture which they regard as 'trashy', or by criticising the programme's apparent anti-feminism, or by pointing out what they regard as faults in its dramatic structure. These people are not decoding *Dallas* by invoking a tragic structure of feeling or a melodramatic imagination. They decode it through different ideological subject-positions, invoking codes of 'quality', 'realism', dramatic criticism, or academic discourse. These critical discourses are either unimportant to *Dallas*'s admirers, or they self-consciously negotiate with them by adopting an ironic attitude to their own pleasure in the programme. This ironic attitude was also found by Gray (1992) in her analysis of women's reactions to their viewing of rented video films. Their reactions depended in part on educational background. More highly-educated women distanced themselves from the films they enjoyed most, by calling them 'trashy' or 'trivial' and thus retained a degree of independence and superiority over their involvement with them. Women with less educational attainment referred to their own tastes and therefore themselves as 'silly' or 'sloppy', accepting a socially devalued identity. But for many of Ang's letter writers, liking *Dallas* is given legitimacy by appealing to the populist discourse which assumes that theoretical judgements about things are not a valid challenge to people's right to enjoy whatever they wish, since pleasures are subjective, different, and all equally valid. This common-sense view is a way of disempowering critical discourses on popular culture and acknowledging the role pleasure plays in our lives. But Ang points out that this common-sense view serves the dominant ideology by assuming that there can be pleasure and choice without political responsibility, and action which is not already given social meaning by naturalised ideological norms of behaviour.

Specific audience groups

Ang's work on *Dallas* is valuable for the insight it provides into how a specific cultural group (Dutch women) negotiate decodings of the programme which correspond to the ways in which they see themselves. Some interestingly different decodings of *Dallas* have been reported by researchers interviewing non-Western viewers of the same TV series. In a series of studies, Katz and Liebes talked to viewers of *Dallas* from different ethnic and cultural groups in several countries. They found there were significant differences in the ways in which viewers in the same group decoded *Dallas*, and differences between the groups. 'Viewers selectively perceive, interpret and evaluate the programme in terms of local cultures and personal experiences, selectively incorporating it into their minds and lives' (Katz and Liebes 1984: 28). As we have seen in the discussions above of *The Cosby Show* and *Dallas*, television programmes are always multiaccentual to some degree and all of TV's signs and codes exhibit some degree of polysemy. In their 1984 study, Katz and Liebes reported that an Arab viewer 'read into' the *Dallas* narrative that Sue Ellen Ewing returned to her father's house with her baby after running away from her husband J. R., rather than going to stay with her lover as the narrative denoted. Although this decoding of the narrative is 'aberrant', it allowed this viewer to accommodate one aspect of the programme into Arab culture more coherently by mapping that culture's expectations of women onto the programme. The ideology and mythic social meanings of the viewer's culture were overlaid on the ideologies naturalised in the narrative. Another respondent, a Moroccan Jew, read *Dallas* as a confirmation that Jewish cultural values were superior to the American ideology represented by the series (1984: 31). In this case, the viewer was decoding *Dallas*'s mythic meanings 'correctly' but not accepting these meanings as 'natural'. For Katz and Liebes, this kind of variation in the decoding of the programme shows that 'people are discussing and evaluating not only the issues in the Ewing family but the issues in their own lives' (1984: 31).

Although the global presence of American programmes in the broadcasting of very different countries is sometimes criticised as the domination or 'hegemony' of American ideology over local cultures, this critique takes too little account of multiaccentuality and the negotiation of meanings by real viewers. The decoding of the signs and codes of TV must be affected by the relationship of the mythic meanings and ideological structure of programmes and ads with the society in which they are broadcast, and with the particular social and cultural positions of viewers. As pointed out in chapter five, global television does not necessarily produce a global audience which decodes TV in the same way. O'Sullivan *et al.* (1994: 287) report that in Fiji in 1993, the TV schedule included for instance, *The Bugs Bunny Show* (US animation), *Police Academy 5* (US film), *My Two Dads* (US sitcom), *MASH* (US sitcom), *The Cosby Show* (US sitcom), *Highway to Heaven* (US drama), *May to December* (British sitcom),

BBC News, *CBS News*, *Porridge* (British sitcom) and *Trainer*
(British drama). The meanings of these programmes for Fijian
audiences are likely to be different from the meanings of the programmes decoded in either Britain or the United States. However, there is an economic and institutional dimension to
globalisation which does have a significant effect on particular
national television cultures. Although some national TV networks outside the United States are large and powerful (Brazil's
RedeGlobo and Mexico's Televisa are the fourth and fifth largest
in the world), Dowmunt (1993: 7) noted that episodes of American series like *Miami Vice* can be obtained by, for instance, Zim-
babwe TV for a special rate of $500 each as part of a package
of material. This is much less money than the cost of Zimbabweans making drama programmes for themselves. Since
imported programmes are watched by a greater proportion of
more affluent white and middle-class black Zimbabweans than
domestically-made programmes, imported programmes are also
favoured by advertisers because this more affluent audience has
greater consumer spending power. The schedules of many Latin
American and African nations contain more than 50 per cent
imported American programmes. But the economic dependency
on American programmes does not automatically produce ideological control.

There are evidently cultural differences in how viewers decode
different semiotic levels of programmes. Katz and Liebes found
that non-Western ethnic groups could identify with the family
relationships in *Dallas* but at the same time they did not identify
with what they perceived as its Americanness. Part of Americanness is the idea of the 'American dream' of financial success
and personal happiness, and Katz and Liebes found that different
cultural groups responded to this naturalised 'background' ideology in *Dallas* in contrasting ways. Jewish members of a kibbutz
in Israel decoded the programme as showing that money does
not bring happiness, while on the other hand members of a
North African cooperative decoded *Dallas* as proving that money
releases people from the troubles of ordinary life (1984, 1985).
In a later study (1987), Katz and Liebes reported that Russian
Jews who had just emigrated to Israel from the Soviet system
decoded *Dallas* as a critique of capitalism produced from within

American capitalist society. For these viewers, the programme was a text unconsciously exposing the contradictions of American ideology. From these examples, it is clear that the mythic meanings in the narrative of *Dallas* are recognised by very diverse groups of viewers. But the status and value of these mythic meanings depends on the viewer's negotiation between the text of the programme and the intertext or structure of social meanings which forms the naturalised cultural world of the viewer.

So different decodings are produced by viewers who occupy different social positions in a particular society, as well as by viewers who live in different nations and cultures. Leal (1990) discussed the collection of domestic objects around the TV set in the home of a working-class Brazilian family who had recently moved from the country to a city. On top of the TV were portrait photographs of dead family members, and relatives who had moved away to other parts of the country. In the edges of the pictureframes were small passport-size photos of relatives who had moved to the city. So in each frame was a sign connoting the rural past (the portrait photograph), and a sign connoting modernity and urbanism (the passport-size picture, produced by an automated machine and used on ID cards, for instance). For a family like this, Leal showed that TV programmes like soap operas were decoded as images of modern urban culture, a confirmation of the family's move to a new life. This move was also signified by the objects which physically rested on top of the TV set. In these social and economic circumstances, the meanings of TV programmes were differently inflected compared to the meanings which were received by affluent middle-class Brazilians. The negotiation of the meanings of TV programmes is affected not only by membership of a national culture, but also by the social status of the viewer in that culture. This point is similar to Ang's more general observation that it is the ideological positioning of women in western society which predisposes them to read *Dallas* in melodramatic terms.

The necessarily short discussion of a variety of television programmes and ads in this chapter has aimed to show the different critical outcomes from using different but related approaches to TV and its audience. Television is an industry and a set of

institutions in which economic factors and professional codes
structure broadcasting and what is broadcast in particular ways.
TV signs and codes are complex and interrelated, and semiotic
analysis can be highly effective in separating the signifying elements of television texts and showing how they are meaningful
in a cultural and ideological context. This issue of how television
constructs a relationship with its viewers can be illuminated by
the analysis of viewer positioning, which also enables us to see
how TV discourses can address different groups of viewers at the
same time. The weakness of these analytical discourses is their
tendency to separate themselves from the experiences of real
viewers. To address this gap in our approach to TV, it is necessary to shift to a quite different kind of critical discourse, that of
audience research or ethnography. The examples of research on
real audiences in this chapter show not simply that signs and
meanings are read differently by different audience groups. More
significantly than this, the meanings which people construct
from their relationships with television (and other media) are an
integral part of their lived experience.

Sources and further reading

Among the many books and essays which use semiotic approaches
to television are Fiske (1987), Fiske and Hartley (1978), Eco (1990),
Selby and Cowdery (1995), and Seiter (1992). An excellent collection of essays on a range of analytical approaches to TV is Allen
(1992) which contains Seiter's essay and the essays by Allen,
Kozloff, Fiske and Collins which are referred to in this chapter. Further studies relating mainly to American TV can be traced in the bibliography compiled by Jacobson (1995).

On the question of audiences and decodings of TV, Fiske (1987)
discusses many of the specific studies referred to in this chapter.
Books on the TV audience include Ang (1989, 1991), Morley
(1992), Drummond and Patterson (1988), Seiter *et al.* (1989) and,
specifically from an ethnographic perspective, Lindof (1987) and
Lull (1988). A very useful discussion of the ways that work on audiences has changed over the last fifteen years or so, in the context of
detailed studies of the *Star Trek* and *Doctor Who* series and their audiences, can be found in Tulloch and Jenkins (1995).

Suggestions for further work

1 Analyse a TV listings magazine detailing programmes on several channels for the same time period. How do the listings inform you of the programmes' genre, form and attractions for viewers? How do the editorial pages in the listings magazine support or multiply the mythic meanings for some programmes?

2 Conduct a detailed analysis of the signs and codes in a short sequence from one TV programme. What contributions are made to narrative progression, viewer positioning, and 'preferred reading' by the elements you have analysed? What are the limitations of this kind of exercise?

3 Select a genre of non-fiction programme focused on a single aspect of contemporary life, like holiday programmes, consumer advice programmes or cooking programmes. What are the mythic meanings that are encoded and what ideologies are naturalised?

4 Analyse a selection of TV ads from different parts of the day (for example, mid-morning and mid-evening). What is the significance of the similarities and differences you find in their address to the viewer, types of product advertised, and relationship to the surrounding programmes?

5 Which current programmes seem to exhibit the greatest degrees of multiaccentuality and polysemy? Do they have any narrative or generic features which could be called postmodern?

6 Compare the visual and narrative codes of two soap operas from different nations (for example Britain and Australia). How similar and how different are their codes? How similar and how different are their ideologies?

7 Compare the breakfast television programmes on two or more TV channels. What does a semiotic analysis reveal about the apparent duration of viewing, and mode of viewing by their audience? Is a specific audience group or subject-position being addressed?

7

Cinema

Introduction

This chapter discusses film signs and codes, the central concerns of semiotic analysis. But like other chapters in this book, there is also a section on the cinema as an economic and cultural institution, since films are made and watched in a commercial context. The vast majority of contemporary films are fictional narratives, and this chapter discusses critical ideas about film narrative with a particular emphasis on narrative structure and on the role of the film viewer in making sense of films. The previous chapter took account of the recent academic research into how particular real viewers watched television, but there is currently little work done on film viewers in this way although the issue is addressed at the end of this chapter. Instead, film theory has concentrated on elaborate semiotic and psychoanalytic approaches to film texts. For this reason, among others, the theory of the film medium has historically been more a complex set of discourses than the theoretical discourses developed for the analysis of the other media discussed in this book. Film theory has also been adjusted and transferred to work on other media, and some of the semiotic and psychoanalytic approaches discussed in earlier chapters originally derived from the writings of theorists working on film.

This chapter is organised around some of the conceptual and theoretical issues in film theory, but it can only claim to be an introduction to a very wide and complicated subject. There are references to a wide range of recent British and American films here, chosen because they are relatively well known and accessible, and most of the sections of the chapter include short discussions of aspects of a few films in more detail. While film and the cultural phenomenon of going to the cinema are the main subjects of the chapter, there is some discussion of film on television, video, and other film-related media products like computer games and film advertising. There is insufficient space here to deal with film history, 'art' film, or to give more than an overview of the complex evolution of theories of film. The Sources and further reading section at the end of the chapter offers guidance on how to fill in these gaps and how to extend your knowledge of the issues discussed briefly here. Many of the points made about signs, codes, narrative and audience relate to the discussion of other media in this book (like television or advertising), and it may be useful to check the index and see how ideas discussed in this chapter can be compared and contrasted with their appearance earlier in the book.

The film business

Films are extremely expensive to make. As well as the actors', technicians' and craftspeople's fees, for instance, there are the costs of buying scripts, building sets, making prints and promoting films. It is very difficult to predict which films will make enough profits to cover these costs, and many films never recoup the expense of making and distributing them. But each year, a few films will make spectacular amounts of money, and these big successes subsidise the cost of the other movies made by a particular film organisation. For instance *Batman Forever* was released in the United States on the weekend of 17–18 June 1995, the most profitable film opening to date. The film took an estimated $53.3 million, opening on 4,307 screens (one in five of the cinema screens in the States) and was seen by an estimated eight million people per day. It broke the record for the highest earnings on the first day ($20 million compared to *Jurassic Park*'s $18.5 million), so although the film is estimated to have cost up to $100 million, not including about $25 million spent on advertising, it is clearly going to make a profit (the *Guardian* Tuesday 20 June 1995:1). A quite different film, the British *Four Weddings and a Funeral* cost only £2.9 million, but between March and November 1994 took over $234 million at cinemas around the world, from the United States to Iceland to South Korea (*Sight and Sound* January 1995: 15). While the makers of *Jurassic Park* always expected the film to be successful, the popularity of *Four Weddings and a Funeral* took the film industry by surprise.

In Europe and the United States the vast majority of films exhibited are American (*Sight and Sound* January 1995, *Chronicle of Cinema* supplement: 126–7). In the sixteen West European countries, just under 60 per cent of all films released in 1992 were American in origin, with American films taking a share of box-office revenue ranging from 54 per cent (France) to 87 per cent (Greece). In a sample of twenty-one countries from all continents representing a total population of about 950 million people, the ten most widely seen films in 1993 were all American. The most popular film was *Jurassic Park*, seen by over 144 million people, with over 60 per cent of its total revenue earned outside the United States. Not only is contemporary American cinema becoming more dependent on global marketing to recoup investment in film production, but the absorption of Hollywood studios by multinational conglomerates (Gulf + Western, Coca-Cola, Sony, Matsushita and News Corporation have all owned film production companies) means that cinema is just one element of a global media industry. The first-run showing of films in cinemas is significant in the profitability of films, but it is not only in cinemas that they are watched. In 1993 British people spent £319 million going to cinemas, but spent £528 million on video rentals, £643 million on buying videos, and £350 million on subscriptions to TV movie channels. When *Four Weddings and a Funeral* is premiered on Channel 4 television it is expected to attract a large enough audience that one minute of advertising time in the film will probably cost about £100,000 (*Broadcast* 1 September 1995: 16–17).

The predominance of American films in the world market is far from new, but one of the more recent developments in the cinema business is the linkage of films to other entertainment media. The Japanese corporations which make video recorders, computers and other home electronic products now invest in the films and associated entertainment products which are produced by Hollywood. A recent example is *Johnny Mnemonic*, a film funded by $30 million from the Sony corporation. Sony has invested heavily in US film production, though so far without making much profit, and wrote off $3.2 billion in film losses in 1994. The reason for this financial commitment is that cinema is only one of a number of image-based technologies which are being brought together as integrated products. The prospect of linking film with interactive video makes cinema itself one aspect of an integrated media industry. In 1994 total cinema box-office takings in the United States were $5 billion, but the value of the US video game market was $10 billion, and these two audiovisual technologies are now merging together. *Johnny Mnemonic* is not only a film, but was simultaneously released as a CD-ROM interactive video game, featuring film scenes shot at the same time as the cinema version for a further cost of only $3 million.

In order to 'sell' a film, to persuade us to note the appearance of a new film and to see it, many promotional techniques are used in addition to direct advertising. The merchandising of products associated with films is one of the most important, with products released before and during the film's exhibition run, like clothing, toys, music, books and computer games. These products both advertise films for people who have not seen them yet, and allow people to 'buy into' the social meaning of a film they have seen (or cannot see, in the case of children too young to be admitted to the film). Many tie-in and spin-off products support the 'narrative image' of the film, the cluster of images and meanings which offer a condensed version of the film's attractions. Film posters and publicity stills contain visual and linguistic signs which encode films' narrative themes, denote the stars of the film, and signify its genre. Figure 9 (p. 178) is a publicity still from *Four Weddings and a Funeral* denoting Rowan Atkinson in a costume and setting connoting 'wedding', and he is widely known (to a British audience at least) as a comedy performer, raising expectations about the film's comic pleasure and its story. Figure 10 later in this chapter denotes Hugh Grant and Andie MacDowell, the stars of *Four Weddings and a Funeral*, where their pose and the composition of the image connote romance, another key genre element of the film. In a similar way, the music videos accompanying film signature tunes often contain a selection of clips which encode the film's meanings in a condensed form. The *Robin Hood, Prince of Thieves* title song 'Everything I Do' performed by Bryan Adams was the top-selling single in Britain for nine weeks, and *The Bodyguard*'s title song 'I Will Always Love You' also made number one in the charts. Both music videos, like Wet Wet Wet's 'Love is All Around' music video from *Four Weddings and a Funeral*, included clips advertising the films and the pleasures they offered to the film audience.

Some products are tied in to films by simply using their name or logo. *Jurassic Park* licensed products, for instance, included watches, slippers, model kits, drinking cups, chocolate eggs, balloons, office chairs, children's socks, children's underpants, stickers, popcorn, Christmas cards, cakes, toothbrushes and children's building bricks. Most of these products used only the film's logo or typographic signs (lettering style and colours). Other means of promotion include press and TV interviews with the stars, TV documentaries on the making of the film, and competitions to win merchandising products. In some cases the cost of promotion exceeds the cost of the film itself, and films need to be analysed not only as self-contained texts but also as intertextual fields of products and meanings. While cinema has historically

9   Father Gerald (Rowan Atkinson) in *Four Weddings and a Funeral*

had an aura of art which set at least some of its products apart from commercial media, mainstream cinema today is as much a popular, industrial and commercial medium as the other media discussed in this book.

Cinema spectators are predominantly in the fifteen to twenty-four age group, the average age of the spectator having fallen since the 'golden age' of cinema-going in the middle of the century. Nearly 20 per cent of British fifteen to twenty-four year olds go the cinema twice a month or more, the largest sector of regular film-goers. Contemporary cinema-goers have to be addressed by particular films which may appeal to them, and they have fairly coherent requirements of films which they may choose to see. Mass market 'family' films are in decline, and tend to be exhibited at particular times of year which follow the patterns of the society in which they are shown, so that family audiences are offered films at Christmas, or during the summer school holidays. Instead of this mass market product, film companies offer a range of films directed to specific types of market focused around a genre, a star, a director or a current issue which is represented in the film's story. This segmentation of the audience is physically signified in multiplex cinemas, where ten films might be shown in overlapping timeslots in ten different auditoria. The selection might include two 'family' films, an action–adventure, a romance with a current star, two teen movies and a foreign 'art film'. Multiplex cinemas tend to emphasise the social experience of going to the cinema, cinema as an event. They have uniformed staff, shops selling merchandising products, cinema ephemera and food and drink, clean purpose-built auditoria, and often tickets are for specific seats to which the cinema-goer is ushered, and tickets can be pre-booked. The whole experience is designed to feel secure, ordered, safe and comfortable, an evening out of which the film is a major but by no means the only part. This chapter is mostly about the semiotic analysis of films, but cinemas and cinema-going can also be analysed in semiotic terms to see how they too encode mythic social meanings.

Cinema spectatorship

This section and the next deal with some of the theory in film criticism which has tried to explain and critique the ways in which films are watched by audiences. These approaches make use of psychoanalytic theories of subjectivity, because our pleasure in films must not only be consciously but also unconsciously produced. Psychoanalysis, because it offers a theory of how our subjectivity is constructed consciously and unconsciously, is useful in explaining the ways that the cinema medium draws on and reinforces the workings of an individual subject's psyche. Psychoanalytic theory can also show how our own individual psychic structure (as masculine or feminine, for instance) allows only certain options for making sense of the film for ourselves. Semiotics and recent psychoanalytic theory share several important assumptions. First, meaning comes not from a natural pre-given state of things, but is the result of the workings of a structure existing in a specific social context. For semiotics, the fundamental structure is language. For psychoanalysis too, it is language which gives us our sense of individual subjectivity, as 'I', and the structure of family and gender relations in society joins with language to construct us as subjects. The subject is therefore a signifier, something whose meaning and position is determined by his or her place in a system which already exists.

The French theorist Christian Metz (1975) proposed that cinema differs from other art forms in that it deploys vision, sound, movement and syntagmatic arrangement all at once, and offers perceptions which are all of absent things, rather than of present ones (whereas in opera and theatre, for instance, actors, music and visual signs are actually present on stage). Thus films are all fictional for Metz, since they all represent something by means of signs, rather than presenting what exists in the spectator's real time and space. The signifier in cinema is thus always 'imaginary'. The three processes Metz identified in cinema spectatorship were identification, voyeurism, and fetishism involving disavowal of lack. I shall outline these three complex processes in turn. While the spectator identifies with represented characters in films, Metz believed that a more crucial identification is with the act of perception itself. Since the spectator knows he or she is in a cinema, he or she is distanced from and master of what is projected on the screen, which seems to be there for him or her alone. So the spectator is identifying with himself or herself as perceiver, with perception itself. The spectator's perception of a film image is enabled by the camera's perception, so that the identification with perception is also an identification with the camera. In addition, the spectator's field of vision is parallel to the cone of projected light from the projector showing the film, and the spectator thus seems even more to be the source of vision, even though the sources are really the camera and projector.

These identifications of the spectator's position with the camera and with the projector seem to place the spectator in an active, producing relationship to what is seen, though of course it is the camera and projector which really produce the image. For Metz, the spectator misrecognises the position he or she is in, seeming to be the image's producer but really being its consumer. The cinematic apparatus of camera, projector, and screen, is set up to encourage the spectator's belief in his or her own transcendent control over what is seen in the cinema, but this is a delusion since the spectator is a consumer of the film and not its producer or source. This argument recalls the discussion of ideology which has occurred in earlier chapters of this book. It has been argued that ideology seeks to persuade us that we are makers of meanings, though in reality connotation and myth 'subject' us to their meanings. For Metz and many other film theorists, the cinematic apparatus has ideological effects by offering the spectator a subject-position of imaginary dominance and control.

Voyeurism, Metz's second way of describing cinema spectatorship, means looking at something which cannot look back at us. The explanation of voyeurism and fetishism in this paragraph and the next will refer to the spectator as 'he', for reasons which I shall explain in the next section. Looking at a desired object or person results in an erotic or sexual pleasure for the spectator who looks. The pleasure of voyeurism in cinema (as elsewhere) depends on the distance between the spectator and what is seen on the screen. The actors are present when the spectator is not (when the film is being made), and the spectator is present when the actor is not (when the film is watched). The spectator does not feel threatened in his voyeurism since the bodies he is looking at are absent while their images are present. In addition, actors rarely look at the camera in films, thereby avoiding a confrontation with the spectator's gaze, so the spectator's transgressive looking is encouraged by the codes of cinema. Fetishism, Metz's third spectating process, is the erotic contemplation of an object or person (often a part of a person, like a woman's legs for instance). Psychoanalytic research discovered that fetishism originally derives from the child's awareness that his mother is 'castrated' and does not possess the phallus (the signifier of sexual power which the father possesses). The desire to cover over this lack in the mother desired by the child leads the child to deny the evident sexual difference and threat which the castrated mother represents, by fixing on a fetish object which stands in for phallic sexual power. The threat is that the same castration might happen to the child as a punishment for desiring the mother sexually, and this crisis for the subject is known as the Oedipus complex.

The fetishistic denial or disavowal of lack is something like 'I know something is lacking or absent, but nevertheless I will believe there is no lack or absence.' Cinema involves fetishism because images of absent people or things are presented as if they were present. Although cinema lacks the reality of actual perceptions, spectators are encouraged to believe that what is seen is effectively present. Pleasure depends on both knowing that film is illusion, but believing it is not. The ability of the technical apparatus of cinema to make an absence present is one kind of fetishism, and representations which themselves cover but reveal lack and absence are fetishistic too. Fetish objects are denoted in films when fascinating and desirable things are presented for the spectator's pleasure (like the Batmobile; parts of Vivian's (Julia Roberts's) body in *Pretty Woman*; or guns). These things displace the spectator's lack onto something signified as present. Their presence denies that anything is lacking, though in their power to do this, fetish objects show that there is a lack. The theory of the cinematic apparatus and of spectatorship concentrates on how film viewers are positioned as subjects, and how cinema supports the psychic structures which turn people into desiring consumers of its film products. The implication of Metz's ideas is that the cinema spectator takes up a masculine subject-position, and the next section explores this further and challenges the assumption.

The gendered spectator

One of the most influential contributions to the critical analysis of film in recent decades was an article by Laura Mulvey (1975). The article argues that the spectator's pleasure depends on an ideological manipulation of film codes, especially as regards the image of women in films, and Mulvey calls for new kinds of film, different from the dominant Hollywood model, which would challenge prevailing ideology and the pleasures which film offers to its audience. The first pleasure that Mulvey identifies for the cinema audience is the pleasure of looking in itself, called 'scopophilia'. Scopophilia is the drive to subject other people to an interested and controlling gaze. In children, scopophilia can often be seen to have an erotic or sexual dimension, as the child tries to glimpse and check out the bodies and sexual organs of other children or adults, as part of his or her curiosity about private and forbidden matters. The same drive persists in adults, sometimes even becoming voyeurism, where sexual pleasure comes from secretly looking at another person with a controlling and objectifying gaze. Looking at a film in the cinema is not a secret pleasure of course. But the world of the film is sealed off from the spectator by being on the screen and not in our own real space, and the film goes on whether we are there or not. It is dark in the cinema, and the bright film image seems like a window onto a different and private world to which we are given access. The spectator is offered scopophilic and voyeuristic pleasure in film by the circumstances of viewing and the narrative conventions that put us in the position of observers able to look in at a story from which we are separated.

The second kind of visual pleasure offered in film is identifying with an image which stands in for ourselves, and we have come across this notion before. As we have seen earlier in this book, the mirror stage, as it is known, is a crucial moment in the formation of an identity for the individual subject. It occurs in relation to an image, where the subject takes a comparable person as an image of a more perfected self, an ideal ego. The subject's imaginary identification with this ideal image, forgetting his or her own real insufficiency, is parallel to the spectator's fascination with the film image, when the spectator forgets everything except the film. The images of other people on the screen have the same fascination as the imaginarily-perfect mirror image which the child perceives in the mirror stage. The mirror image is not the child, it is an image of the child. This other thing, the image, returns to the psyche in the form of the ego ideal, a more perfect person whom the child identifies with. Cinema shows us a vast range of others whom we identify with: the film actors. Film actors fulfil the role of ego ideals, people different from us whom we would like to have and to be. The spectator identifies with images of film actors in the same way that he or she identified with the image of an ego ideal in the mirror stage.

So there are two components to scopophilia in film spectatorship: the pleasure in looking at an image which is made available to our controlling gaze, and the pleasure in identifying with an image that stands in for us. The first of these pleasures is bound up with erotic desire, and the second with the process by which our ego is formed in early life. In the first case, the spectator desires the image of an object which promises to satisfy a sexual aim, and in the second case the spectator desires an ego ideal, the image of a more perfect self. In both kinds of response, the spectator is seeking something which will make good a lack, which will supply something that is missing. We have seen how this lack in being is first signalled in the mirror stage, but it achieves its full meaning in the Oedipus complex, outlined above. Forever afterwards, the child is left with a desire for the other which can never be fulfilled, a lack in being. Whenever the scopophilic look promises to remedy this lack by providing an image of a desired object (an other separate from the subject which promises to supply what is lacking), scopophilia brings with it the threat of castration too. Psychoanalytic theory proposes that whatever is desired takes the place of the original desired object: the mother who was desired by the child but from whom access was prohibited by the father.

Characteristically, it is a masculine gaze which takes women as desired objects, setting women up for masculine scopophilic pleasure in looking. Women have to take up the role of narcissistic exhibitionists, becoming objects for the pleasure of the masculine gaze. As Mulvey puts it, women in film are signs which signify 'to-be-looked-at-ness' (1975: 17). This is extremely common in film, where women are often displayed as desirable objects. But at the same time this gaze at the woman stops the narrative flow of the film, holds things up. The task of the film narrative is then to integrate the image of the woman into the narrative. This is done by making the male character the one who advances the action, controlling the movement of the story. The spectator is thereby encouraged to identify with the active male character as an ideal ego, a desired self, so that the active male character stands in for the spectator. The male character is the bearer of the spectator's look, able like the spectator to gaze at the erotic image of the woman, and giving the spectator, through the spectator's identification with him, the imaginary sense of controlling the action.

These processes go some way to controlling the destabilisation of the film narrative which erotic contemplation of the woman introduces. But there is a fundamental problem. In a patriarchal society, characterised by the dominance of the male gaze over women as objects, the woman representing the desired object must bring with her the threat of castration which always accompanies desire. To dispel this threat, there are several ways that film narrative attempts to do away with the problem that the image of the woman represents. First, the film might be pre-occupied with investigating the woman (as Madonna's character is investigated in *Desperately Seeking Susan* for instance), so that she ceases to be mysterious and threatening. Second, the narrative might take control of the woman by punishing her (as women are punished in *Friday the Thirteenth*, for instance), or rescuing her from her guilt. Or thirdly, the woman could be elevated to the status of a fetish object, an overvalued symbol which covers over the threat it might induce by encouraging excessive scopophilic contemplation (as in the fetishisation of Julia Roberts in *Pretty Woman*). The voyeuristic look both denies castration in its mastery over what is shown, but threatens it by insisting on showing the desired person or object as fully as possible.

The psychoanalytic theories of spectatorship briefly described here were widely accepted and used in film theory for more than a decade, but there are problems with them. One of the problematic issues is the force of cinema's positioning of the spectator, whose response appears to be determined by the film. It seems that the spectator is rigidly positioned by cinema, and has no option but to succumb to the medium's ideological operations on him (or her). Secondly, these theories relate much more easily to the male spectator than the female. In the explanations above 'the spectator' was often referred to as 'he'. The only way out of this problem within the terms of the theory is to argue that women have to align themselves with a masculine spectating position in order to decode the meanings of films. This might possibly be the case, especially since the societies where cinema was developed are patriarchal, putting the male at the centre of things and relegating women to the position of an other, different and subordinate to men. But in response to the dominance of masculine spectatorship and the rigid fixity of the viewer in these theories, a more flexible theory of spectatorship was developed in the 1980s. It made use of the notion of fantasy, and was elaborated by Elizabeth Cowie (1984).

The spectator, Cowie argued, 'enunciates' or produces a fantasy that is supported by the film text. Fantasy is where repressed ideas are allowed into consciousness in a distorted form (as in dreams, for instance). The fantasy therefore covers over a repressed wish but also exposes it. In fantasy, the subject identifies with several figures at the same time, not necessarily with those who the narrative offers as ideals. In *Nightmare on Elm Street* for instance, spectators identify not only with Freddie Krueger's victims and pursuers but also with the 'evil' Freddie himself. The one who fantasises can adopt different roles for identification, and different spectating positions. It is not what happens in the fantasy itself that satisfies the spectator's desire (since by definition desire is what cannot be satisfied), but instead it is the turning into a scenario, the putting on stage of desire which is satisfying. The analysis of film narrative in these terms explains the pleasure produced by the spectator's mobile identifications in films since although the codes of film narrative lay out positions for the spectator, they do not determine which will be taken up, and the theory shows that subject-positions are temporary, shifting, multiple and contradictory. The rest of this chapter discusses film signs and codes, and film genres, paying particular attention to the multiple meanings of signs in film and to the film spectator's multiple points of access to the meanings signified in films.

Film signs and codes

This section builds on ideas which have been discussed in relation to other media in previous chapters. In films, an image of an object, person or landscape will have a denotative dimension. But all images are culturally charged by the connotation procedures available to cinema, like camera position and angle, position of objects or people within the frame, use of lighting, colour process or tinting, and sound. The codes of cinema are particular ways of using signs, the photographic signs, dialogue signs, musical, sound effect and graphic signs which are the resources from which particular film sequences are constructed. Any film sequence can be analysed to discover the relationship between signs in the sequence, and the way that signs from different signifying systems (image, sound) are combined together by means of codes to generate meanings. The meanings of films are generated as much by the connotations constructed by the use of cinematic codes as by the cultural meanings of what the camera sees. Cinema uses codes and conventions of representation which are shared by both film-makers and audiences, so that the audience actively constructs meaning by reference to codes which structure mythic meanings in the social world in which film-going exists.

Christian Metz, whom we encountered above, sought to describe how the systems of signs and uses of codes work in film, and his work on film went through several stages. In his later work, Metz (1974) described cinema as a signifying practice, a way of making meanings in which different codes interact in films or film genres in particular ways. Some of these codes were seen as specific to cinema, like editing, lighting, monochrome or colour, sound and composition. Others derive from other media or from social life in general, like dialogue, characterisation, gesture and facial expression, and costume. For Metz, cinematic codes order elements which exist or could exist in all films, like lighting, while sub-codes are the sets of particular choices made within the larger code system, like the use of low-key lighting rather than high-key in certain films or genres. Clearly sub-codes are mutually exclusive, and form a paradigm from which selections are made, whereas films combine codes and sub-codes together in the unfolding of the text, and are arranged as syntagms of coded signs. Umberto Eco (1977) extended Metz's consideration of codes by arguing that, far from cinema using fragments of reality in order to build its representations, as Metz had once suggested, all images require the operation of cultural codes in order to signify. Eco believed that conventions embedded in society were the precondition for signification. These coding systems, Eco argued in his later work, are elaborated for the purpose of explaining and understanding a textual process, and cannot be seen as determining the meaning of any particular element in a text. Meaning is constructed on the basis of the spectator's continual adjustment and testing of codes rather than simply 'reading off' a meaning from the text, and this suggests the active decoding of signs and the shifting process of signification which earlier chapters of this book have stressed.

There are a wide range of connotations which the use of film's visual properties can introduce. The film stock used will have different properties, either black and white or colour, and with varying degrees of sensitivity to harsh light and deep shadow. The modern camera's depth of field of focus enables objects both close to the camera and far away from it to be in focus. Widescreen processes like Cinemascope and 70mm offer a very wide image in relation to its height. Black and white film might signify the past, and connote nostalgic recreation or harsh documentary realism (e.g. *Schindler's List*), while strong colour can connote surrealism and a fairytale quality (e.g. *Edward Scissorhands*). Wide-screen 70mm is used in the opening of *Star Wars*, for instance, to connote immense scale and spectacle. The positioning of the camera, since it determines the point of view offered to the spectator, is of immense importance in film's signification. Crane shots or overhead shots display the spectacular ability of cinema to take in an entire landscape, particularly when the camera is moving. The camera can be moved along parallel to its subject (tracking), towards or away from the subject (dolly in or out). When static, the camera can be swivelled to one side (panning), or up and down (tilting), or even rolled over. A zoom in or out can be used to concentrate on one character or aspect of the shot. These camera positions and movements can all be used to produce connotations. The power of one character over another can be connoted by a look down from an oppressor's point of view, or a look up from the point of view of the victim. The camera can explicitly take the position of a character to show their point of view, to connote an individual's perception of the action. Changes in the framing of the shot are used to narrow or open out the field of view, to connote a claustrophobic experience or a liberating one respectively. Close-up is a signifier of an emotional high point or a story crisis, and a pan across a landscape finishing on a building is an establishing shot which connotes that the subsequent action will take place there. As noted in the previous chapter, these connotations arise not by nature but from the cultural context in which films are made and watched.

Lighting is most often used to imitate natural light, and thus works as a signifier connoting realism. In most cases, a 'key light' illuminates the figures to be shot, 'fill lights' remove shadows caused by the key light and reveal detail. Both light sources are placed in front of the subject of the shot. Behind the subject, 'back light' enhances three-dimensionality by giving yet more light to the subject, but light which does not fall on the background. The aim of this lighting process ('high-key lighting') is to mimic conventional perceptions of how real environments look. But lighting can also become a foregrounded effect, when light, darkness or particular shadows signify as part of the narrative, and extend lighting's role in emphasising parts of the frame or parts of figures in it. Lighting techniques, whether 'realistic' and unnoticed, or highly atmospheric and 'unrealistic', provide connotations for all film shots.

Sound is also represented by means of signs. Speech or music consist of sounds captured by electronic recording methods and reproduced by mechanical loudspeakers. The film audience receives aural signifiers which are linked to mental concepts, signifieds like musical chords or speech sounds. These are the components of aural signs in film, like words or musical phrases. Modern cinema's impression of reality is heavily dependent on the representation of sounds occurring in synchronisation with the visual events which appear to cause them, known as 'diegetic' sound. Diegetic sound includes the sound of words matched to images of people speaking, or music which is matched to a record being played in the room we see on the screen. Conventions specific to cinema and TV include the use of non-diegetic music, so that the signs of orchestral music heard during a film sequence are read as coming not from the environment represented visually, but from outside the frame, from the implied narrator of the film. This use of 'extra-diegetic' music very often acts as an indexical sign connoting the emotional register of a sequence, and can point out or reveal the emotional state of a character (often in contrast to what the character claims to feel in the dialogue). Music directly communicates emotion which the audience can share individually in the communal space of the cinema, as well as sharing the feeling with the characters represented in the film. Film music constructs a community of feeling based on the responses of each member of the audience.

At the level of the shot sequence, a shot from behind the shoulder of one person, followed by a similar shot from behind the shoulder of another person, is the conventional means for representing a conversation and is called 'shot-reverse-shot'. In this case, there is a clear relationship between one shot and the succeeding one, but cinema narrative always relies on the viewer making links between shots, and links between sequences of shots. Because it is made up of discrete shots and sequences separated by cuts, the position of the viewer is the only place from which the ongoing meaningfulness of the film can be constructed. A film is a very diverse collection of visual, aural and graphic signs, which the viewer works to perceive as meaningful, using his or her knowledge of codes and conventions. Whereas spoken and written language are heavily regulated by the rules of grammar and syntax so that sense can be constructed, cinema has very few hard and fast rules about how its visual and aural signs can be combined to generate meanings. The audience has to do a lot of work in assembling film signs into meaningful units. While language involves similar work, done mostly unconsciously, cinema relies on the viewer's competence at decoding the film by reference to codes, conventions and expectations cued by the film's signs. The film viewer constructs relationships between shots, known as 'montage', and relationships within shots, known as '*mise en scène*'. It is this stitching-together or 'suturing' of one sign with another, one shot with another, which shifts the film spectator through the film and which is the basis for films to narrate their stories.

Film narrative

Contemporary feature films are exclusively narratives. Story is the set of sequenced actions in a film, book, TV programme, etc., and narrative is the term for the process by which the story is told. Story and narrative are common to all human cultures, and always encode a way of making sense of our experience through their structure and form. Much work has been done on narrative, because of its pervasiveness and importance for comprehending our reality. One of the common features which is seen in film narratives is the movement from an initially stable equilibrium, through disorder and conflict, to a new equilibrium. Narrative often takes this circular shape, but the equilibrium of the film's final resolution is not the same as at the beginning, since the situation and/or the hero is changed by the action in the story, and the stability of the resolution may be incomplete. In *Four Weddings and a Funeral*, Charles (Hugh Grant) and his friends are all unmarried, but by the end of the film he has found 'true love'. He and all his friends in the film are denoted in the final sequence in still images which use the conventional codes of wedding photographs, though for Charles and Carrie (Andie MacDowell) the appropriate resolution is precisely not marriage but a relationship which is not 'resolved' in that way. So while the film draws on our expectations about the narrative structure of romance and comedy, in which marriage and the 'happy ending' are appropriate and satisfying resolutions, *Four Weddings and a Funeral* does not end in an entirely conventional way.

One of the pleasures of narrative is that it puts in play and resolves contradictions and problems in our culture. *Four Weddings and a Funeral* does not represent marriage as a narrative resolution for its main characters, and separates the social meaning of marriage from the social meaning of commitment in a relationship. Indeed, the relationship connoted as most committed in the film is between two gay men, who cannot marry under British law. Like myth, narrative plays out and encodes real issues at a symbolic level. Turner (1993: 74) gives the example of the structure of western films involving conflicts between settlers and Native Americans ('Indians'). These mythic narratives are structured by oppositions between one group and the other, and their narrative progression deals with this conflict by means of various narrative functions until it is resolved. The oppositions are often binary and based on the exclusive difference between one set of signs and the other. For instance, here are some of the opposed   characteristics   commonly   found   in   westerns: Settlers/Indians, white/red, Christian/pagan, domestic/savage, helpless/dangerous, weak/strong, clothed/naked. Clearly, these oppositions are value-laden and have an ideological character. The mythic narrative of a western could be read as a way of encoding current mythic ideas around masculine virtue, the exploitation of nature, national identity and the importance of the family, for instance. Westerns, because of the way their narratives are structured, are communicating ideological messages. The recent western *Dances with Wolves* manipulates these value-laden oppositions inherited from previous westerns, and goes

10   Charles (Hugh Grant) and Carrie (Andie MacDowell)
in *Four Weddings and a Funeral*

some way to recasting their ideological value in terms which match the ideology of our own time.

The reuse of oppositions structuring film narratives so that the opposed terms change their meaning, shows that although the same coded oppositions might recur in films separated over a long period of time, nevertheless the value of the terms opposed to each other can change. There is no invariant value system which will always be represented or read in the same ways at every time or in every place. Rather, the value of signs in film depends on the social context pertaining at the time the film was made, at the time the film is seen, and by whom it is seen. The codes and conventions which enable the viewer to make sense of the film will change and evolve, and the viewer will decode the meanings of film narratives by invoking his or her experience of his or her own culture, including the film conventions circulating in that culture as well as codes of expression recognised from 'natural' social behaviour. For instance, the gestural codes and the bodily and facial expressions of actors in silent films belonged to conventions which connoted emotional realism when they were made and watched. These conventions derived from the stage-acting conventions of melodrama. To a contemporary audience, these gestural signs might now be decoded as artificial, excessive and unrealistic. Some of these coded signs might even be incomprehensible to a contemporary audience, except as signifiers of 'pastness', because the codes to which the gestures belong are no longer naturalised.

In Britain, audiences are familiar with conventions used in American cinema, and relatively unfamiliar with conventions used in, for instance, Indian cinema. British audiences recognise the insubordinate, physical and witty behaviour of Bruce Willis in *Die Hard* as a coded representation of masculinity and heroism. This behavioural code has crossed the Atlantic and become part of the audience's repertoire of conventional knowledge used for understanding films in the action–adventure genre. The English villain in *Die Hard* also exhibits an uptight viciousness which codes him as a terrorist, and is comprehensible to British audiences not as a critique of Britishness but as a convention of this type of film. In the British film *Peter's Friends*, Britishness is represented as a rather repressed and verbal way of behaving, which

is opposed to the flashiness and self-deception of the only American character in the film. In this comedy of manners, coded representations of nationality are different, though both films rely on
conventional codes which are familiar on both sides of the
Atlantic.

The meanings of films will obviously depend on how the visual
and aural signs of any particular film narrative are structured,
how the film marks out character roles by invoking conventional
behavioural codes, and the coded oppositions between connoted
ideas. An audience's reading of the film, however, is not only
generated by what is within the frame. Every film is viewed in a
particular social context, some of which is produced by the film's
industrial and commercial context, and some of which is not
controllable in the same way. For instance, *Bram Stoker's Drac-
ula* might be read as a film about Aids because of the prominence
of blood and contamination in the narrative and the existence of
the Aids virus in the culture. The advertising and promotion of
a film will enfold it in a network of various meanings deriving
from texts, conventions and objects which are already in circulation, and more or less controlled by the film's producers. The
mythic meanings of film stars, for instance, are not only constructed in films but in other media like newspapers, fan magazines, and TV appearances, so that the star exhibits
characteristics which may easily be different to those of the character he or she plays in the film. The star as sign affects the
meanings constructed by the viewer of the character in the film
text. The star might even be deliberately cast so that their star
persona alters the representation of the character in the script,
creating a double or ironic meaning (like the casting of Arnold
Schwarzenegger in *Kindergarten Cop*). Films exist in a complex
social context, where the mythic meanings circulating in a culture affect the ways they are decoded, and where the film text is
not the only source of meanings.

Cinema has developed some narrative conventions which are
specific to it. For example, in comedy films a bang on the head
can cause loss of memory, and another bang can restore it. Ellip-
sis, the omission of parts of the story, is an accepted code which
allows film narratives to cut from a character getting into a car
to the same character getting out in another location without

needing to show the journey. There are film conventions which are highly ideological in character, and have persisted in film as well as in other media. For a long time, conventional ways of shooting men and women in films have been different. Women's bodies, and parts of their bodies, are objects of voyeuristic interest for the camera. Women can be lit to emphasise pose and facial shape, remaining static while the camera displays their attractiveness, or they can be placed in a narrative situation which enables them to display themselves (e.g. sunbathing or taking a shower). It has been rare to see men represented in the same way (though perhaps scenes depicting fights enable men to be displayed). Conventions for representing women, as discussed in chapter two and earlier in this chapter, display the woman as an object offered for possession by a male gaze, for the desire of both men and women and for narcissistic identification. But now as our contemporary culture turns bodies of both genders more and more into commodities and sites for consumption, film images of men have begun to deploy similar conventions.

Film genre

Genre analysis is a method of study which aims to classify types or groups of films, showing that the film industry and the film audience respond to films by recognising the codes and conventions which enable an individual film to be comprehended. Recent film comedies have made much use of conventions taken to an extreme for comic purposes. The *Naked Gun* sequence of films exposes and plays with police–thriller conventions, the multiple endings of *Wayne's World* parody the convention that the story will end with a resolution (and virtually marriage, in the manner of earlier film comedies). But it is not only in comedy that conventions are exposed. In *Unforgiven*, the conventionally marginal women characters of westerns are the motor of the story, and several recent westerns focus on a woman as their main character in an action–adventure plot. In *Thelma and Louise*, women are the central characters of the conventionally male genre of the road movie. These are examples of films which work against the known conventions of different film genres. The signs which cue the recognition of a particular film as belonging

to a certain genre are many and varied. The visual style of the
film's title graphics, the accompanying music, the stars of the
film, its setting, story structure, narrative style including its lighting patterns, colour system, types of discourse in the dialogue,
emphasised camera shots, can all offer the audience a set of
expectations which inform the coding systems brought to the
film by the audience, and into which the film company can slot
the film in its marketing and promotional discourses. As well as
placing a film in a certain genre, it is even possible to position
the film by raising generic expectations which will not be met, so
that the film reacts against generic expectations by raising them
in the first place (often the case in comedy films which parody
the generic expectations of 'serious' films, in the way that *Hot
Shots* parodies *Top Gun* and other films).

It is clear that identifying a film's genre relies on identifying
particular signs within a film, the relationship between signs,
and their membership of one or more codes. But the analysis of
a particular film will involve comparing and contrasting the signification in a film with that of other films and with texts in other
media. This is part of the study of intertextuality, which we have
already encountered in previous chapters. No film will be seen by
a spectator outside of a context which includes other films they
have seen, films they have seen advertised, or heard about from
other people. The concept of genre reminds us that films are not
self-contained structures of signs, but texts which exist within a
broader social context. Every film will exist in relation to two
contradictory impulses, repetition and difference. To ensure comprehensibility, a film will repeat the signifying practices of other
films, their conventional signs and established codes, and conventional narrative structures of disequilibrium and resolution.
Part of the pleasure of seeing a new film is the viewer's ability to
recognise and predict meanings appropriately. But every film will
also need to be different, to find new ways of using existing signs
and codes in order to offer the pleasure of the new. Genre connects individual film texts to the industrial commercial context of
cinema, and to the study of film audiences. For the industry,
genres allow films to be marketed in ways which inform potential audiences about the pleasures offered by the film, since
posters, advertising, etc. contain coded signs which cue genre

expectations. If a previous film has been commercially successful, further films in the same genre including sequels can be expected to repeat the same success by addressing a similar market. Within the narrative of a particular film, signs and codes will relate the film to existing generic expectations to ensure comprehensibility. The film audience will possess competencies to decode and enjoy films in certain genres, and are likely to watch new films in genres which they are familiar with.

The study of genre relates each film to other films, but this study of intertextuality can also be extended to relating films to other media texts. In contemporary culture there is a blurring of the boundaries between cinema and other media. There are a range of contemporary films which are based on comic-book characters for instance, including the three *Batman* films, *Dick Tracy*, *Judge Dredd*, and *Tank Girl*. These films are able to draw an audience already at least minimally familiar with their scenarios, and provide opportunities for spectacular visual effects. But in this kind of action–adventure film there is an evident difference from the pleasures of 'classical Hollywood cinema' films for the spectator. As in *Speed*, *True Lies* and the *Die Hard* series for example, identification with a heroic ego ideal, narrative resolution and conventions of realism seem less important than self-conscious spectacular effects. There are many examples of contemporary action–adventure films which abandon classical narrative structure in favour of a series of plot climaxes which occur in quick succession, and which organise their stories in terms of a progression from one 'level' of story to another. This is sometimes a direct result of films' relation to computer games: some films are based on games, others are subsequently marketed as games, for example *Super Mario Brothers*, *Streetfighter*, *The Terminator* and *Mortal Kombat*. For the younger cinema audience accustomed to enjoying graphic novels and computer games, cinema makes links between film spectatorship's pleasures and the pleasures familiar in these other media.

The consequences for cinema spectatorship include the diminished significance of narrative resolution in favour of episodic structure and moments of narrative-arresting spectacle and thrill, the denotation of technology in films and the display of the technologies used in the cinema medium, and the spectator's identifications in fantasy with multiple characters or with the film's spectacular scenario. This form of spectator competence both responds to and promotes the competencies required by computer games. The CD-Rom game version of *Johnny Mnemonic* allows the user to take on the role of either the hero or Jones, a cyberdolphin programmed by the US Navy. Rather than following a single narrative sequence, clicking a mouse or operating a keyboard controls character movements (kick, punch, block, etc.) which produce alternate plot events in response to the user's decisions. The film therefore becomes a mythic intertextual world supported by the related but different fictional narrative of the game, and vice versa. Computer games have always reused the signs, narratives and mythic worlds of other media texts. There are computer games based on *Star Trek*, for instance, which invoke the mythic world of the TV series although the TV series was made thirty years ago, before computer games were invented. Now however, some films (and some TV programmes) both share the forms of subject-positioning in computer games and are marketed together with games. In addition to an increased intensity of intermedia crossover, entertainment experiences are becoming further interrelated in their subject-positionings and modes of pleasure.

Genre study arose in film studies as a response to the study of *auteurs*, directors whose work seemed to possess the marks of individual creativity which were discriminated in the academic study of literature by 'great' authors. While some directors of commercial Hollywood feature films were endowed with the distinction of being *auteurs*, the prevailing discourse of *auteur* criticism left out of account a great mass of popular cinema. The study of genres shows that all films exist within a context, rather than being the inspired and unique expression of one person's creative imagination. Genre study also allows us to consider a much wider field of films for study in addition to those which film critics have labelled as 'great', and is particularly useful in discussing popular cinema since many of its products are genre films (horror, westerns, thrillers, epics, science fiction, etc.). The intertextuality of contemporary media culture, and the polysemy of many media texts, means that elements of several genres may be encoded in a single film. The recent *Waterworld*, for instance, includes the swinging on ropes and the villain's eyepatch of pirate films, the search for lost treasure of swashbuckler films like the *Indiana Jones* series, the apocalyptic scenario of ecological films like the *Mad Max* series, and many elements from the codes of other genres including romances and medieval films, all wrapped up in action–adventure. Part of the pleasure in watching a film like this is the spectator's ability to recognise these generic codes and to enjoy their reuse and manipulation, shifting in fantasy between the subject-positions which each code invites him or her to take up.

Cinema audiences

For many years the academic study of cinema has been based on the assumption that films can be studied as relatively self-contained texts. Although it has been recognised that films are obviously set in a social context of making and viewing, until very recently there has been little substantial work on how real viewers understand and enjoy films. Semiotic theories of meaning can allow the critic to assume that there are 'correct' readings of the signs in film, and the psychoanalytic theories of the cinema experience and film spectatorship deal only with the general and fundamental structures in the human psyche which individual films mobilise. The dominance of these two theoretical approaches in film study has yielded a very rich (and very complicated) critical discourse, of which brief glimpses have been given in this chapter. As we have seen earlier in this book, the discourse of semiotic analysis and related approaches to the media has been challenged by more empirical studies of media reception, variously known as audience studies or ethnography. This kind of research is not 'more correct' than semiotic research, since it adopts a different discourse, and asks a different set of questions. But even in a book on semiotic approaches to the study of the media, it is important to see how the questions of audience and reception might contextualise, redirect or critique semiotic analysis. In academic film studies in the 1980s and 1990s, there has been much discussion of the place of audience research, but very few studies of contemporary film audiences have yet been published.

Many of the studies of film viewers have been carried out from a feminist perspective. This is because of the problem in the psychoanalytic theory of spectatorship discussed above, that it has argued that women film-goers have to identify with the masculine control exercised by film narrative over women characters, or with the submissive and narcissistic women characters themselves. Either women film-goers take up a masculine subject-position, or they identify with a devalued version of feminine identity. Mulvey and other theorists have moved away from the psychoanalytic account of gendered spectators and have recently looked for traces of resistance to the masculine domination of film subjectivities (de Lauretis 1984, Modleski 1988, Mulvey 1989), for active female audience responses to films (Pribam 1988, Hansen 1991), and at the place of film viewing in the lives of real women (Pribam 1988). The majority of this work discusses viewers' responses to Hollywood films in the 'golden age' of cinema, roughly 1930–55, since it is films from this period that were used to illustrate the psychoanalytic theories of the spectator. Therefore the specifics of few of these studies directly relate to the contemporary films referred to in this chapter.

Nevertheless, the results of this research point to some similarities between the ways in which films are read by viewers and the ways in which television and other media are experienced and used, as outlined in earlier chapters of this book. The key issues here include the recognition that film viewing is set in a particular historical, geographical and cultural moment for individual viewers. Ethnic or racial background has significant impacts on the relationship between viewer, film, intertextual environment and the social meaning of enjoying films or cinemagoing. Watching films and going to the cinema have social uses in the lives of film viewers, and enable them to gain social status, negotiate membership of social groups or subcultures, relate to family members and conceive of their own identity in particular ways. However, as Judith Mayne (1993) has argued, the tendency of ethnographic research on individual film viewers or small groups of viewers is to overvalue the apparently subversive and critical ways in which viewers watch and enjoy films. Rather than ending up with a spectator passively positioned by the cinematic apparatus and by film narrative, research on real viewers seems sometimes to be 'constituting a viewer who is always resisting, always struggling, always seemingly just on the verge of becoming the embodiment of the researcher's own political ideal' (Mayne 1993: 61). Thus the apparently passive spectator of 'classical' film theory can simply be exchanged for an active one, and in each theoretical discourse the film viewer is of interest only as a justification of the analyst's argument.

Ethnography has emerged as a reaction against semiotics's and psychoanalytic theory's analysis of the spectator as a category or construct rather than a real person. The theory of the spectator was devised in part as a way of critiquing the social and ideological role of cinema in perpetuating mythic social meanings and the formation of individual subjects by dominant ideologies. This theoretical and political discourse about spectators assumes that the responses of real film viewers always exceed or differ from the response of the spectator constructed by films and the cinematic apparatus, because the social and psychic history of individuals is always particular and in some respects unique. Ethnographic studies of audiences focus on these particular and sometimes unique aspects of individuals, and the discourse of audience study thus links film viewers to society and ideology in useful ways. But as Mayne's critical remarks above indicate, every analytical discourse is constrained by the discursive codes which it uses, and which themselves encode the mythic significance of what they analyse. It remains to be seen in film studies whether the active viewer negotiating the meanings of the films he or she sees is more than a signifier of the researcher's desire for a new radical discourse.

Sources and further reading

Good introductions to film theory including semiotics, the theory of ideology and psychoanalytic criticism are Turner (1993), the more complex Lapsley and Westlake (1988) and Andrew (1984). Monaco (1981) also deals with film history, technology, and many other topics in a single volume. Stam *et al.* (1992) is entirely devoted to film semiotics and related theoretical issues like narrative and spectatorship, and covers a very wide range of terms and ideas. The collections edited by Easthope (1993) and Mast and Cohen (1985) contain some of the formative essays (by Mulvey and Cowie for instance) which are discussed in this chapter, and Easthope's collection also has short essays at the beginning that introduce key theoretical currents. The collection of essays edited by Collins *et al.* (1993) explores theoretical approaches in relation to detailed analyses of recent films, and many of the essays make use of semiotics to some degree. Mayne (1993) debates the issues around studies of film audiences, while also discussing the psychoanalytic and semiotic traditions in film criticism. Bacon-Smith and Yarborough's essay (1991) is an interesting use of ethnographic methods to discuss viewers' reactions to the *Batman* film and the other texts (like comics) which relate to the film, and can be compared to other essays in the same volume which adopt different approaches to the *Batman* phenomenon, including the discourses of semiotic and ideological analysis.

Suggestions for further work

1   Analyse the posters advertising three films you have not seen which are playing at your local cinema. How does the poster inform you about each film's genre, stars, and attractions? If you later see the film, how much correspondence is there between the narrative image on the poster and your experience of the film's attractions and pleasures?

2   Compare the reviewing discourses used about the same film in different media (for example local and national newspapers, film magazines like *Empire*, TV film review programmes). What assumptions about the audience, the film medium, stars, directors, and genres are being made? Why is this?

3   If you have played a computer game based on a film, which aspects of the film's narrative codes and *mise en scène* have been included in the game? What characteristics of this interactive medium determine the choices which have been made?

4   Analyse one sequence from a film, discussing technical codes, narrative codes, signs of genre, spectator positioning and any other issues which seem useful. What are the limitations of this kind of close analysis?

5   Gather as many examples of media coverage of a current film star as you can. How coherent and consistent are the various codings of this star's social meanings? How closely do they relate to the character roles recently played by the star?

6   Compare the representations of women or of Native Americans

in some recent westerns and some westerns of the 1950s. How much change in ideological assumptions do you find?

7 Analyse a film which intertextually borrows conventions from other film genres (for example *Aliens*, *Waterworld* or *Blade Runner*). How do these conventions affect the ways in which the film may be decoded?

8

Conclusion

Semiotics has changed since it was inaugurated at the beginning of this century. This final section briefly considers some of these shifts and outlines how the semiotic analysis of the media might take account of some of the new media technologies and experiences which are currently appearing in Western culture. From a semiotic point of view, all of social life is a continual encounter with assemblages of signs, from the public experiences of advertising posters, shop windows and diversely-dressed strangers in the street, to the more private experiences of watching TV, choosing what kind of décor to use in the home, or playing a computer game. As we become increasingly accustomed to living in a culture infused with media, semiotics is a particularly effective means of taking stock of this situation. One version of semiotics, structuralism, would even claim that what we call 'I', our very sense of identity, is itself a function of the traffic in signs which surrounds and permeates us. The notion that social life is saturated by media messages, and experiences mediated by media texts, is part of the labelling of the present epoch as 'postmodern' (see chapter six). Rather than simply celebrating a postmodern or virtual experience of reality, or simply condemning the proclamation that reality has evaporated into shifting clouds of signs, semiotics asks how our experience of the media and of our social existence makes sense.

The question of how individuals make sense of their involvements with the media has recently been addressed by a different discourse to that of semiotics: the discourse of audience research which has been discussed in several chapters of this book. In the contemporary diversification of audiences brought about by the proliferation of media and of new ways of interacting with them, there is a temptation be overoptimistic about the extent to which individuals make meanings on their own terms, and for their own individual purposes. It is tempting to assume that individual users of the media, simply because they are all different, and belong to different subcultural groups in society, can subvert the meanings of media texts in ways that some audience researchers and other academic critics would like to value as radical or even revolutionary. This optimistic view is in one sense relevant and important because it challenges the assumptions of structuralist semiotic research; that fixed meanings are structured into texts and signs by universally known codes and a fixed repertoire of ways of positioning the audience. But it does not challenge the more recent semiotic approach (progressively adopted in this book) which assumes that signs and texts have several meanings at once (polysemy), a kind of excess or proliferation of meanings which enables them to be used by audiences in different ways (multiaccentuality). Indeed, research on the uses and role of the media in the lives of individual subjects shows that what media texts and the makers of media products do is to systematically channel this excess of meaning as much as they can, although this enterprise can never entirely succeed.

The institutions of the media and the media products they produce try to impose order on meaning, against the ever-present threat posed to meaning by polysemy and by multi-accentual decoding practices on the part of actual audiences. Just as audiences are only relatively free to produce new and different meanings, so media texts and their producers are only relatively successful at delimiting the decodings of signs which audiences can produce. In this situation, semiotics is still an essential analytical perspective for studying the media. Semiotic analysis shows how the meanings of signs in texts are at once constrained by codes and ideological structures, but also how signs can be read in different ways because they always depend for their meaning on their relationship to the other signs in the same text and on their relationship with the signs in other texts (intertextuality). To sum up this perspective, meanings are perpetually being made but are at the same time perpetually being fractured from within and scattered by their interactions with other meanings. Every text is only meaningful when an individual subject decodes it himself or herself, and every text presupposes a reader (or viewer) for whom its signs will make sense. Since signs and texts have multiple, polysemic meanings, and can be decoded multiaccentually by readers taking up different subject-positions, the individual subject who decodes a media text must be perpetually constructed and reconstructed in different ways in the process of making sense of signs. Just as the meanings of media texts are continually being fixed and continually shifting again, so too the identity of the individual subject must be fixed and shifted.

Thinking about meaning and subjective identity in this way, as always existing in a tension between order and dispersion, position and fluidity, is particularly useful in relation to the new computer-based media. As far as the individual subject is concerned, communicating with others on the Internet allows subjective identity to be both constructed in an ordered form, but for the identity thus constructed to be an imaginary and temporary persona. Computer network technologies link individual subjects together by remote means, but so remotely that their communication with each other loses the concrete and material character of previous ways of interacting. Logged on to the Internet for some kinds of communication, you can adopt a persona and become another kind of subject when communicating by these electronic means, perhaps deciding to adopt a different gender identity, for instance. The individual subject becomes a collection of signifiers, which whoever reads the message has to reconstitute into the mythic person which the message's codes and signs appear to reflect. The subject becomes a sign separated from its referent (the person formed by the specific cultural, historical and political contexts in which they live), and becomes a subject in a virtual global community formed by the communications network. Perhaps the distinction that structuralist critics like Barthes made, between sign and referent, text and author, subjective identity and physical body, has become virtually the case.

Just as the subject becomes a sign separated from his or her physical body and cultural reality, the word processors and computer terminals used for communicating make texts virtual too, divorced from the concreteness of paper, film, and their connection with particular local contexts. Texts are digitised and can move around the electronic networks of the world, to be reconstituted and used in all kinds of ways by whoever can access them. So the meanings of individual subjects and of texts in these new media are controlled by the signifying activities of their producers and the patterns of access to information associated with the technological apparatus. But their meanings are dispersed and released from control by the multiple ways in which they can be decoded by receivers in different cultures and local contexts.

Internet communications allow the sender to represent him or herself by signs, as well as being a receiver and decoder of signs. This kind of interactivity is a stage further than the interactivity of games and information programmes in the computer medium. There are already computer games on CD-Rom disk which allow the user to make decisions about the narrative progression and outcome of a game. This is a form of interactivity which is limited only by the number of decision points included in the game, the number of alternative combinations of narrative segments which can be accommodated on the disk, and the investment in the programme by the makers of the game. Similarly, there are already cable TV systems which allow the home viewer to make decisions about which film he or she wishes to view from among a huge selection all available at the same time, and there are experimental TV services in which alternate endings of programmes or alternate narrative sequences in films can be selected by remote control.

From the perspective of the user, one of the advantages of these new ways of interacting with screen-based media is that positionings encoded in the semiotic structure of texts are multiple and can be exchanged one for another. The 'traditional' media texts like TV programmes or magazines can be decoded in different ways by audiences, but the images, linguistic signs and sounds which the reader or viewer decodes are not subject to change in themselves. You cannot change what is on the page or on the screen. New interactive media offer their users the chance to change the text, and thus to create new texts for themselves. However, the contemporary value given to viewer choice and interactivity in computer games or Internet communications rests on naturalised assumptions about their users. Each of these

technologies are needless unless the user grants primary involvement and attention to them, and to the texts which the new
delivery technologies bring into the viewer's private domestic
space. It is necessary to be interested, and to care about the outcomes and narrative progression of a film or a game, and to keep
making choices in order to exploit and enjoy interactivity. New
technologies are predicated on the assumption of an active
viewer, and a social subject who wants to be involved with the
latest entertainment products. The user of interactive technologies may not be a passive consumer of a fixed repertoire of meanings, but he or she is nevertheless required to work hard at being
a kind of viewer constructed in and for the entertainment products he or she has bought into.

The same problem already exists in the proliferation of TV
channels and the common use of videorecorders. While 'channel
surfing' and 'zapping' are not insignificant, one of the attractions
of contemporary entertainment media is the luxury of passivity
and consumption, rather than the 'work' involved in actively
constructing a text for oneself made up of fragments of other
texts, either from the available TV programmes and ads at the
same point in time, or by editing videotape into a personal
'scratch' video. When videorecorders were invented, it was
thought that people would make tapes of bits of their favourite
programmes, becoming in a sense producers rather than consumers. When video cameras were invented, it was assumed that
people would make their own movies, rather than filming family
holidays or playing with their new piece of technology. While the
creativity of the user in making new semiotic assemblies of texts
for themselves has occurred to a limited extent, the patterns of
technology use seem to be similar to existing ones, rather than
the technology creating new forms of independent media producer (rather than consumer) and new forms of control over
texts and meanings.

Similarly the Internet at the moment is explored and enthused
about by those people (overwhelmingly men) who have used it,
but like multichannel television, curiosity about what is available
and how it works is not the same as the development of the new
forms of social interaction and new forms of subjectivity which
some enthusiasts proclaim. One of the chief effects of these tech-

nologies comes from their base in the home. Using the new entertainment and communications media depends on having the
expensive technology in your own domestic space, and the profits of technology producers depend on the widespread sales of the
equipment. As with previous media technologies like television,
the economic drive of the interactive media business is towards
the increasing 'privatisation' of experience. The user is an end
point in a huge network, and in this sense is like the TV viewer
who is an individual receiver of TV broadcasts which are also
being watched by a multitude of other individuals all separated
from each other. But on the other hand, many of the network
services on the Internet substitute for the social activities which
go on outside the home. The social world is itself simulated by
the interactive conversations of e-mail and the pages of the
World Wide Web, sometimes literally in the case of virtual shopping malls, virtual town halls or virtual cinemas. Interacting
with people and texts remotely like this offers the user freedom
to enjoy different and fluid identities, but social experiences and
subjective identities which are all mediated by systems of signs
may have disadvantageous alienating effects.

In commercial terms, it is extremely difficult for providers of
networked information on the Internet to find out who is using
it and how it is being used, though plans are being made to
gather this data by providing interactive sites in which users log
on with their names or other contact information. Indeed for
advertising, the Internet has been hailed as a new and better way
to target consumers in their homes with information which can
be tailored especially for them. Advertisers, broadcasters and
film-makers are concerned about how to target particular groups
of people accurately, so car manufacturers and film companies,
for instance, set up home pages advertising their products. As in
the case of traditional kinds of advertisement where jokes, puns
and puzzles are used to create involvement and activity for the
viewer, these Internet ads offer a game, a quiz, or some other
kind of interactivity, in order to involve the viewer with the
advertised product and its mythic brand identity. Semiotic studies of the new computer-based media will need to develop ways
of understanding these media which may have much in common
with the semiotic analysis of ads, as well as using methods devel-

oped for the study of fictional narratives in screen-based media like television.

Perhaps the key contribution of semiotics to our understanding of social life comes from its reversal of common-sense assumptions. Rather than thinking of language as an instrument for expressing thought, Saussure's linguistics enabled us to see that thought is constituted by language. Barthes and other structuralist semioticians insisted that rather than human culture being built on an essential human nature, it is our culture which gives us our assumptions about what human nature is. What had been thought of as the foundation of things was understood as a superstructure, and what had been thought of as a superstructure became a foundation, with all of the shaking-up of established ideas which this reversal implies. As semiotics evolved as a discipline, post-structuralist semiotic thinkers argued that this world-shaking discourse about culture and society could not be the universal science of everything which it seemed to be, because semiotics is itself a discourse rather than a value-free and scientifically valid truth of things. So the great promise of semiotics became impossible to achieve. Instead of moving ever further towards a few underlying truths, semiotics has moved outwards to become one of many components in the methodologies of many intellectual disciplines, including media studies but also psychoanalysis, anthropology, art history and architecture, for instance.

At this point, there is no synthesis between the different discourses of media studies. In some respects, this is an advantage rather than a disadvantage, because it compels the analyst of the media to recognise the stakes and limitations of the various discursive frameworks in which he or she works. That is the most prominent feeling for me at the end of writing this book. The book is designed to be used in a teaching and learning situation, which is itself a particular context in which some discourses are naturalised as legitimate while others are not. Perhaps it might seem that a book to be used in an educational context should have a single and consistent discourse, and appear to argue for a seamless methodology which would enable its reader to go out and do his or her work using this methodology as a tool to achieve results more efficiently and effectively. However, I do not

think that books should work this way. This book does not stick
to one consistent discourse, since while concentrating on semiotics it shows both that semiotics is not a single and consistent
body of ideas, and that it cannot always account adequately for
some of the features of media culture which are evidently important. In this respect, I hope that this book fulfils the role of an
introduction relatively well by demonstrating that there is much
more to be said and discovered beyond what is contained in these
pages.

Sources and further reading

Poster (1994) is an interesting essay on new computer-based communications media, which also discusses how semiotic theories have
evolved and might account for a postmodern media culture. Poster
has also written a book (1990) on related issues. In the same volume
as Poster's essay, Collins (1994) discusses the media in a postmodern context, with interesting sections on contemporary cinema. He
too has written a full-length study of popular media culture of today
(1989).

Select bibliography

Allen, R. (ed.) (1992), *Channels of Discourse, Reassembled: Television and Contemporary Criticism*, London, Routledge.

Allen, R. (1992), 'Audience-oriented criticism and television', in *Channels of Discourse, Reassembled: Television and Contemporary Criticism*, London, Routledge, 101–37.

Althusser, L. (1971), 'Ideology and ideological state apparatuses: notes towards an investigation', in *Lenin and Philosophy*, London, New Left Books, 121–73.

Alvarado, M. and J. Thompson (eds) (1990), *The Media Reader*, London, BFI.

Andrew, D. (1984), *Concepts in Film Theory*, Oxford, Oxford University Press.

Ang, I. (1989), *Watching Dallas: Soap Opera and the Melodramatic Imagination*, trans. D. Couling, revised edition, London, Routledge.

Ang, I. (1991), *Desperately Seeking the Audience*, London, Routledge.

Bacon-Smith, C., and T. Yarborough (1991), 'Batman: the ethnography', in R. Pearson and W. Uricchio (eds), *The Many Lives of the Batman: Critical Approaches to a Superhero and his Media*, London, Routledge/BFI.

Ballaster, R., M. Beetham, E. Frazer, and S. Hebron (1991), *Women's Worlds: Ideology, Femininity and the Women's Magazine*, London, Macmillan.

Barthes, R. (1973), *Mythologies*, trans. A. Lavers, London, Granada.

Barthes, R. (1977), 'The photographic message', in *Image Music Text*, trans. S. Heath, London, Fontana, 15–31.

Barthes, R. (1977), 'Rhetoric of the image', in *Image Music Text*, trans. S. Heath, London, Fontana, 32–51.

Baudrillard, J. (1983), *Simulations*, New York, Semiotext(e).

Branston, G. and R. Stafford (1996), *The Media Student's Book*, London, Routledge.

Blonsky, M. (ed.) (1985), *On Signs: A Semiotics Reader*, Oxford, Blackwell.

Butler, J. (1990), *Gender Trouble: Feminism and the Subversion of Identity*, London, Routledge.

Cho, M., and C. Cho (1990), 'Women watching together: an ethnographic study of Korean soap opera fans in the U.S.', *Cultural Studies*, 4:1, 30–44.

Cohen, S. and J. Young (eds) (1973), *The Manufacture of News: Social Problems, Deviance and the Mass Media*, London, Constable.

Collins, J. (1989), *Uncommon Cultures: Popular Culture and Post-Modernism*, London, Routledge.

Collins, J. (1992), 'Postmodernism and television', in R. Allen (ed.), *Channels of Discourse, Reassembled: Television and Contemporary Criticism*, London, Routledge, 327–53.

Collins, J. (1994), 'By whose authority? Accounting for taste in contemporary popular culture', in D. Crowley and D. Mitchell (eds), *Communication Theory Today*, Cambridge, Polity, 214–31.

Collins, J., H. Radner, and A. Preacher Collins (eds) (1993), *Film Theory Goes to the Movies*, London, Routledge.

Cook, G. (1992), *The Discourse of Advertising*, London, Routledge.

Corner, J. (1995), *Television Form and Public Address*, London, Edward Arnold.

Cowie, E. (1984), 'Fantasia', *m/f*, 9, 71–105.

Culler, J. (1976), *Saussure*, London, Fontana.

Culler, J. (1983), *Barthes*, London, Fontana.

Dahlgren, P. (1985), 'The modes of reception: for a hermeneutics of TV news', in P. Drummond and R. Patterson (eds) *Television in Transition* London, BFI, 235–49.

Dowmunt, T. (ed.) (1993), *Channels of Resistance: Global Television and Local Empowerment*, London, BFI/Channel 4.

Drummond, P., and R. Patterson (eds) (1988), *Television and its Audience: International Research Perspectives*, London, BFI.

Dyer, G. (1982), *Advertising as Communication*, London, Methuen.

Eagleton, T. (1983), *Literary Theory: An Introduction*, Oxford, Blackwell.

Easthope, A. (ed.) (1993), *Contemporary Film Theory*, Harlow, Longman.

Eco, U. (1977), *A Theory of Semiotics*, London, Macmillan.

Eco, U. (1990), 'Interpreting serials', in *The Limits of Interpretation*, Bloomington, Indiana University Press, 83–100.

Fairclough, N. (1989), *Language and Power*, London, Longman.

Ferguson, M. (1983), *Forever Feminine: Women's Magazines and the Cult of Femininity*, London, Heinemann.

Fiske, J. (1982), *Introduction to Communication Studies*, London, Methuen.

Fiske, J., and J. Hartley (1978), *Reading Television*, London, Methuen.

Fiske, J. (1987), *Television Culture*, London, Routledge.

Fiske, J. (1992), 'British cultural studies and television', in R. Allen (ed.) *Channels of Discourse, Reassembled: Television and Contemporary*

Criticism, London, Routledge, 284–326.

Fowler, R. (1991), *Language in the News: Discourse and Ideology in the Press*, London, Routledge.

Galtung, J., and M. Ruge (1973), 'Structuring and selecting news', in S. Cohen and J. Young (eds) *The Manufacture of News: Social Problems, Deviance and the Mass Media*, London, Constable, 62–72.

Glasgow Media Group (1976), *Bad News*, London, Routledge & Kegan Paul.

Glasgow Media Group (1980), *More Bad News*, London, Routledge & Kegan Paul.

Glasgow Media Group (1986), *War and Peace News*, Milton Keynes, Open University Press.

Goffman, E. (1979), *Gender Advertisements*, London, Methuen.

Goldman, R. (1992), *Reading Ads Socially*, London, Routledge.

Gray, A. (1992), *Video Playtime: The Gendering of a Leisure Technology*, London, Routledge.

Gurevitch, M. (1991), 'The globalization of electronic journalism', in J. Curran and M. Gurevitch (eds) *Mass Media and Society*, London, Edward Arnold, 178–93.

Hall, S., C. Critcher, T. Jefferson, J. Clarke and B. Roberts (1978), *Policing the Crisis: Mugging, the State, the Law and Order*, London, Macmillan.

Hall, S., D. Hobson, A. Lowe and P. Willis (1980), *Culture, Media, Language*, London, Hutchinson.

Hansen, M. (1991), *Babel and Babylon: Spectatorship in American Silent Film*, Harvard, Harvard University Press.

Harrison, M. (1985), *TV News: Whose Bias? A Casebook Analysis of Strikes, Television and Media Studies*, Hermitage, Policy Journals.

Hartley, J. (1982), *Understanding News*, London, Methuen.

Hawkes, T. (1983), *Structuralism and Semiotics*, London, Methuen.

Hebdige, D. (1988), *Hiding in the Light: On Images and Things*, London, Routledge.

Hermes, J. (1995), *Reading Women's Magazines*, Cambridge, Polity.

Hutcheon, L. (1987), 'The politics of postmodernism, parody, and history', *Cultural Critique*, 5, 179–207.

Jacobson, R. (1995), *Television Research: A Directory of Conceptual Categories, Topic Suggestions and Selected Sources*, Jefferson, McFarland.

Katz, E., and T. Liebes (1984), 'Once upon a time in Dallas', *Intermedia* 12:3, 28–32.

Katz, E., and T. Liebes (1985), 'Mutual aid in the decoding of *Dallas*: preliminary notes from a cross-cultural study', in P. Drummond and R. Patterson (eds) *Television in Transition*, London, BFI, 187–98.

Katz, E., and T. Liebes, 'On the critical ability of television viewers', paper presented at the seminar 'Rethinking the Audience', University of Tubingen, February 1987.

Kozloff, S. (1992), 'Narrative theory and television', in R. Allen (ed.), *Channels of Discourse, Reassembled: Television and Contemporary Criticism*, London, Routledge, 67–100.

Lacan, J. (1977), 'The mirror stage', in *Écrits: A Selection*, trans. A. Sheridan, London, Tavistock, 1–7.

Lapsley, R., and M. Westlake (1988), *Film Theory: An Introduction*, Manchester, Manchester University Press.

de Lauretis, T. (1984), *Alice Doesn't: Feminism, Semiotics, Cinema*, London, Macmillan.

Lavers, A. (1982), *Roland Barthes, Structuralism and After*, London, Methuen.

Leal, O. (1990), 'Popular taste and erudite repertoire: the place and space of television in Brazil', *Cultural Studies*, 4:1, 19–29.

Lewis, J. (1985), 'Decoding television news', in P. Drummond and R. Paterson (eds) *Television in Transition*, London, BFI, 205–34.

Lewis, J. (1991), *The Ideological Octopus: An Exploration of Television and its Audience*, London, Routledge.

Lindof, T. (ed.) (1987), *Natural Audiences: Qualitative Research of Media Uses and Effects*, Norwood, Ablex.

Lorimer, R., with P. Scannell (1994), *Mass Communications: A Comparative Introduction*, Manchester, Manchester University Press.

Lull, J. (ed.) (1988), *World Families Watch Television*, London, Sage.

Macdonald, M. (1995), *Representing Women: Myths of Femininity in the Popular Media*, London, Edward Arnold.

Mast, G., and M. Cohen (eds) (1985), *Film Theory and Criticism*, Oxford, Oxford University Press.

Masterman, L. (1984), *Television Mythologies: Stars, Shows and Signs*, London, Comedia.

Mayne, J. (1993), *Cinema and Spectatorship*, London, Routledge.

McCracken, E. (1993), *Decoding Women's Magazines: From Mademoiselle to Ms.*, London, Macmillan.

McNair, B. (1994), *News and Journalism in the UK: A Textbook*, London, Routledge.

Metz, C. (1974), *Language and Cinema*, trans. D. Umiker-Sebeok, The Hague, Mouton.

Metz, C. (1975), 'The imaginary signifier', *Screen*, 16:2, 14–76.

Mitchell, J. and J. Rose (eds) (1982), *Feminine Sexuality: Jacques Lacan and the École Freudienne*, trans. J. Rose, London, Macmillan.

Modleski, T. (1988), *The Women Who Knew Too Much: Hitchcock and Feminist Film Theory*, London, Methuen.

Moi, T. (1985), *Sexual/Textual Politics: Feminist Literary Theory*, London, Routledge.

Monaco, J. (1981), *How to Read a Film*, Oxford, Oxford University Press.

Morley, D. (1992), *Television, Audiences and Cultural Studies*, London, Routledge.

Mulvey, L. (1975), 'Visual pleasure and narrative cinema', *Screen*, 16:3, 6–18.

Mulvey, L. (1989), *Visual and Other Pleasures*, Macmillan, London.

Myers, G. (1994), *Words in Ads*, London, Edward Arnold.

Myers, K. (1986), *Understains ... The Sense and Seduction of Advertising*, London, Comedia.

O'Sullivan, T., B. Dutton and P. Rayner (1994), *Studying the Media: An Introduction*, London, Edward Arnold.

Philo, G. (1987), 'Whose news?', *Media, Culture and Society*, 9:4, 397–406.

Pierce, C. S. (1958), *Selected Writings (Values in a Universe of Chance)*, ed. P. Wiener, New York, Dover Press.

Poster, M. (1990), *The Mode of Information*, Chicago, University of Chicago Press.

Poster, M. (1994), 'The mode of information and postmodernity', in D. Crowley and D. Mitchell (eds), *Communication Theory Today*, Cambridge, Polity.

Pribam, D. (ed.) (1988), *Female Spectators: Looking at Film and Television*, London, Verso.

de Saussure, F. (1974), *Course in General Linguistics*, eds. C. Bally, A. Sechehaye and A. Riedlinger, trans. W. Baskin, London, Fontana.

Schlesinger, P. (1978), *Putting 'Reality' Together: BBC News*, London, Constable.

Seiter, E. (1992), 'Semiotics, structuralism, and television', in R. Allen (ed.) *Channels of Discourse, Reassembled: Television and Contemporary Criticism*, London, Routledge, 31–66.

Seiter, E., H. Borchers, G. Kreutzner, and E-M. Warth (eds) (1989), *Remote Control: Television, Audiences and Cultural Power*, London, Routledge.

Selby, K., and R. Cowdery (1995), *How to Study Television*, London, Macmillan.

Social Trends, (1992) survey 22, London, HMSO.

Stam, R., R. Burgoyne, and S. Flitterman-Lewis (1992), *New Vocab-*

ularies in Film Semiotics: Structuralism, Post-Structuralism and Beyond, London, Routledge.

Tunstall, J. (1983), *The Media in Britain*, London, Constable.

Tulloch, J. and H. Jenkins (1995), *Science Fiction Audiences: Watching Doctor Who and Star Trek*, London, Routledge.

Turner, G. (1993), *Film as Social Practice*, London, Routledge.

Umiker-Sebeok, J (ed.) (1987), *Marketing and Semiology*, Amsterdam, Mouton de Gruyter.

van Dijk, T. (1988), *News as Discourse*, Hillsdale, Erlbaum.

Vestergaard, T. and Schrøeder, K. (1985), *The Language of Advertising*, Oxford, Blackwell.

White, R. (1988), *Advertising: What It Is and How To Do It*, London, McGraw-Hill.

Williamson, J. (1978), *Decoding Advertisements: Ideology and Meaning in Advertising*, London, Marion Boyars.

Winship, J. (1987), *Inside Women's Magazines*, London, Pandora.

Whitaker, B. (1981), *News Limited: Why You Can't Read All About It*, London, Minority Press Group.

Index

Numbers in **bold** type indicate definitions of key terms. Numbers in *italics* refer to illustrations. Material in the Sources and further reading and Suggestions for further work sections of the book is not included in the Index.